"In this book, Michael Baltutis displays an i[illegible]
practices, and history. It will serve as an excellent introduction to the complex tradition today known as Hinduism."

Jeffery Long, *Elizabethtown College, USA.*

What is Hinduism?

This book is an engaging introduction to the complex religious tradition of Hinduism. Central to its focus is demonstrating the fundamental diversity within Hinduism through the multiplicity of its core beliefs and traditions.

Chapters are divided into four historical categories – Vedic, Ascetic, Classical, and Contemporary Hinduism – with each examining one deity alongside one key term, serving as a twin focal point for a more complex discussion of related key texts, ideas, social structures, religious practices, festivals, and concepts such as ritual and sacrifice, music and devotion, and engagement and renunciation. The organization of this book requires that we see deities not simply as divine entities who preside over one part of the Hindu world. Rather, their complexity requires each to be seen as a larger cultural category whose related persons, concepts, and practices provide a vivid lens through which Hindu devotees see and continue to readapt to the world in which they live.

With study questions, glossaries, and lists of key contemporary figures, this book is an essential and comprehensive resource for students encountering the multiplicity of Hinduism for the first time.

Michael Baltutis is Professor of Religious Studies at the University of Wisconsin Oshkosh, USA, where he teaches courses on the religions of Asia. He is the author of *The Festival of Indra: Innovation, Archaism, and Revival in a South Asian Performance* (2023).

What is this thing called Religion?

The Routledge Religion *What is this thing called?* series of concise textbooks have been designed for use by students coming to a core area of the discipline for the first time. Each volume explores the relevant central questions with clear explanation of complex ideas and engaging contemporary examples.

Available in the series:

What is Mormonism?
A Student's Introduction
Patrick Q. Mason

What is Antisemitism?
A Contemporary Introduction
Linda Maizels

What is Religious Ethics?
An Introduction
Irene Oh

What is Hinduism?
A Student's Introduction
Michael Baltutis

For more information about this series, please visit: https://www.routledge.com/What-is-this-thing-called-Religion/book-series/WITTCR

What is Hinduism?

A Student's Introduction

Michael Baltutis

Routledge
Taylor & Francis Group
LONDON AND NEW YORK

Designed cover image: Michael Baltutis

First published 2024
by Routledge
4 Park Square, Milton Park, Abingdon, Oxon OX14 4RN

and by Routledge
605 Third Avenue, New York, NY 10158

Routledge is an imprint of the Taylor & Francis Group, an informa business

British Library Cataloguing-in-Publication Data
A catalogue record for this book is available from the British Library

Library of Congress Cataloging-in-Publication Data
Names: Baltutis, Michael C., 1975- author.
Title: What is Hinduism? : a student's introduction / Michael Baltutis.
Description: 1. | New York : Routledge, 2024. |
Series: What is this thing called religion? ; vol. 4 | Includes bibliographical references and index. | Identifiers: LCCN 2023055734 |
Subjects: LCSH: Hinduism.
Classification: LCC BL1202 .B257 2024 | DDC 294.5--dc23/eng/20240108
LC record available at https://lccn.loc.gov/2023055734

ISBN: 978-1-138-32270-7 (hbk)
ISBN: 978-1-138-32608-8 (pbk)
ISBN: 978-1-003-47503-3 (ebk)

DOI: 10.4324/9781003475033

Typeset in Sabon
by Taylor & Francis Books

Contents

Illustrations

Figures

Acknowledgments

I am honored that the editors at Routledge Press asked me to write this book. Amidst the usual work of university teaching, research, and service, and the unusual occurrence of the global pandemic beginning in 2020, we all had hoped that this book would have been published a few years earlier. Hopefully, the delays were worth it and this book will serve as a useful source for students and instructors throughout the world who might also have the opportunity to use other books in the larger Routledge series of which this book is a part: "What is this thing called Religion?"

Writing this introductory text has been an absolute pleasure as it has taken me out of my comfort zone, as I hope it will for its readers also, reminding me of the many interlocking facets of the diverse Hindu tradition that I rarely have the opportunity to write about. As with any study, this book's content is as much autobiographical as it is "objective," as if such a thing were even possible in the academic field of Religious Studies. My selection and interpretation of topics is based on the education that I have received, the questions I have asked and conversations I have had, and the places, practices, and festivals I have had the wonderful opportunity to travel to, witness, and participate in throughout the Hindu world.

During and since earning my PhD at the University of Iowa, I have traveled to South Asia on numerous occasions and I hope to bring many of those experiences to the readers of this book. Accompanying a somewhat linear history of Hinduism from ancient times to the present day, this book will spend time in those places where I myself have spent time, from the Hindu temple closest to me as I write this book – in the tiny town of Kaukauna, Wisconsin – to the frenetic goddess-oriented worship services of Caribbean Hindu communities in Queens, New York, to the majestic cave temples of Ellora in western India, to the city-wide festivals of Kathmandu, Nepal.

Although it is impossible for me to thank everybody who has contributed to my academic development along the way, I am honored to name those whose influence has been the greatest.

Walter Neevel, whose undergraduate courses at the University of Wisconsin, Milwaukee, interested me in learning about a culture that was not my own and helped me to understand the relationships of these concepts across cultures.

Fred Smith and Philip Lutgendorf, whose graduate courses at the University of Iowa helped me to think about these concepts in more nuanced ways, to translate them into other languages, and to consider the complex relationships between text and practice. My first host family in Pune, India, while on the inaugural Sanskrit program with the American Institute of Indian Studies, who taught me to take all stories “seriously, but not literally,” as I now repeatedly tell my students. Sailesh Rajbhandari, Monalisa Maharjan, and Alok Tuladhar for all of their assistance and companionship in Nepal. Karen Pechilis and Sushil Mittal, who recommended and have retained me as the Book Review Editor for the *International Journal of Hindu Studies*, an opportunity that has led to wonderful conversations with so many people I never otherwise would have met.

Financial support for this book has come from the Kenneth J. Grieb Professorship and a Faculty Development Grant from the University of Wisconsin, Oshkosh. Both of these grants supported trips to New York City where I visited with gracious hosts at temples throughout the city; all of these places will make appearances throughout this book, and my hosts deserve special thanks here. Mangalnidhi Swami, at the BAPS Swaminarayan Temples in Edison and Robbinsville, New Jersey. Tejas Jivrajani and his family, for hosting me for several days in their home outside Robbinsville. Urdhva Raval, at the BAPS Swaminarayan Temple in Flushing, Queens. Kaustabha Das, at the Bhakti Center at the original ISKCON headquarters in Manhattan. Sharda and Perley Kutayiah, at the Shri Shakti Mariammaa Temple in Queens. Ravi Vaidyanaat Sivachariar, at the Ganesh temple at the Hindu Temple Society of North America. Roshan Bhattarai and Nandakumar Thirunarayan, at the Shri Shirdi Sai Baba Temple in Flushing, Queens.

Many thanks to the publishers at Routledge for their extraordinary patience in the delivery of this manuscript and to the readers who have made this a more readable and accessible text.

Introduction

Multiplicity – the One, the Many, and the Multiple

In 1955, *LIFE* magazine began a six-part series entitled "The World's Great Religions." Within a larger standard issue covering that week's events, each issue included a smaller photojournalistic piece on one of six religious traditions. (The "Religions" sections of these six issues would be published together as a single hardcover book with the same title in 1957.) This series was intended to "present each religion's basic philosophy and practices" and "to present to the Western world those religions which play such a great part in the lives of so much of the world" (57). The first issue in the series contained a twenty-four-page section on Hinduism and displayed on its cover a young girl in traditional festival dress, jewelry, and forehead *tika* mark celebrating a "vigil at Indian Festival of Lights." Underneath the term "HINDUISM" in all capital letters and in a massive font on the section's first page, the magazine's authors offered the following overall description of the tradition: "India's people seek the one true reality through an ancient and mystic religion of exotic ritual and pure philosophy" (58).

With its focus on the "sublime" object of the religion – "to achieve union with the eternal spirit which the Hindus usually call Brahman" (58) – the editors of *LIFE* magazine reinforced a popular, though not totally incorrect, oversimplification of a complex religious tradition. Implying that Hinduism is concerned more with the transcendent world beyond than with the domestic life with which most Hindus are immediately concerned, the authors ignored the diverse actions, concepts, and goals that have long been part of the Hindu tradition. And as it would not be until 1965 that American immigration policy would welcome families from India and from Asia as a whole, this issue offered many Americans their first taste of Hinduism as it is found in India. Thus, this single issue of a popular American magazine raises relevant questions in the study of Hinduism that continue to be instructive many decades later: What is (and is not) Hinduism? How does Hinduism change as those who practice it move out of India and into a religiously pluralistic – yet predominantly Christian – nation such as the United States? And how might Hinduism point out certain flaws within the typical ways that we think about religion? In other words, what *is* this thing called Hinduism?

DOI: 10.4324/9781003475033-1

We see a difficulty in defining Hinduism within the legal system of British India. An 1862 court case legally determined that devotion to gods and goddesses, as is typically found in Hindu temples, was illegitimate, whereas true Hinduism was "ancient, ascetic, individualistic, transcendent, world-denying, and had the singular goal of *moksha*" [liberation] (Haberman 2006: 28). The early British sometimes awkwardly referred to Hindus as "Gentoo"; by using this term that resembled "Gentile," the British attempted to keep their ideological distance from local populations by considering them unorthodox or even heathen (as, biblically, Gentiles are opposed to orthodox Jewish communities). Nineteenth-century scholars operating within the structure of the British Empire reaffirmed not only the dichotomy between East and West but also the "true" nature of Hinduism (and Buddhism) as a "philosophy, not a religion." Such flawed imperial definitions have, in many contemporary circles, remained untouched for well over a century.

All of these questions become even more difficult to answer as Hinduism, in both popular and academic discussions about religion, mostly defies categorization as a "world religion." Whereas Christianity and Islam are largely dependent upon a set of central beliefs (orthodoxy), Hinduism is more like Judaism in that it focuses on sets of proper domestic and public practices (orthopraxy). Such practices establish intimate connections between religion and culture (and language, and economy, and landscape). Amidst the diverse ways that Hinduism has traveled outside of South Asia – especially due to British imperial policy in the nineteenth century and to changes in American immigration policy in the twentieth century – we will see how the religion always carries with it elements of the region's diverse cultures.

Most generally, such elements as poetry, the visual arts, and dance have long been used within sacred and secular arenas throughout South Asia and the diaspora to reflect and maintain elements of Hindu culture. For example, inherent within the Hindu religious tradition are several specific gestures that are frequently used also outside of explicitly religious spaces: touching the feet of an important person or deity and the *namaste* greeting with palms placed together in front of one's chest. Whereas touching the feet of another always communicates a social hierarchy between participants, the *namaste* greeting is more flexible: communicating a sense of equality and community between people, this gesture also reinforces hierarchy when performed before the icon of a deity when praying for divine assistance.[1]

Similarly, the landscape of South Asia itself is often incorporated into the tradition. Water, for example, is more than just a natural element; it represents a cultural feature that regularly appears throughout the Hindu tradition. Water in general is a life-giving metaphor in creation stories, rivers are feminine objects of devotion that anchor pilgrimage places where funeral rituals take place, and the ocean is the ultimate male destination of those rivers. In fact, the very word "Hinduism" is related to a river. The Indus River that runs through contemporary Pakistan provides the names of both India and Hinduism. Based on the Sanskrit word *sindhu*, Hinduism simply translates as "the religion of India."

This use of cultural elements as part of the religious tradition means that Hinduism, maybe more than other religious traditions, is in a perpetual state of creative flux. While this flexibility might represent a problem for those just acclimating themselves to the study of a fundamentally different worldview, for Hindus this flexibility represents an opportunity to think about the world through a number of different lenses simultaneously.

The central theme: multiplicity

This book will focus on this diversity within Hinduism wherever we find it. To illustrate one facet of this diversity, I will begin with a tangent to an otherwise unrelated religious tradition and then consider the ways that this example might assist us in our study of Hinduism. In her study of the Haitian Vodou tradition celebrated in Brooklyn, New York, anthropologist Karen McCarthy Brown writes of the *lwa*, the Vodou spirits, who, "unlike the Catholic saints whose names they borrow, are characters defined by contradiction. The Vodou spirits," Brown continues, "represent the powers at work in and on human life. The wholeness of the spirits – their ability to contain conflicting emotions and to model opposing ways of being in the world – gives Vodou its integrity as a religion" (Brown 2001: 98).

Despite the many differences between the cultures of Haitian Vodou and South Asian Hinduism, the similarities between their respective pantheons are many and striking. This comparison encourages us to think about Hinduism, its deities, and its practitioners in relationship to other cultures and other peoples around the world. Like the Vodou *lwa*, Hindu gods and goddesses are not simply remnants of a bygone era. Rather, Hindu deities are active beings whose stories, rituals, and artistic representations have maintained real power "in and on human life" and continue to provide a similar integrity to the diverse forms of the Hindu religion.

Another important similarity with the Vodou *lwa* in Brown's description is in the complexity of the Hindu pantheon. Brown writes of the "wholeness" of the Vodou spirits who are "defined by contradiction [through] their ability to contain conflicting emotions and to model opposing ways of being in the world." In other words, an individual spirit or deity is hardly limited to one single function, in the ways that we often think about the gods and goddesses of the moribund Greek, Egyptian, and Babylonian pantheons – "Diana is the goddess of the hunt," "Ptah is the creator god," or "Ishtar is the goddess of fertility." In Haitian Vodou, practitioners assert that there are seven, twenty-one, or even more forms of Ogou, the *lwa* whose many appearances embody at different times the entire spectrum of emotions: he is fierce, shy, brave, a liar, a beggar, a sorcerer, as well as an unreliable drunkard (96). Among these many forms of Ogou, Brown writes, "none of the various Ogou is good or evil, right or wrong, in a simple, unqualified way. Each contains his own paradoxes of personality, which are teased out in possession-performance and in song" (97). These many forms of Ogou reflect a "static" diversity, as he embodies different characteristics and personalities at one time. He also embodies, however, a "dynamic" diversity, as his personality changes as the needs of Haitian people have changed; once a protector of hunters and ironworkers, he is now associated most with soldiers and the military, both roles visible in the ritual sword that he wields during his possession events.

This introductory aside to the spirits of Haitian Vodou provides us with a model, or at least an analogy, for our approach to Hinduism, so very different from the Protestant Christianity that has come to define "standard" religiosity in the United States. As with the worship of Haitian spirits, through which "the cosmos became thoroughly socialized" (100), the worship of Hindu deities provides people with opportunities to access different parts of their own personalities – as individuals and as members of families, larger communities, societies, and nations – and to see the world through a variety of lenses.

This complexity also requires that we, as students and scholars of religion, avoid simplistic language that seeks a single simple "essence" of Hinduism and that thus limits our own perceptions of Hindu deities, practitioners, and cultures.

Rather than thinking of Hindu gods and goddesses as passive symbols that simply exist somewhere in the universe, we will consider them here as complex cultural entities. These active divine agents both "establish powerful, pervasive, and long-lasting moods and motivations" in Hindu practitioners, as the anthropologist Clifford Geertz once wrote about religion, while also supporting a local society's ethical, economic, legal, and political systems. Living within the fluid culture of a global Hinduism, the "wholeness" of gods and goddesses requires that we see them as embracing this sense of "contradiction" and as working in tandem with the equally diverse and complex human beings who venerate them.[2]

Many scholars in various sub-fields of South Asian studies have addressed this unique feature of the seemingly limitless, apparently contradictory, and sometimes overwhelming diversity of Hindu forms of the divine. Diana Eck, in her book *Darśan*, a slim but influential study of Hindu imagery, uses the term "polytheistic imagination" as a foil to the Western "myth of monotheism" (1998: 22). Eck argues that whereas people in European, American, and Islamic societies tend to think of matters of ultimate importance in the singular (one nation, one God, one prophet, one book), South Asian societies have long thought in terms of polycentrism and pluralism, even when affirming the existence of an ultimate divine singularity.

Other scholars have picked up on this concept of the polytheistic imagination, addressing the ways that multiple versions of the same story might all be considered "true" (Flueckiger 2015: 8–9). Art historians have studied how standard visual forms of Hindu deities are depicted with multiple heads, arms, and eyes (Srinivasan 1997: 3). And scholars of ancient Hindu ritual have used such terms as "resemblance," "cosmic homology," "association," "duplication," and "identification" to show how Hindu texts have established systematic connections between and among the elements of ritual, the human body, culture and society, landscape, and the cosmos as a whole.[3]

I will use term *multiplicity* throughout this book to refer to the diversity that is unique to Hindu forms of the divine. I hope to use this simpler term more holistically, allowing us to make sense of the related sets of images and ideas that might initially seem confusing to a student not yet familiar with the Hindu tradition. As a working definition, *multiplicity* refers to the ability for multiple – and seemingly contrasting – images, performances, narratives, and viewpoints to be interchanged, substituted, and held simultaneously within a single culture. This concept highlights the emphasis that Hindus have traditionally placed on imagery, practice, and narrative, cultural forms that are inherently more flexible than the doctrinal unity often found within forms of Christianity that some American students might be more familiar with. Such flexibility, moreover, does not signal opposition to or logical contradiction within the Hindu tradition, but rather shows how a number of related features might be sited along a continuum. For example, the many goddesses of the Hindu tradition occupy a broad spectrum between gentle and fierce forms while still possessing features of both. In other cases, this flexibility shows a dynamic tension between significant social locations: an individual might function as a regular householder with a house and a family, or they may become a renouncer who gives up all attachments to the trappings of domestic life.

The simplest examples of multiplicity can be found in various types of enumeration. Significant sites throughout India and the Himalayas comprise the Four Places of Pilgrimage (Char Dham); long and repeating cycles of time are subdivided into the Four Eras (yuga); a set of six philosophical systems are often said to comprise the entire thought of Hinduism; cities, sages, and rivers are placed in groups of seven; forms of the elephant-headed god Ganesh, Mother Goddesses, and Protectors of the Directions (Digpala) are placed in groups of eight; and the names of many deities are chanted in rounds of 108. Although these lists are fixed and well known, they also imply a degree of flexibility as new members can be added to these lists. For example, to the collection of the four ancient texts of the Vedas, later authors sometimes add a "fifth Veda," especially the long epic *Mahabharata* or the *Natyashastra*, a treatise on music, dance, and drama that describes its audience as universal. What Diana Eck writes about the repetition of locations throughout the sacred geography of India might be applied to all of these different types of examples: "Any place that is truly important is important enough to be duplicated and sited in multiple places" (Eck 2013: 436).

Beyond simple enumeration, the complexity of the Hindu tradition extends to include apparent logical contradictions in fundamental points of belief. As a key example, it might seem logical to ask what Hindus believe about the afterlife and to anticipate the answer we already expect: "Hindus believe in the cycle of reincarnation." Although reincarnation is the primary model of the afterlife in early philosophical texts, when we observe the many ways that Hindus throughout South Asia ritualize death, it becomes clear that another model is simultaneously at work. In addition to a general belief in the cycle of rebirth and redeath, Hindus also actively celebrate, at multiple occasions throughout the festival calendar, the long life of their ancestors who have successfully reached heaven and who now watch over them.

This ancestral model of the afterlife is reinforced throughout the festival season in Kathmandu, Nepal, where the living repeatedly celebrate, embody, and feed their ancestors, especially those who died within the previous year. During the Gai Jatra ("Cow Festival") in July, children dress as renouncers, as Krishna, and especially as the cow Vaitāraṇī who leads the spirits of the deceased across the river to the proverbial other side (Figure 0.1). During the September Indra festival, many of these same family members will walk the boundaries of the city of Kathmandu lighting lamps, carrying incense, and visiting shrines. And for the *shrāddha* ritual later in October, married couples will perform an ancient rite on the riverbank when, assisted by a (Hindu or Buddhist) priest, they feed rice balls to three generations of their ancestors (Figure 0.2).[4]

The tendency towards the multiple has led the authors of one introductory text to write, "For Hinduism, the meaning of 'tradition' is cumulative, not unchanging" (Hawley and Narayanan 2006: 4). For this example of the afterlife,

Figure 0.1 Discarded masks from the Gai Jatra cow festival with the cow Vaitarini on the front and Ganesh on the reverse. Kathmandu, Nepal

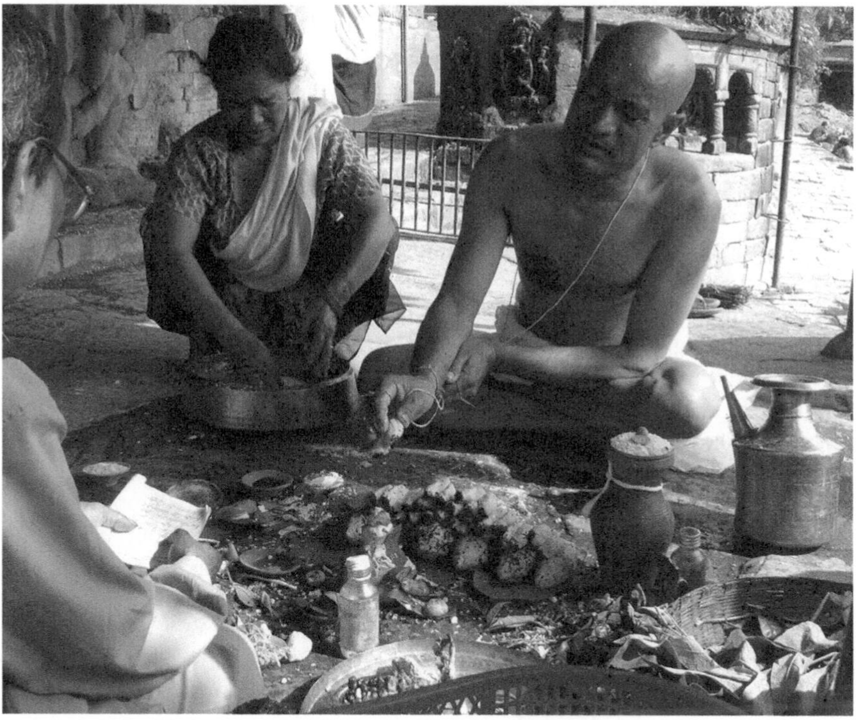

Figure 0.2 Annual shraddha ritual for remembering and feeding the ancestors. Bhaktapur, Nepal

we simply have to acknowledge that Hinduism allows for both models simultaneously, at least in part because the concept of reincarnation and the *shrāddha* rites emerged at different times and among different communities, and both fulfill fundamental social and emotional needs. Another author considers Hinduism in the form of an Indian banyan tree: as its many branches grow downwards, put down roots, and appear as new trunks, the tree becomes its own ecosystem that is interconnected and polycentric, though "forming a multifaceted unity" (Lipner 1996: 110). (I find the inverse metaphor of a river with many contributing tributaries also to be helpful.) This emphasis on complexity might serve as a productive interpretive structure both for students who have no prior familiarity with the Hindu tradition and for those students of Indian heritage who may have struggled attempting to explain their tradition to non-Hindu friends and colleagues. This multiplicity, once acknowledged, eliminates any confusion in navigating an unfamiliar cultural system and clarifies the connections between the many and complex facets of the Hindu tradition.

As this book will use Hindu deities as a way to think through the larger Hindu tradition, let's also look at one particular deity, the god Vishnu, who provides another example of multiplicity. Taking ten avatars that each appear on earth in a different historical era when dharma (cosmic order) is in decline,

Vishnu illustrates a marked contrast from his Christian counterpart, where salvation results from the belief in the one God sending his one Son for the ultimate salvation of the entire world once and for all. The Hindu regard for Vishnu is seen not in the strict belief in his singular existence but in the knowledge, recitation, and pure enjoyment of the different versions of his many stories passed down via oral, written, illustrated, epic, devotional, comic, and virtual sources. This is hardly to say, however, that Hindus have not engaged in vigorous theological debate: by defending a philosophical and sectarian position devoted to Shiva, Vishnu, or the Goddess, authors have supported the social, religious, and political communities to which they belong (Fisher 2017: 13).[5]

It is not enough, however, to simply treat Hinduism as a "unity in diversity" where Hindu authors, philosophers, and practitioners offer different acceptable solutions to the same human problems. Such a perception of Hinduism as a singular unified religion simply draws us back to the "myth of monotheism" that is more typical of Western traditions. Similarly, it is also not sufficient for students and scholars to treat Hinduism as an ancient religion that has thoughtlessly accumulated numerous elements over time without editing or processing. The concept of multiplicity encourages us to recognize the agency of Hindu authors and actors over centuries and millennia. Rather than viewing the Hindu tradition as a static series of timeless structures, this book sees Hinduism as a lived and organic tradition where Hindu agents respond to changing conditions creatively and conscientiously by translating culturally relevant transcendent mysteries into new verbal and physical forms.

Previous introductory textbooks have notoriously stumbled over the proper way to communicate the complexity of the Hindu tradition. In a review essay of ten such textbooks, P. Pratap Kumar speaks from his own experience in teaching these texts, each of which – in part, due to their reliance upon technical and Sanskrit-language vocabulary – is excessively complex for an undergraduate audience.[6] But his primary problem with all of these texts is, simultaneously, their simplicity: each follows a master narrative that begins with, returns to, and revolves around the orthodox, ancient, and Sanskrit-language textual tradition of high-caste Hindu brahmins.[7] Such a focus, Kumar asserts, provides readers with "no insight into the Hindu practice on the ground" (123). He suggests as a solution to this problem the inclusion of local and regional performances that work outside of, and thus problematize, the singular orthodox textual tradition.[8]

I will attend to Kumar's warning by including in this book many regional variations of Hinduism. In addition to the texts, rituals, festivals, systems of ethics, and other components typically associated with a world religion, this book will also attend to the ethnographic labor of scholars of religion and cultural anthropologists working on the ground in South Asia. My use of the term "South Asia" here and throughout this book is meant to extend the geographic area where Hinduism has traditionally been practiced beyond India (especially beyond north India), where much scholarship on Hinduism takes place. My own continued research in Nepal, including a book on Hindu festivals in Kathmandu, will help to extend the geography of this book. Despite its close cultural, historical, and religious affinity with India, the perceived remoteness of Nepal's Himalayan setting has rendered its diverse cultures virtually absent from most religion textbooks and introductions to Hinduism.

Moreover, as Hindu families have moved from South Asia to the United States, Europe, south and east Africa, southeast Asia, and the Caribbean, they have adapted their practices to fit their new homelands. An introduction to Hinduism would be incomplete without a consideration of these relatively new global forms of Hinduism and the diverse ways these diasporic communities have connected themselves both to their new worlds and to other Hindu communities back in India and throughout the world. Rather than relegating these communities to separate chapters, this book will attend to both Nepal and the Hindu diaspora throughout the entire book, incorporating these diverse Hindu forms into a fluid narrative that includes elements from ancient, medieval, and modern Hindu traditions, and from Indian, Nepali, and diasporic Hindu communities.[9]

While the fluid system described in this chapter makes defining Hinduism difficult, we can offer a description that will help us further navigate the coherent system of cultures we will encounter in this book, without reducing the complex culture of Hinduism to any one thing.[10] We will consider Hinduism to represent a South Asian religious system whose rituals and narratives establish proper relationships among and between humans and the gods, the performance of which leads to ultimate salvation. Not every element of Hinduism introduced in this book will directly reflect all parts of this simple description, but its focus on relationships will help guide us through a sometimes overwhelming quantity and diversity of unfamiliar ritual and narrative actors. Moreover, as we consider religion to be a facet of local culture alongside art, literature, and music, this description will always remind us that it is human actors who create, maintain, and change their relationships with the gods.

The concept of multiplicity means that we should expect to see different types of relationships maintained in a variety of ways. Some relationships, such as the traditional Hindu caste system, signal their greater hierarchical nature through displays of austere respect, while others signal a greater amount of equality through a rhetoric of intimacy (devotion, erotic love, and even deity possession). Although the ultimate goal of salvation also takes multiple forms – becoming an ancestor (*pitṛ*) after death, attaining eternal life in the realm of the gods (*devaloka*), or achieving ultimate liberation (*mokṣa*) from life – this salvation in the afterlife is always connected to the ritual maintenance of proper relationships in *this* world. The Hindu focus on proper relationships has remained constant throughout the tradition, despite the changing vocabulary, sets of physical gestures, and types of offerings that have defined these relationships. As each chapter will handle a different Hindu god or goddess, this book will introduce and reiterate these relationships – with various specific (groups of) gods and goddesses, ancestors, demons, and renouncers – as they occur in different historical periods.

The historicity of Hinduism

Before providing an introduction to the contents of this book, I would like to make a few introductory comments on the inherent limitations in (and opportunities of) our capacity to present a linear history of Hinduism.

The "cumulative" nature of Hinduism means that themes, images, and practices seen in one chapter will plant the seeds for those that will develop in complex and unexpected ways in subsequent chapters. Although older forms of religious practice will naturally wane as they are gradually replaced by more contemporary forms, they still survive in cultural memory and can be fully or partially revived to meet certain cultural needs. For example, the first chapter of this book will introduce the Purusha, the Cosmic Person whose story of sacrifice told in the Rig Veda reflects the dominant theme of sacrifice (*yajña*) detailed throughout the early Vedic texts. The strength of this Vedic metaphor encouraged its application to the non-dual form of Shiva in the philosophical texts of the Upanishads (in Chapter 2) and to the universal form of Krishna in devotional texts (in Chapter 4). Moreover, the very authority of Vedic ritual, though not practiced in most parts of South Asia today, remains largely intact. Surviving in some small pockets in south and west India, its mantras continue to be used in Hindu marriage rites and its ritual fires continue to be kindled in Hindu temples throughout the world today.

Also historically important is the simple idea that subsequent texts and practices often directly respond to preceding ones. In the text of the *Bhagavad Gītā*, Krishna introduces readers to the concept of the Three Yogas or the Three Paths (*tri-mārga*) of Action, Knowledge, Devotion. These three techniques refer to ritual action, philosophical understanding, and the emotional relationships forged between people and deities. This structure provides a way for understanding how Hindu authors have categorized their tradition, while also articulating a dynamic and cumulative development of the tradition over time. Ritual action develops into a robust philosophical understanding of ancient Vedic rites and their ultimate meanings, while devotional attitudes, emotions, and practices emerge later as a mode of Hindu practice accessible to all. Although in a sectarian text whose authors are making theological arguments about proper Hindu understanding and practice, the tri-marga provides readers of this book with one model to understand the historical trajectory of Hinduism from the earliest times to the present day, as forms of all three of these yogas remain intertwined with one another.

This trajectory, however, is notoriously difficult to precisely date. For example, the mammoth Sanskrit epic *Mahabharata*, of which the *Bhagavad Gita* is an integral part, was long seen as having been the result of a long process of writing and editing by multiple authors. Its composition was long dated from 500 BCE–500 CE, though later scholars narrowed that range by a few centuries. Newer scholarly trends, however, see this same large epic as having been written over a much shorter period of time, its final draft a Hindu devotional response to a series of political events occurring in the third century BCE. The truth is, more than likely, somewhere in the middle. And some traditional Hindu scholars have connected the authorship of the epic by the sage Vyasa to his earlier role as the "divider" of the Vedas and his authorship of even later narratives. Although his single lifetime in this scheme would stretch over many centuries and millennia, Vyasa's singular authorship of many Hindu texts tells us something about the unity with which many Hindus see their many central texts.

Sacred texts from around the world, most notably the Bible and Qur'an, were often composed against the background of cultural contact and political strife. Hindu texts are no different, as this cultural contact had significant influences on larger Hindu cultural trends. Contact in fifth-century-BCE urban India with communities that would become the religions of Buddhism and Jainism also produced the Hindu texts of the Upanishads; contact with Buddhists in the sixth century CE resulted in an outpouring of early medieval literature; contact with Muslim communities (especially those practicing its mystical branch of Sufism) as early as the tenth century, and with the Islamic Mughal dynasty beginning in the sixteenth century in north India, extended forms of Hindu devotional poetry, practice, and pilgrimage; and contact with Western scholars and British imperial officials in the nineteenth century – especially in Calcutta, the capital of British India – stimulated the Bengali Renaissance and widespread religious change throughout India. In these moments of cultural contact, Hindu authors and ritualists worked to translate Hindu concepts across cultures as they also reinforced and adapted those concepts for Hindu communities.

Structure of the book

Leading you through a full-semester introductory course in world religions, Asian religions, or Hinduism specifically, this book will use Hindu deities as a particular way to think about Hinduism. Each chapter will name one particular deity in its title along with one key term; together, they will serve as a twin focal point for a more complex discussion of related key texts, ideas, social structures, religious practices, festivals, and concepts such as ritual and sacrifice, music and devotion, and engagement and renunciation. Each chapter can thus be read as a microcosm of Hinduism, tracing the history of one set of related concepts from its beginning through to the present day. It will show the innumerable forms that these deities take and the many ways that they have operated within daily Hindu life and in relationship to Hindu communities: these deities are of the family, neighborhood, village, and nation; they are married and single; civilized, royal, and rustic; male, female, adult, and child; animal, stone, river, and tree; gentle and fierce; universal and local.

After a brief introduction that provides the reader with a specific example of how that deity operates within Hindu life, each chapter will detail the relevant textual and performative traditions associated with that deity. These related traditions comprise one facet of global Hinduism, found throughout India,

South Asia, and the wider Hindu world, and sometimes generated in moments of contact with the Western world. The organization of this book requires that we see deities as complex divine individuals, each of whom – especially the gods Shiva and Vishnu, and the goddess Devi – operates as a larger cultural category whose related persons, concepts, and practices provide a vivid lens through which Hindu devotees see and continue to readapt to the world in which they live.

The nine chapters of this book will trace the history of Hinduism using four historical categories: Vedic, Ascetic, Classical, and Contemporary Hinduism.[11] Chapter 1, "Indra and the Vedas: ritual knowledge, royal power, and fertility in ancient India," will detail the texts and practices of the Vedas. With the earliest portions of the Rig Veda written around 1500 BCE, the Vedas represent the earliest religious and literary forms that come to be a part of Hinduism. Despite the many archaeological finds in the Indus River Valley in what is now Pakistan – small stone seals with writing in undecipherable characters, beadwork, and the footprint of its cities – "[p]ractically nothing is known about religious life" in this culture that precedes the Vedas (Michaels 2004: 31). Since it is currently impossible to know if the culture practiced by the people of the Indus cities bears any relationship whatsoever to that of the early Vedic peoples, this book will begin in earnest with the poetry and practices enshrined in the texts of the Vedas.

With roots in the Vedic tradition, the Ascetic period acquires its own identity with the Upanishads, late Vedic philosophical texts that overlap considerably with the rise of the equally ascetic traditions of Buddhism and Jainism, with which the Hindu authors of this period were in conversation (500 BCE–200 BCE). Chapter 2, "Shiva and *yoga*: transgression and liberation on the banks of the Ganges River," will detail the role of the ascetic, a standard character in Hindu narratives who renounces regular connections with the world socially, economically, sexually, and culinarily. The men (and sometimes women) who emulate Shiva perform ascetic techniques as they fully and permanently renounce the world. Equally part of the Hindu world, male and female lay people with families and worldly concerns will have the opportunity throughout the Hindu festival calendar to also focus their attention, however temporarily, on the spiritual rather than the mundane material world.

Detailing four of the main gods and goddesses of Classical Hinduism, the next four chapters (Chapters 3–6) will describe Hindu devotional texts and practices that represent the predominant ways that Hinduism is practiced today. The first pair of chapters in this section focus on Ram and Krishna, two avatars (incarnations) of Vishnu, while the second pair of chapters details devotion to the goddesses Lakshmi and Durga. The long duration assigned to Classical Hinduism (200 BCE–1800 CE) is hardly meant to communicate the lack of dynamism of this period. Rather, each of these four chapters will investigate the many vigorous debates that authors, poets, ritualists, and rulers engaged in – and continue to engage in – as they have variously aligned themselves with powerful and practical gods and goddesses.

The fourth and final section on Contemporary Hinduism will cover two major Hindu gurus from the recent past (1800 CE–present). The first, Swaminarayan, lived in the late eighteenth and early nineteenth centuries in western India. His concerted and largely successful attempts at social and religious reform in western India dovetailed with similar efforts by others throughout India at this same time. Greatly supported by officials in the British Empire, his reform resulted in what is now called Swaminarayan Hinduism, a popular global movement rooted in the efforts of the guru.

The second chapter in this section will detail another religious figure considered a Hindu guru. Mātā Amṛtānandamayī, commonly known as Amma (Mother), represents one of the most famous living gurus. Steeped in the Hindu tradition of her native south India, her global movement is less rooted in one particular place or among one particular people, as is Swaminarayan Hinduism. Drawing devotees from across the globe as she maintains an intense travel schedule, Amma uses the more universal language of love and compassion to alleviate the suffering experienced by all people in so many ways.

This book will conclude with a consideration of Kamadhenu, the mythological Hindu cow, as a lens through which to view several issues prominent throughout the contemporary Hindu world, namely environmental sustainability and political nationalism.

Each of this book's chapters will separately contribute a response, though hardly a final answer, to the questions that the books in this series ask: How does Hinduism change as it moves out of South Asia? How might Hinduism point out certain flaws within the ways that we think about religion? And, ultimately, what *is* this thing called Hinduism? By extending our focus beyond the orthodox textual record to Hinduism's many local narrative and performative traditions, and beyond India to Nepal, to the greater South Asian region, and to the global Hindu diaspora, I hope to paint a vibrant portrait of Hinduism that is more comprehensive than usual for such a text, all the while focusing on the culture, humanity, and multiplicity inherent throughout the Hindu tradition.

*

I offer here a few final notes as a sort of user's guide to this book. Throughout this book, I will default towards using plural non-gendered pronouns (they/them/theirs) when referring to Hindu people in general, even though there are times when texts specifically refer to men. For example, when texts detail the lives of male renouncers who have given up domestic life to live like a yogi in the wilderness, we should not assume that women have never done such a thing, even if the majority are male. And when the texts state a preference for the birth of sons rather than of children in general – it was sons who have long carried on the family's reverence for its ancestors – we are not to assume that daughters were universally shunned.

In the absence of a modern ideal of gender equality – one that virtually none of us actually live up to – it is often too easy to presume that a culture with distant and ancient roots is fundamentally different from our own, wherever we might be as we are reading this book. My purpose here is to make familiar the Hindu tradition, lived by millions of people for thousands of years and now all across the globe. One of the ways that a culture becomes familiar is by considering the people who follow and wrestle with their tradition rather than presuming that they are disconnected from the modernity that we consider ourselves to be a part of.

Among these issues of understanding across culture, the translation of Hindu concepts from their South Asian roots for a Western audience is complicated in multiple ways. First, South Asia is composed of many local and regional cultures whose different languages ground these concepts in slightly varying cultural systems. Second, these concepts change over time, so that a single concept – especially one that crosses regional and linguistic boundaries – acquires and sloughs off different meanings and associations. In addition to English translations that attempt to accommodate all of these nuances, we must also transliterate words from different South Asian scripts to the Roman script that we use in the West; in doing so, we must make certain accommodations to understand how a word is to be pronounced. The standard way of doing this is to add diacritic marks to many vowels and consonants.

For example, the name of the deity कृष्ण is properly transliterated as Kṛṣṇa with dots underneath the vowel /r/ and the consonants /s/ and /n/; to assist readers of this book in pronunciation, however, I will use the spelling Krishna without these diacritics. The spelling of some words can also appear different when translated from textual Sanskrit to a related spoken South Asian language, such as Hindi or Nepali, and even more so when translated to one of the languages of south India, such as Kannada and Tamil. Since this book has undergraduate students as its primary audience, I will aim for consistency and simplicity by standardizing spelling as much as is possible; often, I will use the proper spelling with full diacritics with the first use of a word, eliminating most of these diacritics in subsequent uses. (I will often retain /ā/, the long /a/ sound that resembles the vowel sound in "mom" or "father," to differentiate it from the short /a/ sound as in "luck.") Certain variations and inconsistencies will inevitably remain, as they do across the many books written on the Hindu tradition.

Since this book will regularly address the ways that Hindu organizations represent themselves on the Internet, I include links to temples and other organizations throughout this book. I encourage you to search these sites and to look for other related institutions to see how Hindu organizations closer to where you live present themselves to a global audience. You must, of course, also exercise patience and ingenuity when the links I provide here ultimately change.

Finally, each chapter will include a brief works cited list that includes three accessible sources from that chapter; all sources referred to in each chapter are included in a complete bibliography at the end of the book. Each chapter will also include a short list of key terms; several chapters will also include a related section that includes contemporary people discussed in that chapter, and every chapter will conclude with a few study questions that you can use to think about broader issues contained in that chapter.

Notes

1 Fuller 2004 introduces his book with a brief passage on the opposing valences of the *namaste* gesture, which acknowledges the simultaneous equality and hierarchy between people and the gods.
2 This complex relationship between humans and deities is sometimes called "co-agency." See Baltutis 2009 for an example of how co-agency works for the deity Bhairav and his local community in Kathmandu, Nepal. See Geertz's full definition of religion in his essay "Religion as a Cultural System" (1973/1993).
3 Smith 1989; Flood 1996: 48; Patton 2005; Eck 1998; Michaels 2004: 7.
4 Adding another layer of multiplicity to the *srāddha*, Ann Gold (2000) describes in her ethnography *Fruitful Journeys* the overlapping terms that local Rajasthani pilgrims use to describe the entire cycle of life: likened to the embryo in the womb of a pregnant woman, these rice balls become children (*putra*), wandering ghosts (*pattar*), and finally the ancestors (*pitri*).
5 Flueckiger (2013: 53) uses the term multiplicity in a similar way to describe the easy ways that south Indian Hindus tell varying stories of the goddess.
6 Kumar 2010.
7 Fuller 2004, more than most, grounds his book in his own ethnographic work in south India, as does Flueckiger 2015; Huyler 2002 is primarily about devotion, which typically receives a single chapter in most books.
8 Falk 2006 does this by including chapters such as "In the home" and "Among the poor and oppressed."
9 This inclusion of Hinduism from the diaspora draws on Flueckiger 2015, extending her specific attention to Atlanta's Hindu community to additional places around the globe. Although most textbooks include some version of "Hinduism in the West," they do so typically through a cultural lineage based on the written works and social organizations derived from Bengali brahmins of the nineteenth century. Knott 2000/2016 and Olson 2007, especially, take up similar questions in their introductions.
10 Similarly, Hawley and Narayanan (2006) describe Hinduism as embodying "a range of practices and sensibilities" (9) that result in a certain coherence, and they name five characteristics (with examples) that have developed "out of a history of conversation, elaboration, and challenge" (12): doctrine (*dharma*), practice (*puja*), society (*varna* and *jati*), story and performance (*Ramayana*), and devotion (*bhakti*).
11 Axel Michaels (2004) divides the history of Hinduism into six eras, describing the predominant practices of each era: Prevedic, Vedic, Ascetic Reformism, Classical, Sects, and Modern.

References

Dalrymple, William. 2010. *Nine Lives: In Search of the Sacred in Modern India.* New York: Alfred A. Knopf.

Eck, Diana L. 1998. *Darśan: Seeing the Divine Image in India.* New York: Columbia University Press.

Kumar, P. Pratap. 2010. Introducing Hinduism: The Master Narrative – A Critical Review of Textbooks on Hinduism. *Religious Studies Review* 36 (2): 115–124.

Key terms

dharma
diaspora

multiplicity
South Asia

Study questions

1 In what general and specific ways is Hinduism connected to the larger South Asian culture of which it is a part?
2 What does a comparison with Haitian Vodou help us to understand about the complexity of the Hindu pantheon?
3 How does the term "multiplicity" help us to see Hinduism as a religion different from the Protestant Christianity that often serves as the "standard" religion in the West? What are some examples of multiplicity?
4 What is the significance of the geographical term "South Asia" rather than "India"? What might this help us to anticipate about a study of Hinduism?
5 What are the roles of human beings in constructing, maintaining, and shaping the Hindu tradition?

1 Indra and the Vedas

Ritual knowledge, royal power, and fertility in ancient India

Poets of the early Vedas told many different stories that we might classify as "creation stories." Each story reinforces one aspect of the Vedic world and highlights the creative power of one or another deity (or pairs or groups of deities). The most clear creation story is that of the self-sacrifice of the Purusha, the cosmic Person; this story details the fundamental separation of the world into its distinctive tripartite structure of earth, middle realm, and heaven. Most often, however, it is the god Indra who is named the world's creator. His destruction of the water serpent Vṛtra in Rig Veda 1.32 presents one of his most recognizable creation stories. In yet another hymn in the Rig Veda (2.12), a fifteen-verse panegyric that compiles many different stories that affirm Indra's existence and power, verse 2 provides another way that Indra created the world: "He who made firm the tottering earth, who made still the quaking mountains, who measured out and extended the middle realm, who propped up the heaven – he, my people, is Indra."

Indra creates these spaces for humans and gods with a wooden post (*stambha*), alluded to in the Sanskrit verb for his action of "propping up" (*astambhṇāt*) the heaven. The stambha, also referred to as a skambha, is similarly wielded by Varuṇa, also a royal deity like Indra, who "with his skambha held apart the two world-halves" (RV 8.41.10b).[1] The skambha is also wielded by Vishvakarma, the carpenter, smith, and sculptor of the gods. With Vishvakarma's identity also as priest, sage, and sacrificial victim, the Rig Veda's hymns to Vishvakarma connect the creation of the world to the proper performance of the Vedic fire ritual (10.81–82), a theme common throughout the Rig Veda. In the later text of the Atharva Veda, the skambha operates independently when it too creates the world: "Skambha established these two, heaven and earth. Skambha established the wide middle realm. Skambha established the six wide directions. Skambha entered and pervaded this whole world" (AV 10.7.35). Although Indra is rarely worshipped today, his festival is still celebrated in Nepal's capital city of Kathmandu, where citizens celebrate the creative power of the (erstwhile) king of Nepal and of the city's resident ancestors, with the focal point of the festival a forty-foot-tall wooden post installed immediately outside the city's royal palace (Figure 1.1).[2]

DOI: 10.4324/9781003475033-2

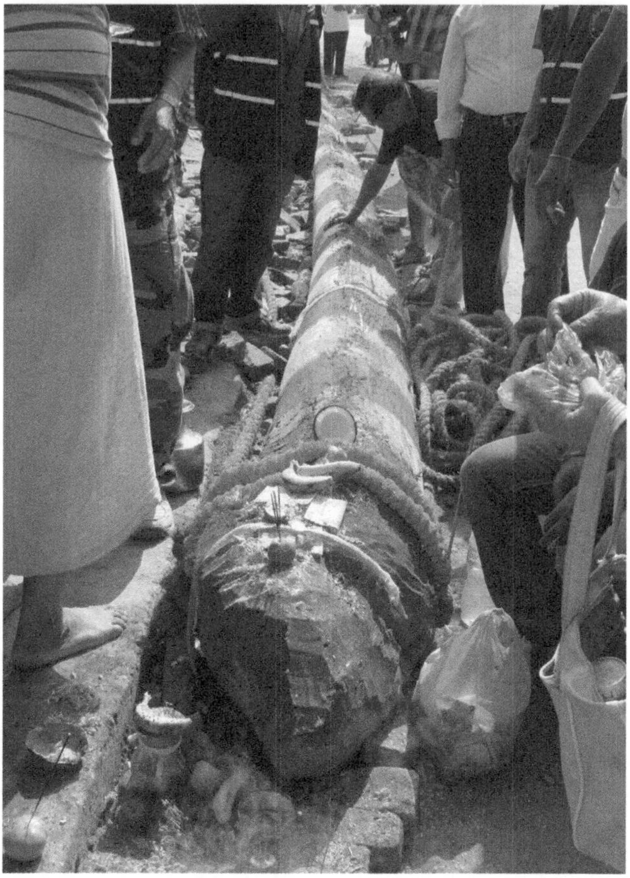

Figure 1.1 People welcome the wooden festival post into the city for the Indra festival. Kathmandu, Nepal

These creation stories are part of the Vedas, the root texts against which all South Asian religious and philosophical traditions measured themselves. Whereas Buddhism and Jainism eventually rejected the authority of the Vedas – the Sanskrit term *veda* means "knowledge" – they are so key to the foundations and origins of what we call Hinduism that scholar Brian K. Smith asserts, Hinduism is "the religion of those humans who create, perpetuate, and transform traditions with legitimizing reference to the authority of the Veda" (1989: 29). By using the singular term "the Veda," Smith acknowledges the relatively unified intellectual system that we find in this body of Sanskrit-language poetry and literature and the consistent ways that its authors prescribe ritual performances, tell stories of the gods, and wrestle with a variety of philosophical issues.

In the nineteenth century, F. Max Müller coined the term "kathenotheism" to describe the unique Vedic system of divine multiplicity, "a successive belief in single supreme gods" (Müller 1878/1976: 271). It is this principle that allows for multiple deities to act as creators. In her own study of Hinduism in India, Diana Eck summarizes Müller's theory of the Hindu gods as such:

> Each is exalted in turn. Each is praised as creator, source, and sustainer of the universe when one stands in the presence of that deity. There are many gods, but their multiplicity does not diminish the significance or power of any of them.
> (Eck 1998: 26)

Although certainly not all of these lofty characteristics can be equally ascribed to each and every Vedic deity, the high degree of multiplicity in this earliest stratum of Hinduism makes it more difficult to focus on just one deity. Although this chapter is named for Indra, it will follow three important Vedic deities: Agni, the god of the ritual fire; Indra, of warrior-kings; and Soma, of the ritual drink that inspires the Vedic poets.

This chapter will focus on the text of the Rig Veda, the oldest Sanskrit-language text in existence and one that has long been regarded as the first text of the large and open Hindu textual canon. Noting the individual and groups of Vedic gods and goddesses who alternately stride to the forefront of this text, this chapter will explore how the Rig Veda highlights themes of ritual knowledge, royal power (*rājan*), and fertility in ancient India. By focusing on these themes, as well as those themes we might expect in the study of a "world religion" – an ethical system, beliefs about the afterlife, and the secular, social, or political life of the Vedic people – I hope to show how this body of literature contributed to the Vedic worldview, how it provided some of the themes still seen in contemporary Hinduism, and that it should be considered among the world's great literature.

The Rig Veda

The Rig Veda belongs to a body of literature that is often referred to in a sort of shorthand as "the Vedas" or "the four Vedas." The four Vedas are really four collections (*saṁhitā*) that contain hymns (Rig Veda), songs (Sāma Veda), ritual instructions (Yajur Veda), and passages handling a mix of domestic, royal, and magical rites and spells (Atharva Veda). In addition to these fairly standardized collections, different Vedic schools produced their own texts within three other categories: ritual texts (Brāhmaṇa), mystical forest texts (Āraṇyaka), and philosophical texts (Upanishad), followed later by other works detailing ethics and public and domestic rites (various categories of Sūtra). Many authors from various schools subsequently composed over many centuries "Vedic limbs" (Vedāṇga) and Appendices (Parishishta) to clarify and augment the sometimes arcane and archaic materials contained in these ancient texts. All of these texts are divided into two broad categories: the final category of the Sūtras and later texts are "remembered" (*smriti*), whereas the earlier texts are "heard" (*shruti*), a sort of mystical designation that connects the Vedic "seers" (*rishi*) directly to the sounds of the Vedas. These texts are also categorized according to their ritual application: a *mantra* is a poetic verse chanted by one of a number of priests during the performance of a Vedic ritual, while a *brāhmaṇa* is a prose passage that offers narrative explanations of the texts and rites that comprise the ritual.

The Vedic narrative tradition begins with the oldest of these texts, the Rig Veda, which will be the main focus of this chapter. The earliest hymns of the Rig Veda were composed between approximately 1500 and 1000 BCE by different families of poets who lived in the Punjab region of what is now northwestern India and northeastern Pakistan; the full text as we have it today was compiled a few centuries later farther east in north India. Memorized and accurately passed down via oral tradition for centuries, the Rig Veda contains 1,028 hymns distributed among ten books. Books 2 through 7 are each composed by poets of a single different family and are arranged, somewhat like the Qur'an in Islam, according to the number and length of hymns in each book; Book 8 resembles those family books but contains hymns from two different families; Book 9 contains 114 hymns dedicated solely to Soma, the ritual plant and purifying drink central to the Vedic rite; and Books 1 and 10, the two longest books, each contain 191 hymns and represent somewhat later collections compiled from a number of different families. The later tradition further systematized the hymns of the Rig Veda by attributing three characteristics to each hymn: the god or goddess or pair or group of deities to whom it is dedicated, its family or specific author, and the poetic meter they used.

Composed some 3,500 years ago, the Rig Veda is among the oldest texts in any Indo-European language. Although written in an archaic form of the Sanskrit language, it still represents, as all religious texts and traditions do, one facet of a living religious and cultural tradition. The oldest representation of South Asian literature in existence, the Rig Veda presents us with many of the basic terms, concepts, and deities that will ground later and contemporary forms of Hinduism, Buddhism, and Jainism, though these forms will undergo changes – sometimes sudden, usually gradual – over the course of time.

The text is also an aspect of human culture from a long-bygone era. The hymns of the Rig Veda were composed by poets who observed and wondered about the world around them and who wrote about that world using the specific images, sounds, and symbols from the historical, cultural, and ecological settings that their audiences would understand and appreciate. Since their use of multiplicity is occasionally opaque and overwhelming, its literary devices are not all necessarily clear to us today. A close study of the Rig Veda (and of any other religious text), however, allows us to see what was of great concern to its authors and their audience at a particular moment in time and how they provided some sense to that world in the language of their culture.

Whereas the Hebrew Bible, for example, focuses much of its attention on the theme of exile, tracing the movement of its people through gardens, the wilderness, and cities as they long to establish a permanent relationship with God in the land he had promised them, the Rig Veda is largely structured around metaphors of ritual knowledge, royalty, and fertility. These three radically overlapping themes are associated with different gods and goddesses found throughout the hymns of the Rig Veda and reflect the economy of the semi-nomadic Vedic people. Seeking to carve out and extend their influence in the pre-urban late Bronze and early Iron Age of ancient South Asia, the early Vedic ritual differed markedly from the later Classical Hinduism that venerated icons of the gods in permanent temples of stone and brick. Reflecting their desire and need to preserve fire, the Vedic ritualists venerated fires kindled in temporary altars and lauded the natural elements required to navigate the sometimes dangerous world around them.

The Vedic ritual system

The Rig Veda is populated by the earliest pantheon of Hindu deities. Opposed to the Indo-Iranian or Persian Zoroastrian pantheon that divides into the demonic *daiva* and divine *ahura*, the Rig Veda retains this antagonistic duality but presents a more complicated pantheon that also shows internal change over time or even competing notions simultaneously. Presenting a political opposition in which the *deva* are divine and the *asura* demonic, the Rig Veda also casually asserts that some gods – most notably, the royal Varuṇa – are devas who are also asuras. This sort of ambiguity, though probably producing some cognitive dissonance for Western readers, shows how historical changes have produced overlapping and seemingly contradictory elements in an otherwise orderly system.

The Rig Veda includes a large pantheon (of mainly male gods with a few goddesses) who represent different facets of the Vedic world. We might consider as one category of gods those who represent key features of the natural environment, such as the Sun (Surya), the Dawn(s) (Ushas), the Rainstorm (Parjanya), and the dual male-female Heaven-Earth (Dyaus-Prithivi). Another more abstract category is comprised of the Ādityas, solar siblings who are children of the sky goddess, Aditi. These deities represent embodiments of social, ethical, and economic components of Vedic life: Mitra and Varuṇa, often depicted together, represent beneficial social alliances between and among Vedic peoples; Āryaman embodies the cultural values of marriage within the Vedic Ārya clans; Bhaga and Amsha ensure the proper share of the goods of life; and Daksha provides "dextrous" skill to priests and sacrificers.

One other group of deities, or at least super-human beings, are the vrātyas. Always described as being part of a *gaṇa*, a group or "gang" with often sinister overtones, this wandering band of competitive warriors displays some diversity within the Vedas. Whether they are Aryan or non-Aryan, they are powerful outsiders who, though often regarded unfavorably, are still connected to the core ritual system of the Vedas. Moreover, their power is related to their performance of powerful acts of renunciation, namely restrictions on food and sex. These acts of renunciation associate them with the god Shiva, who is repeatedly named in the most prominent Vedic text that details the vrātyas, and with the many types of renouncers who will continue to stand outside of later orthodox Hindu society.[3] Shiva and the outsider renouncers who follow him will be the subject of the next chapter.

Very few members of the Vedic pantheon will survive beyond the Vedic period, falling out of existence as social, economic, and political realities changed. Most of them have been renamed, reconceived, or simply replaced by members of the Classical Hindu pantheon we will encounter in subsequent chapters. These changes are only part of what leads to the Rig Veda reading as sometimes fragmentary and discontinuous. Many hymns contain multiple stories, these stories can be told from multiple perspectives and in multiple voices, and the "tone, imagery, and reference" can change mid-verse, as Wendy Doniger notes in the Introduction to her translation (1981, 18).

With some proper names appearing only once in the entire text and some words clearly imported from other languages, the Rig Veda sometimes leaves us with no context to understand the text's full mythological life. With the possible exception of the vratyas, the text's close focus on the ritual system performed by the Vedic elite provides us with virtually no other information about the other and more common forms of religious life that inevitably existed: rituals performed by women, at particular local places, and to other gods and goddesses outside of this system. Despite breaches in continuity with earlier Indo-European narratives, with later Classical Hindu conceptions of the world, and even among the 1,028 hymns contained within it, the Rig Veda still contains a "solid mythological corpus behind the hymns" and presents a number of consistent elements through which we can achieve a fundamental understanding of the ancient Vedic worldview (Doniger 1981: 18).

One of these continuities is the Vedic ritual system itself. Practiced by only an elite few with sufficient resources, this system has been passed down both orally and via the literary heritage of the Vedic texts and has come to represent our only concrete knowledge of the culture of this early period. Built upon the simple rite of offering edible materials into a sacred fire maintained in the house of the ritual's patron, a qualified married man, the Vedic system came to offer both complex solemn (*shrauta*) and simpler domestic (*grihya*) versions of many of its basic rites. The three basic types of Vedic rite are the offering of clarified butter into a ritual fire (*ishti*), the animal sacrifice (*pashubandha*), and the Soma pressing (*somayāga*). Hundreds of different variations, additions, and substitutions to these rituals are prescribed throughout the corpus of Vedic ritual literature, many of which are performed at chronological junctures: at sunrise and sunset, at the full and new moon, and at the transition points between the three seasons (spring, monsoon rains, and autumn).

Increased complexity in the rite requires a larger coterie of priests. The simplest domestic offering can be made by just a qualified and initiated householder, whereas the most complex solemn rites require the work of up to seventeen priests. This large group includes representatives fulfilling duties associated with each of the four Vedas and a *brahman* who, though remaining silent throughout the entire ritual, ensures that all rites are performed and all mantras chanted properly; he corrects and offers expiation (*prāyashcitta*) for those that are not. (Touching water is one of the simplest and most common ways to acknowledge and atone for an incorrectly performed rite.)

The term *brahman* that here names the priest in the ritual's supervisory role also possesses many other meanings. Some of these applications will be relevant in later phases of the Hindu tradition, but in the context of the Vedas the term also refers to the ritual speech (*mantra*) intoned by those priests overseen by the *brahman* priest. (Thus, the *brahman* oversees the *brahmins* who speak *brahman*.) These mantras can only be properly spoken, sung, and chanted by priests and householders who are properly initiated, a correct performance that generates heat-energy, variously known as *brahmavarcas, tejas*, and especially later as *tapas*. Related to Agni – the ritual fire and the god of fire – this heat-energy builds up inside performers and signals their ritual expertise. Such skill requires the sort of asceticism that will become the key feature in the later veneration of the god Shiva, as devotees restrict themselves from the pleasures of the world and, simultaneously, purposefully expose themselves to certain hardships, either temporarily or permanently.

Whereas later Classical Hinduism is based upon the worship of fixed images of the gods in permanent temples, Vedic ritual possesses neither images nor temples. Rather, the Vedic people who practiced semi-nomadism as they led their cattle to greener pastures performed their outdoor rituals on the ground in a space that they built and organized anew for each rite. And, despite the absence of any physical representations, the gods are still very present. Invited to sit upon grass seats placed near the ritual fire, the gods become present through the recitations of Vedic mantras, as they consume the food and drink of the ritual. This earliest form of ritual guest reception came to influence the temple Hinduism of a later era, when gods and goddesses are presented with large feasts that they ritually consume and then return to priests, patrons, and audience members as a divine blessing.

The construction of Vedic ritual spaces and of the brick fire altars that comprise this space reflects early knowledge of mathematics and geometry. Made into the shape of a multi-layered bird for some larger rituals, the basic layout requires three fires. The square Offering Fire in the eastern part of the ritual space represents the main fire into which offerings to the gods are made. At the half-moon shaped Southern Fire, offerings are made to the ancestors to keep dangerous influences at bay. Finally, offerings are made to household deities in the circular western Domestic Fire (Gārhapatya), where the patron's wife is positioned and where she serves as a symbol of family, fertility, and fecundity. In the center of the ritual space sits the *vedi* reserved for the deities and a small circular space for the storage of ritual offerings (Figure 1.2).

The married couple remains the basic ritual unit in many contemporary Hindu rituals, including many of the rites of passage (*saṃskāra*) that are first seen in the later Sūtra sections of the Vedas. In addition to their wedding, the construction of their house, and rites of passage for their children, husband and wife are also present together at the rites for the ancestors (*shrāddha*) where they offer food, in the forms of rice balls (*piṇḍa*), to feed three generations of their ancestors who reside in heaven. The rice balls are, like many items in Hindu rituals and festivals and like the very remains of the deceased at cremation rites, consigned to water after they have served their ritual function.

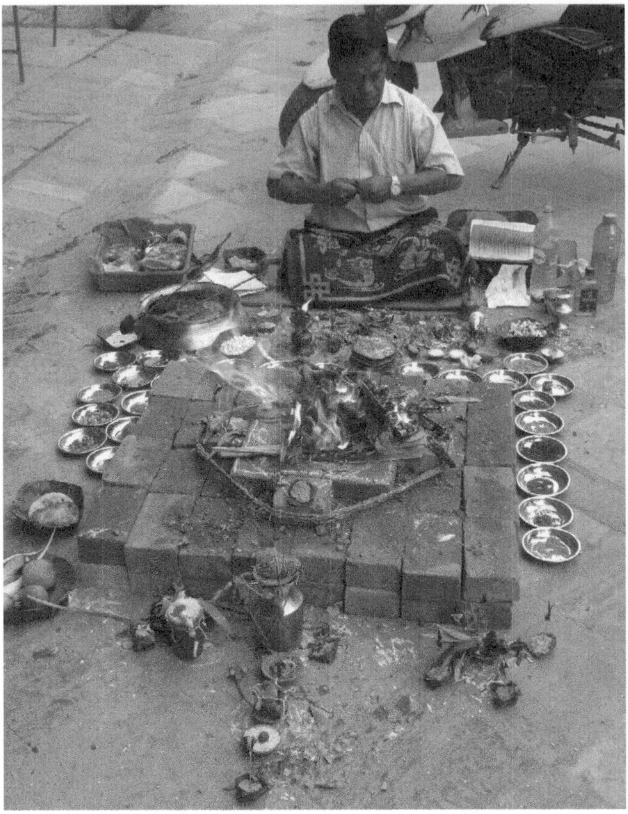

Figure 1.2 Accompanied by animal sacrifices, a Buddhist priest performs a Vedic-style fire ritual in front of the mask of the fierce Bhairav as part of the Indra festival. Kathmandu, Nepal

Agni (fire)

As the fire is the centerpoint of all Vedic rituals, it should come as no surprise that the very first hymn of the Rig Veda is devoted to Agni, the god of fire. (The name Agni denotes both the ritual fire and the god of fire; the name is cognate with the English words *ignite* and *igneous*.) This hymn serves as a fitting opening to the text: it represents the first of a set of three hymns to the three deities invoked during the successive pressings of the soma plant (the second is to the wind god Vāyu and the third is to the twin Ashvins). With a clarity and simplicity not seen in other such hymns, the first five verses of this opening hymn each begin with variants of the word Agni. I have reproduced a translation of the entire first hymn below, with the first verse written also in the Devanagari script in which authors typically write Sanskrit; transliterated into Roman script and then translated into English, I have underlined the name Agni at the beginning of this first verse (Jamison 88; Doniger 99).[4]

अग्निमीळे पुरोहितं यज्ञस्य देवमृत्विजम् । होतारं रत्नधातमम्॥

agniṃ īḷe purohitaṃ yajñasya devaṃ ṛtvijaṃ । *hotāraṃ ratnadhātamaṃ* ॥

1 I praise Agni, the household priest, the god and priest of the sacrifice, the *hotār* priest, and the keeper of great wealth.
2 Agni earned the prayers of the ancient sages (*rishi*), and of those of the present, too; he will bring the gods here.
3 Through Agni one may win wealth and growth from day to day, glorious and most abounding in heroes.
4 Agni, the sacrificial ritual that you encompass on all sides – only that one goes to the gods.
5 Agni, the priest with the sharp sight of a poet, the true and most brilliant, the god will come with the gods.
6 Whatever good you wish to do for the one who worships you, Agni, through you, O Aṅgiras, that comes true.
7 To you, Agni, who shine upon darkness, we come day after day, bringing our thoughts and homage
8 to you, the king (*rājantam*) of sacrifices, the shining guardian of the Order (*rita*), growing in your own house.
9 Be easy for us to reach, like a father to his son. Abide with us, Agni, for our happiness.

Spoken from the first-person perspective of the poet, this first hymn establishes some of the groundwork for the Vedic worldview, showing us what is important to the poets and their audience. And, appropriately, this verse includes the very first example of multiplicity that communicates Agni's multifarious nature: often referred to as "the seven-tongued one," Agni possesses multiple identities that connect him to nature, to the Vedic ritual, and to its complex priesthood. As the priests bring the gods to mind during their chanting of Vedic mantras, so also Agni brings the gods down from heaven to participate in the earthly sacrifice (v. 2) at the same time that he conveys the offering upwards to the gods in heaven (v. 4). A messenger between humans and the gods, Agni establishes proper relations with, between, and among the three realms of the universe: the earth governed by Agni, the sky by Vayu, and the atmosphere or the middle realm by Indra. This set of three gods will reoccur several more times in Vedic literature where together they represent, as the poets frequently state, "All This" (*idam sarvam*).

More than just focusing on the gods, however, this hymn also highlights the pragmatic benefits bestowed upon those who properly sacrifice. In the final verse of this first hymn of the Rig Veda, the poets highlight the domestic side of Vedic ritual as they request that Agni live with us for our happiness and desire that Agni "be easy for us to reach, like a father to his son" (v. 9). The human beings who perform these rituals do so in order to keep the gods on their side and to acquire all good things: the children, wealth, and long life that people in all cultures seek. The final two verses of this hymn to Agni (vv. 8–9) provide us with a number of Vedic concepts that become staples throughout the post-Vedic Hindu world: royal power ("king of sacrifices"), cosmic order ("shining guardian of the Order"), and creation, family, and fertility (parents and children).

One of the most famous of all Vedic hymns is the Purusha Sukta. This "hymn to the Person," a later hymn that appears in the tenth and final book of the Rig Veda (10.90), brings all of these themes together. Deeply rooted in the culture and ideas of the Vedas, it details the creation of the universe by means of the self-sacrifice of the cosmic Person, as "the ruler of immortality" was bound to a wooden post as a *pashu*, a sacrificial animal. With one thousand heads, eyes, and feet, the Purusha physically encompasses the entire universe, and from his sacrifice the entire universe emerges: the three seasons of the year; the physical and verbal elements of Vedic ritual; the three gods Agni, Vayu, and Indra, who rule the three levels of the universe; and, for the first time in Vedic literature, the components of the later four-*varna* social caste system.[5]

The three main themes of the Vedas – ritual knowledge, royal power, and fertility – are frequently separate and often maintained by a variety of otherwise unrelated deities. Overlapping in complex ways that are sometimes difficult for us to understand, these themes frequently come together in the person of Indra.

Indra, Part 1: the creation of the world

Some later Vedic hymns question what we can precisely know about the earliest moments of the universe and its creator. Describing the primordial elements of darkness, energy, desire, and the waters, the famous Nāsadīya ("non-existence") hymn asserts that human thought is at the core of the universe and questions whether it is possible for us to know how this world came into being. In the hymn's final verse, the poets ask whether even the Overseer of the world knows or does not know (*veda yadi vā na veda*) (10.129.7). The early Vedic tradition is not concerned with telling a single creation story, as does the biblical creation story in the book of Genesis. Rather, the Rig Veda develops its multiplicity by telling a number of stories about various deities who are responsible for different facets of the world's formation.

Indra's creation of the world with the stambha pole represents one part of his larger narrative, as poets elaborate on the related themes of ritual knowledge, royalty, and fertility. Reflecting what little we know of Vedic politics, Indra is the king (*rājan*) of the semi-nomadic Vedic Āryan people who throughout the Rig Veda are composed of a federation of five tribes (*pañcha-janāḥ*). Thus, whereas Agni's royalty in the Rig Veda's first hymn establishes him as a priestly leader of the Vedic sacrificial system, Indra's royalty in these hymns reinforces his identity as a political and military leader who protects his people through the violence of war and his patronage of Vedic priests. Although the human king is often identified as Indra during times of war, he also becomes the god Varuṇa during stable agricultural times and is thus responsible for the maintenance of society via the waters of creation governed by Varuṇa. It is probably for that reason that both Indra and Varuṇa are seen as creating the world in such similar ways. In several hymns of the Rig Veda, these two gods are referred to together and represent one of the most prominent of the Vedic dual divinities (Indra-Varuṇa) (Gonda 1974)..

Despite Indra's precipitous and legendary fall from grace in later Hinduism, more hymns of the Rig Veda are dedicated to him than to any other deity. Stories of Indra, in which he is often referred to as Maghavan (the Beneficent), make up some of the most detailed narrative material in the entire Rig Veda. A hymn detailing Indra's releasing the cows from the cave (3.31) ends with little ambiguity over the identity of Indra and the audience's desire for Indra to protect and remain close to them: "For success in this battle where there are prizes to be won, we will invoke the generous Indra, most manly and brawny, who listens and gives help in combat, who kills enemies and wins riches" (v. 22) (Doniger 154).

Indra is most known, however, for the oft-repeated story of his victory over the serpent deity Vṛtra (the Obstacle), for which he comes to be known as Vṛtrahan (the slayer of Vṛtra). In one of the most famous hymns in all of the Rig Veda (RV 1.32), Indra's powers of creation and destruction are put on full display. Here, his defeat of Vṛtra provides not only a metaphor for the larger and ongoing cosmic struggle between the devas and asuras but also signals Indra's identity as a creator of the world.

1 Now I shall proclaim the heroic deeds of Indra, the first that the mace-wielder performed. He smashed the serpent (*ahan ahiṃ*). He pierced an opening for the waters. He split open the bellies of mountains.

2 He smashed the serpent (*ahan ahiṃ*) who lay upon the mountain; Tvaṣṭar fashioned the roaring club for him. Like lowing milk-cows, the flowing waters rushed straight down to the sea.

3 Wildly excited like a bull, he took the Soma for himself and drank its extract from the three bowls. Indra the Generous [Maghavan] seized his weapon the mace and killed the firstborn of serpents.

4 Indra, when you killed the firstborn of serpents and overcame the magic of the magicians, at that very moment you brought forth the sun, the sky, and dawn. Since then you have found no rival.

5 Indra smashed Vṛtra (*ahan vṛtraṃ*), the greatest obstacle, whose shoulders were spread apart (like a cobra), with his mace, his great weapon. Like the trunk of a tree whose branches have been lopped off by an axe, the serpent lies flat upon the ground.

6 For, like a drunken non-warrior, Vṛtra challenged the great hero who had overcome the mighty and who drank Soma to the dregs. Unable to withstand the onslaught of his weapons, he whose rival was Indra was shattered, his nose crushed.

7 Without feet or hands he fought against Indra, who smashed his mace upon his back. The steer who wished to become the equal of the bull, Vṛtra lay broken in many places.

8 Over him as he lay there like a broken reed the swelling waters flowed for man. Those waters that Vṛtra had enclosed with his power – the serpent now lay at their feet.
9 The strength of Vṛtra's mother ebbed away, for Indra had hurled his weapon at her. Above was the mother, below was the son; Dānu lay down like a milk-cow with her calf.
10 In the midst of the channels of the waters that never stood still or rested, the body sank down. The waters flow over Vṛtra's private parts; the rival of Indra sank into long darkness.
11 The waters stood still. They had the Dāsa as their husband, the serpent as their herdsman, and were imprisoned like the cows imprisoned by the Paṇis. When he killed Vṛtra he uncovered the hollow of the waters that had been covered over.
12 Indra, you became the tail-hair of a horse when Vṛtra struck his fangs at you. You won the cows, great warrior, and you won the cows and Soma; you released the seven streams to flow.
13 The lightning and thunder and fog and hail that Vṛtra had scattered about were useless to him. When Indra and the serpent fought each other, Indra the Generous [Maghavan] remained victorious for all time to come.
14 What avenger of the serpent did you see, Indra, that fear entered your heart when you had killed him and when you crossed the ninety-nine streams [*srvantīḥ*] like the frightened eagle crossing the realms of earth and air?
15 Wielding the mace in his arms [Vajrabāhu], Indra is the king of that which moves and that which rests, of the tame and of the wild. Only he rules over the different peoples as their king [*rājan*], encircling all this as a rim encircles spokes.

Set during the season when Indra wages war against the enemy Dāsas, this hymn narrates a military attack against Vṛtra, a mythological serpent (or "dragon" in some translations) and the husband of the female waters (v. 11). This hymn contains themes and images common to creation hymns found throughout the world, especially across the ancient Near East. In the Babylonian *Enuma Elish* and in various creation stories found in certain passages of the Bible, the god who represents the authors and audience of the hymn slays a demonic and serpentine enemy in an act of violence that results in the release of cosmic waters and the creation of the world. And so it is with this hymn, whose authors repeatedly mention Indra's fundamental act of destruction, twice using the exact same phrase, "He smashed the serpent" (*ahan ahiṃ*), at the beginning of two of the hymn's first three lines and beginning verse 5 with the similar phrase, "He smashed Vṛtra" (*ahan vṛtraṃ*).

The conclusion of this hymn provides a far-reaching metaphor of Indra's kingship. As the *Enuma Elish* narrates how the gods elected Marduk as the king of Babylon after he fulfilled his promise to defeat the female serpent Tiamat, with whose own bloody carcass he created the world in general and Babylon in particular, this Rig Vedic hymn narrates how Indra, too, becomes a model for earthly kings, as the hymn concludes with Indra the king (*rājan*) "encircling all this as a rim encircles spokes" (1.32.15).

The concentric metaphor of the rim encircling its many spokes replicates a number of similar circular structures seen in Vedic and post-Vedic texts and practices. In later narratives and images, the devotional cow-protecting female gopis encircle Krishna in their group *ras lila* dance. In tantric texts, the multiple fierce mother goddesses support the goddess Durgā in battle. These same mother goddesses are represented as smaller wooden poles that surround Indra's pole in his annual festival and in shrines that mark the boundaries of cities in Nepal's Kathmandu Valley. In these stories, performances, and structures, the powerful center of the circle is connected to the hub of the royal palace, reinforcing the traditional focus on royalty.

Indra, Part 2: royalty (*rājan*), Cosmic Order (*rita*), and Truth (*satya*)

The rhetoric of royalty that is integral to literature, ritual, and art throughout Hindu South Asia is first seen in the Vedas. Requesting that the gods attend their rituals and that they pass by the rituals performed by others, Vedic hymns contain the seeds of rivalry and violence that accompany the exercise of power everywhere. This antagonism becomes enshrined in many rituals and festivals that draw on the language of the Vedas.

The late Vedic Mahāvrata festival celebrates the new year with a focus on chariot races and the symbolic destruction of one's enemies with bow and arrow. The Indra festival of the late monsoon season associates the king with Indra who crushes Vṛtra and creates the universe by propping up the sky with a wooden post. The autumnal festival of the goddess Durgā identifies the king with the goddess, who similarly destroys the demonic enemies who threaten the gods in heaven and universal order on earth. And the royal coronation, last performed for King Gyanendra of Nepal in 2001, is suffused with the weapons of war.

The literary if not historical roots of the violent warfare seen in later Hindu narratives might be found in the Battle of the Ten Kings, narrated most fully in RV 7.18. In this hymn, the poet tells the story of King Sudās who achieved victory over an alliance of neighboring kings in northwest India and lauds Indra who, assisting Sudās against his enemies, "split open all their fortified places, their seven strongholds, with his might" (v. 13) (Jamison 904). Sudās appears to signal his military victory with the celebration of yet another royal Vedic ritual, the horse sacrifice (*ashvamedha*). A kingdom-wide festival that celebrates creation and fertility as much as it does royal power, the Indo-European horse sacrifice is developed in great detail (as are most Vedic rituals) in the later ritual texts of the Brāhmaṇas. One passage among the many scattered hymns detailing Sudās's victory in the Rig Veda foreshadows the travel of the victorious king's horse throughout the conquered region: "Release the horse of Sudās, to gain wealth. The king will smash the obstacle to the east, to the west, and to the north. Then he will sacrifice on the best part of the earth" (3.53.11) (Jamison 539).

In the post-Vedic Hindu world, the horse sacrifice remained more important in its rhetoric than in its actual performances. Combining warfare and rivalry with orthodox ritual and animal sacrifice, the power of its symbolism provided a flexible series of metaphors that authors could adapt to their own circumstances. The epic Ramayana tells the story of Indra's theft of King Sagara's horse sacrifice in order to highlight the prominence of the Classical deity Shiva and the veneration of ancestors. The epic Mahabharata narrates an account of the horse sacrifice near its conclusion to prescribe a new form of religious practice (*dharma*) that is rooted in non-violence and donations of food. And the Brihadāraṇyaka Upanishad, a philosophical text of the late Vedic period, reappropriates the elements of the horse sacrifice as a way to reconsider the creation and maintenance of the world.

As might be expected of the Rig Veda, royal power is not just the military power of kings but also the related power of the cosmos itself.[6] The poet's assertion in the first hymn of the Rig Veda that Agni is "the shining guardian of the Order (*rita*)" (1.1.8) posits Agni as responsible for the maintenance of the entire universe. Replaced in later Hindu thought by the term *dharma* that focuses more closely on moral and ethical order, the term *rita* has an expansive semantic range that brings together many facets of the nearly infinitely interlocking pieces of the Vedic religious system. In a sense, the entire text of the Rig Veda is about the maintenance of order on both cosmic and human levels and, especially, the influence of the Vedic sacrifice over the actions of the gods.

In RV 1.33, the hymn that immediately follows Indra's smashing of Vṛtra, Indra breaks open the Vala cave guarded by the Panis and releases the cows. As Indra adjudicates between the warring armies of the Vedic Āryas and the non-sacrificing Dāsas, the hymn's authors focus on the material success of human beings, suggesting that human sacrificers "go up close to Indra, seeking cattle" (1.33.1). Multiplicity is especially rich here, as the cows explicitly reflect the other good things that Indra provides: the donations of cows (*dakshina*) that sacrificers give to priests at the morning pressing of soma, the rays of the morning sun at dawn, and the flames of the sacrificial fire.

Winning these things as frequently with ritual speech as with his vajra weapon, Indra is as much a priest-king as he is a warrior-king. In eradicating the Panis and winning these good things, the poets write of Indra's preferences: "From heaven on high you sent fire burning down on the Dasyu; you favored the recitation of the presser [of soma] and the praiser [of hymns]" (1.33.7b) – whereas the first part of this half-verse praises Indra's military violence, the second lauds the priests who earn these victories for their human patrons. Yet another hymn of the Vala cave connects Indra directly to the priesthood; here in RV 10.108, he is identified as the divine priest, Brihaspati; attended by several bands of poets and priests, Indra, "sharpened by soma," will indeed win the cows (v. 8) (Jamison 1572).

It is through powerful, truthful, and often complex, confusing, and even riddling ritual speech that Order is maintained and the world kept in balance. In the Vala hymn mentioned above, the poet refers to how the seven rishis found the path of Order as they shepherded the cows down the mountain (3.31.5). The poet of the notoriously difficult Riddle Hymn (1.164) relates Order (*rita*) to Speech (Vāch) and then to the ritual fire, musing, "When the first born of Order [Agni] came to me, I won a share of this Speech" (v. 37). And in a hymn to Varuṇa (2.28), the poet addresses this royal deity as "the emperor of Order" who forgives moral fault and relieves fear while also possessing the related powers of healing dropsy (a swelling of the body caused by the accumulation of excess water) and of causing rivers to flow (Doniger 217–218; Jamison 441).

Indra's acts of destruction are meant simultaneously to emphasize his ensuing acts of creation. Numerous images of fertility appear throughout RV 1.32, few more frequent than the cow who provides a crux of the homological system of identifications and equivalences present throughout the Rig Veda (Jamison 120–122). Although the idea of cows as sacred in India is a relatively recent development, marshaled especially by Gandhi during the freedom movement of the twentieth century and continuing with some ecological sustainability movements in the twenty-first century, this hymn shows the more common and specific Hindu notion of the cow as a maternal symbol of fertility. Likening the sound of the cosmic waters rushing down the mountain to the lowing of cattle, verse 2 describes the multiple rivers flowing to meet together. Later devotional Hindu authors will further this image of the multiple (feminine) rivers flowing to meet the single (masculine) ocean. After releasing the waters formerly pent up by the obstructive Vṛtra, Indra then "brought forth the sun, the sky, and the dawn" (v. 4), the latter who is always feminine and often plural. In his deathbed scene, the broken and dying Vṛtra is shown with waters flowing over his "secret place" (v. 10), as he desires to be like Indra, whom the authors liken to a bull, the male counterpart of the cow, and who is "bursting with seed" (v. 7).

Bovine imagery continues throughout the hymns of Indra. Reminding us again of the defeat of female monsters in other creation stories – of Tiamat by Marduk and of Rahab by the biblical God – Indra follows up his victory over Vṛtra with his defeat also of the serpent's mother Dānu whose carcass Indra lays above that of her son, "like a cow with her calf" (v. 9). Aligning the creation of the world with military victory, Indra's defeat of a primal enemy in this hymn further serves as the inspiration for the Vedic king (*rājan*) and his ability to successfully rustle cattle from enemy neighbors. And several accounts of Indra's defeat of the Panis and the release of the cows/waters name Indra as the "lord of cows" (*patir gavām* in 3.31.4; *gavām gopatir* in 10.108.3). His release of the cows is not only the release of the waters but also the creation of the sun, dawn, and fire, a set of links that connects him simultaneously to Agni, the god of fire, and to Soma, the ritual liquid of the Vedic ritual.

Images of water also permeate these early hymns, as they anticipate the significance of water throughout Hinduism – cremations, veneration of ancestors, and ritual bathing, which all occur in sacred rivers such as the Ganges. Culturally significant on a number of different levels, references to the waters that Indra releases through his act of smashing Vṛtra in RV 1.32 simultaneously reinforce the text's themes of fertility. As the cosmic waters (*āpaḥ*) low like cattle when they descend from the mountain, they represent the natural element required for the survival of all plant, animal, and human life and allude to the seasonal monsoon rains (and the threat of their absence) that uniquely provide life to the South Asian subcontinent. The Seven Rivers, as they are referred to in verse 12 (*sapta-sindhūn*), are recognizable on any modern map as the Indus River and its tributaries that flow through the Panjab, crossing what is now the border between India and Pakistan, and represent the earliest homeland of Vedic communities.

Soma: water, goddesses, and fertility

In addition to highlighting water as an important natural element, this hymn to Indra also alludes to water as a metaphor for the Vedic ritual system. The regular references to the waters of creation allude to the liquid offerings of Soma that are produced during Vedic ritual and are referred to on three separate occasions in this hymn. In verse 12, Indra's victory over Vṛtra resulted in him winning cows, Soma, and the Seven Rivers; in verse 6, Indra drank Soma before seizing his vajra and slaying Vṛtra; and verse 3 adds the ritual detail that Indra drank "three bowls" of Soma, referring to the three-day Soma ceremony.[7]

Pressed between two stones, filtered through a cloth, mixed with water or milk, and poured into and drunk from wooden cups uniquely constructed for each priest, the soma juice not only helped Indra to defeat Vṛtra but also enlivens the priests who recite the text.[8] The identity of soma has been much debated and possibly may never be settled upon, with the most common hypotheses suggesting a local mushroom or the stimulant ephedra. That the Vedas themselves allow for many different and ready substitutions signals either the early loss of the identity of the soma plant or the absence of any single botanical substance.

The poets of the Rig Veda use a number of metaphors when writing about soma. As the plant is carried on a small chariot and the juice pressed out three times daily during the rite, Soma is compared to the three-wheeled war chariot of the twin Ashvins. The Vedic texts more frequently use metaphors of fertility and plenty for the drinking of soma. Also connected to the soma rite via the Ashvins are the liquid food offerings of *madhu* (honey) and, in the Pravargya rite, a pot of boiling milk, an object that will occur again in the south Indian Pongal festival to the goddess. These two offerings provide a few of the only clear examples of non-Vedic rites that were later brought into the Vedic ritual system. Due to their independent importance, connections to the Ashvins, and similarities to the offerings of soma juice, the soma rite was seen as the most logical place to incorporate them (Jamison 58, 81).

The Rig Veda makes clear that the Pravargya – and by extension the soma rite – is associated with fertility. Book 7 of the Rig Veda concludes with two Pravargya hymns to Parjanya, the god of rainstorms and thunder whose name soon becomes an epithet of the storm-god Indra. In the first and longer of these two hymns, the poets use the image of the bull as they did for Indra in 1.32; after praying to Parjanya as the bull who inseminates each and every plant, the poet asks that "there be joy-bringing rain for us" and that the plants be "well-berried"

(7.102.5–6). The second and much shorter hymn states simply that Parjanya, who "creates the embryo of the plants, of the cows, of the steeds, and of women," receives the "honeyed" offering the ritualists make (7.103).

Before concluding with a long and somewhat unrelated hymn containing divine requests to punish evildoers, Book 7 includes a rain charm for frogs, where the noisy main characters serve multiple metaphorical functions (7.103). The enlivening of the frogs in the monsoon rains is attributed to Parjanya himself; their repetitive croaking replicates both the sound of the chanting of priests at the soma ritual and the Vedic system of memorization between teachers and students; and the frothy mess of eggs (they are "hundreds of cows") that male and female frogs together create brings to mind "the hot ritual milk-drink" of the Pravargya ritual.

Whatever the source of the soma juice, its effects are not in question. One Vedic author, intoxicated with soma, describes himself as higher than both the five Vedic tribes and the two halves of the world as he praises his own abilities: "I will win a cow and a horse [...] I surpassed the sky and this vast earth [...] I am huge, huge! flying to the cloud [...] carrying the oblation to the gods" (10.119). Each verse of this hymn concludes with the refrain: "Have I drunk of the Soma? Yes!"

The logical extension of the fertility that soma brings, exemplified in the Pravargya rite, prefigures the later Hindu narrative of the fight between Hindu devas and asuras at the beginning of the world over the substance of *amrita*, the purifying elixir of immortality. Cognate with its English translation "immortality," *amrita* resembles the ambrosia drunk by the Greek gods on Mount Olympus. In one key Rig Vedic passage, the author writes, "We have drunk soma and have become immortal. We have gone to the light and found the gods" (8.48.3). Seeking immortality, the Vedic priests and poets come to resemble the victorious Indra who creates the world with his simultaneous use of soma, cows, the waters, and divine ritual speech.

The feminine language and imagery in these hymns of fertility continues throughout the Rig Veda. Several hymns personify ritual recitation and even normal and truthful speech as a woman, one of the few full goddesses in the Rig Vedic pantheon. In 10.71, she is known as Jñānam ("Wisdom," typically pronounced Gyānam) and is praised for her beauty and speech. The primary vehicle for the Vedic chanting of priests during the ritual, she is also known as Vāk or Vāch, from which we get the English word "voice."

Hymn 10.125 begins with a list of many of the groups of Vedic gods who don't retain much of their power after the Vedic period – the fierce Rudras, the solar Vasus and Ādityas, the royal pair Mitra and Varuṇa, Indra and Agni, the twin Ashvins, the artisan Tvaṣṭar, the charioteer Pūshan, and the god of luck Bhaga – before praising Speech as a queen (*rāshtri*, related to *rājan*, king) who, pervading earth and sky, also becomes a creator of the Vedic universe. Described as a goddess through whom people are able to eat, see, breathe, and hear, Speech is established as a requirement not only for the ritual but also for human survival. This hymn points to later philosophical texts, which we will discuss in the following chapter, that argue that Brahman – the male counterpart of the goddess, the priestly speech that calls the universe into existence – represents the very essence of the universe.

Vāch further contributes to the identity of the later Classical goddess Sarasvati. Her name representing a now dried-up tributary of the Indus River, Sarasvati is later closely associated with the god Brahmā who, often also said to be the creator of the world, chants the four Vedas with his four mouths.[9] And it is for this reason that on her festival day in late winter as the spring season approaches, schoolchildren throughout South Asia perform a *puja* ritual to her.

Conclusion

This chapter began by quoting Brian K. Smith's definition of Hinduism: "the religion of those humans who create, perpetuate, and transform traditions with legitimizing reference to the authority of the Veda." One of many definitions that attempts to encompass the entire religious tradition of Hinduism, its focus on the Vedas recognizes the legacy of this most ancient textual and ritual tradition. Some of the more spurious modern applications of the term – Vedic astrology, Vedic mathematics, or Vedic flying machines – represent rhetorical strategies to push the ancient origins of Hinduism even farther back in history. But more authentic components of Vedic culture survive and remain relevant in contemporary Hinduism.

The text of the Rig Veda was transmitted to the West within the setting of the British Empire in India. A complex period in Indian history that lasted nearly two centuries (1757–1947), the empire gradually made itself responsible for the majority of India's legal, political, and economic functions. Much European scholarship on India at that time also greatly benefited from the patronage of the empire, as scholars produced translations of important religious works in order to learn more about the Indian society over which they came to rule.

Drawing on the Orientalist and philological scholarship of such Victorian authors as William Jones from the late 1700s, Max Müller ("kathenotheism") began editing the fifty-volume *Sacred Books of the East* series in 1879. The majority of the texts in this series were translated from Indo-Iranian languages and were part of the Hindu, Buddhist, and Persian Zoroastrian religious traditions of south Asia. (Other translations were made of the Chinese texts of the Daoist and Confucian traditions and of the Qur'an, the central text in Islam.) The attention given to this literature by Western scholars, many of whom saw the roots of Western culture in ancient India, contributed to a complex relationship with Hinduism as it came to be discussed in India. Müller also published a full transcription and English translation of the Rig Veda, the first into any Western language.

As this book uses Hindu deities as a way to think through larger and more complex aspects of Hinduism, we should take note of the transition away from the large and diffuse Vedic pantheon led by Indra, Agni, and Soma. Nearly completely disappearing in the post-Vedic period, the Vedic pantheon still bears the seeds of the forthcoming Classical pantheon; playing small and supportive roles in the Rig Veda, three of the most important deities in Classical and contemporary Hinduism get their start there. Multiple forms of the protective Shiva, Indra's assistant Vishnu, and the goddess Devī will all go on to occupy the natural and cultural roles previously filled by the multitude of Vedic deities outlined in this chapter. These new deities ensure that the very human themes of ritual knowledge, royal power, and fertility carry on. Taking on a multitude of new and different forms, these newly anointed gods and goddesses will come to be venerated as physical and anthropomorphic icons in permanent urban temples and domestic shrines, some of which maintain the presence of a Vedic-style ritual fire.

Authors of the later epic and devotional texts that focus on this new pantheon will use archaic forms of the Sanskrit language that resonate with the authority of the Vedas. They will apply the structure of individual Vedic stories to new content and characters (especially of Indra defeating Vṛtra), they will set new stories within hermitages (*āshrama*) of Vedic study and practice, and they will use the performance of Vedic sacrifice as a literary device to introduce elements of military and spiritual conflict.

Similarly, elements of ritual outside of the Soma rite outlive the end of the Vedic period. Most prominent are the survival of the domestic rituals present in many hymns in Book 10 of the Rig Veda that outline initiation, marriage, and funeral rites. These rites will come to be systematized as a set of rites of passage (*saṃskāra*) that each person will go through in their lifetime. All of these new applications highlight strategies that authors and ritualists have used to ground new communities of Hindu practice in the ancient authority of the Vedas.

Finally, and despite shifts in the ancient Indian economy that spurred changes in Hindu religious performance, the Vedic ritual system has survived intact in some places in the contemporary Hindu world. Among families and communities that have been performing the Vedic rites continuously for centuries, the most famous is that of the Nambudiri brahmins of Kerala in southwest India. At risk of dying out completely, their rites have been studied extensively and their multiday Soma rite represents the core of Frits Staal's 1975 documentary, *Altar of Fire*.[10] Other communities have developed what we might call revivalist performances, performed in India and throughout the Hindu diaspora. Adapting to local cultures by adding devotional songs, public lectures, and other rites that invite general participation, these rites append to traditional Vedic rituals new elements that assist their audience in understanding the content of these rarely performed ancient rituals.

Notes

1 The Sanskrit verb that names Indra's action of separating the worlds (*vi-dhārayan*) is related to the later key Hindu concept of *dharma*.
2 Baltutis 2014 and 2023.
3 Book 15 of the Śaunakīya Atharvaveda Saṃhitā.

4 The translations that I provide here are based on those in Doniger 1981 and Jamison and Brereton 2014, though in consultation with the original Sanskrit I have simplified and clarified them at certain points. I have simplified citations to Jamison and Brereton 2014 as "Jamison [page #]." Brereton and Jamison 2020 offers a more accessible introduction and guide to the Rig Veda.
5 The varna ("color") system represents one of two components of what is often referred to as "the caste system," a complex social system to which we will devote more time in subsequent chapters.
6 The Sanskrit term for king (*rājan*) is linguistically related to the Latin *rex* and the English *regal* and *royal*.
7 Jamison and Brereton 2014 offer a completely different translation here, stating that Indra drank soma among a group of deities, possibly the Marut storm-gods, who are here referred to as the Trikadrukas.
8 The Museum of Sacrificial Utensils in Pune, India, contains a collection of these ritual cups and other Vedic ritual objects.
9 The Indra-Vṛtra hymn uses a similar word here when it describes how Indra flees in fear across "the ninety-nine rivers (*sravantīḥ*)" after slaying Vṛtra (RV 1.32.14).
10 Knipe 2015 represents another study of contemporary Vedic ritual, here in the Godavari River delta in the neighboring state of Andhra Pradesh.

References

Baltutis, Michael. 2023. *The Festival of Indra: Innovation, Archaism, and Revival in a South Asian Performance*. Albany, NY: SUNY Press.

Brereton, Joel and Stephanie Jamison. 2020. *The Rigveda: A Guide*. New York: Oxford University Press.

Doniger, Wendy. 1981. *The Rig Veda: An Anthology*. London: Penguin.

Key terms

Agni, Vayu, Indra
brahman
devas and asuras
rishi
three realms
veda/Vedas

Study questions

1 What roles does Indra play in the early Vedic religion?
2 What themes in the Rig Veda anticipate the later religion of Hinduism? How might these themes change as Indian society moves from rural to urban?
3 How does Vedic religion embody themes of multiplicity?

2 Shiva and *yoga*

Transgression and liberation on the banks of the Ganges River

On April 3, 2015, the Supreme Court of California was presented with a case challenging the practice of eight-limbed Ashtanga Yoga as taught in the Encinitas Union School District. At issue was whether or not this particular brand of yoga, as its teachers were presenting it to kindergarten and elementary public school students, promoted a fundamental component of the Hindu religion. The plaintiffs – parents of children in the district who brought this case to trial – argued that "the yoga program both advances/endorses Hinduism and inhibits/disapproves of other religions, including Christianity." A successful challenge would mean that this yoga program represented a violation of the Establishment Clause of the First Amendment of the constitutions of California and the United States.[1]

Like the issue of *LIFE* magazine with which I opened this book, this court case, whose final judgment I will return to at the end of this chapter, reiterates similar basic issues in the Western understanding of Hinduism and of religion in general: What is (and is not) Hinduism? How does Hinduism change as its practices and those who practice it move out of India and into a religiously pluralistic nation such as the United States? And how might Hinduism point out certain flaws with the ways that we think about religion? In other words, what *is* this thing called Hinduism?

This chapter will consider the god Shiva, the central Hindu deity associated with yoga. Tracing his presence from late Vedic texts, to the earliest Hindu philosophical treatises of the Upanishads, and through later devotional literature and practice, this chapter will detail Shiva's engagement with the earliest forms of what these authors flexibly refer to as yoga. To be more clear, however, it is actually the *disengagement* of Shiva and of those who follow him that defines their presence in and their desired exit from the world in which we live.

This disengagement from the world defines much of yoga. Like ascetic traditions found throughout the world's religions, yoga constitutes a discipline or training of the mind and body towards a spiritual goal. Incorporating techniques of meditation that restrain one's senses from the outside world, that renounce the world's fleeting pleasures, and that violate standard ethical and cultural boundaries, yoga, like many forms of monastic Buddhism, represents a body of thought and practice by which a person seeks ultimate liberation from this world of suffering.

DOI: 10.4324/9781003475033-3

The word *yoga* is as flexible as the many practices that fall within this category. The Three Paths (*trimārga*) of Action, Knowledge, and Devotion that we saw in the introduction to this book and that we will use as a general framework for the Hindu tradition as a whole are sometimes referred to as the Three Yogas. For example, the Path of Action is referred to both by the term *karma-mārga* as well as *karma-yoga*. An additional fourth yoga can be added to this trifecta, the *rāja-yoga* of Patanjali's eight-part system that is connected both to tantra, a system of power often related to the worship of Hindu goddesses, as well as to the Postural and Meditational techniques of modern yoga.

The term *yoga* is also related to the English word "yoke," meaning "to join." Techniques of yoga connect one to the divine, though the texts often offer multiple interpretations, or none at all, of how this term might be applied. The word yoga also functions similarly to "religion"; related to the word "ligament," "religion" is a word that essentially means to "re-join" and often communicates similar human and divine connections. It is for these linguistic and other religious reasons that the California yoga case cannot be summarily dismissed and why it reached all the way to the state Supreme Court.

> This chapter will use the common Sanskrit adjective "Shaiva" to refer to texts, images, and practices that refer to Shiva. Similarly, subsequent chapters will use the terms "Vaishnava" to refer to religious elements related to Vishnu and "Shākta" for those related to forms of the goddess, Shakti.

Shiva and Ganesh

To understand the place of Shiva, renunciation, and yoga within a larger Hindu culture, we will begin with a story. Complex and somewhat shocking to an audience not raised in the Hindu tradition, the well-known story of how Shiva's son, Ganesh, obtained his elephant head introduces a number of key interlocking facets of the Hindu tradition (Figure 2.1).

Desiring the privacy for her morning bath that her husband Shiva regularly denies her, Parvati creates a young boy from the dirt of her body. Unaware of who this boy is guarding the doorway, Shiva threatens and quickly beheads his wife's son. Seeing her decapitated son, Parvati demands that her husband revive him. Entering the forest with his army of ghosts and ghouls, Shiva beheads the first animal he sees – an elephant – and fulfills his promise to his wife: he brings her son back to life by placing the elephant head atop the boy's body.[2] Popular poster-art images of the entire family adorn houses and temples ignoring this background tension, as most family portraits do, showing the family as living happily ever after, which they do.

Ganesh's story helps us understand the many dynamic complexities within the figure of Shiva. The name Ganesh identifies him literally as "the *īsha* of the *gaṇa*," or what might be translated as "the lord of the gang" (Figure 2.2). This

Figure 2.1 Wall painting of Ganesh. Varanasi, India

Figure 2.2 Ganesh as leader of the gana, at the foot of a statue of Shiva and Parvati. Kathmandu, Nepal

name is a nod to his father who is frequently shown leading a gang of terrifying ghosts, ghouls, and vampires, such as those who accompanied him to the forest and beheaded the elephant. In a different story that picks up on themes similar to those in Ganesh's story, Shiva's father-in-law Daksha invited everybody but Shiva to his Vedic sacrifice, afraid that Shiva would also invite his unruly gang. Incensed with being shut out yet again, Shiva decapitated Daksha – his wife Parvati's father – eventually replacing his severed head with that of a goat.

Stories of beheadings abound in Hindu literature. Rama beheads the demon Ravana in the culminating victorious moment in the classical epic Ramayana; the goddess Chinnamastā cuts off her own head as a tantric blessing and offering to her devotees; and stories of Bhairav, a fierce form of Shiva, frequently involve acts of decapitation and re-capitation, stories often celebrated with temple displays of only Bhairav's head, mask, and crown of skulls. Such stories stretch all the way back to the Vedic ritual, where the head (real or symbolic) symbolized "a treasure or secret that is the essence of the universe," and the acquisition of the head signals victory to those who possess it (Heesterman 1985: 47).

The many dynamic forces involved in Ganesh's story point us towards the first of many fundamental oppositions held in tension throughout the developing Hindu tradition. The battle for the essence of the universe in the form of the boy's severed head operates against the background of a domestic disagreement between husband and wife. Synthesized in later texts on proper dharma, the tension between the domestic householder and the yogic renouncer will remain fundamental to Shiva's identity. Remaining on the boundary between domesticity and danger, Shiva forever embodies this opposition, simultaneously holding within himself the identities of householder and renouncer and forever providing a place for those who reside on the margins of the Hindu tradition.

Before detailing the complex figure of Shiva, it is helpful to know how the elephant-headed Ganesh continues to be worshipped. One of the more popular forms of Ganesh worship is in the western state of Maharashtra, especially in the cities of Mumbai and Pune. In the 1890s, the political activist Lokmanya Tilak revived the largely domestic Ganesh Chaturthi festival as a response to a British ban on political gatherings. Desiring to unite Indians, and especially all Hindus, in opposition to British colonial rule, Tilak cultivated the public festival seen today. Focusing on massive unfired clay images of Ganesh displayed and paraded throughout the city, the festival ends with their mass *visarjan*, their collective disposal in a nearby body of water. Hardly a god for those on the margins, Ganesh stands squarely in the center of this festival, becoming, as Tilak proposed, a "god for all people."

Shiva as the fierce Rudra and Bhairav

Shiva embodies the structural opposition of householder and renouncer, leading author Wendy Doniger to refer to him as the "erotic ascetic." Performing yoga and meditation high in the Himalayan mountains distant from human habitation, Shiva provides a model for intensely devoted followers who similarly seek to renounce the world and attain enlightenment (*moksha*). At the same time, however, Shiva is also a husband and father. While regularly appearing with the *damaru* drum of creation and destruction, numerous serpents on his body, the Ganges River in his hair, and his begging bowl and walking stick identifying him as a renouncer, he meditates on Mount Kailash alongside his wife Parvati, their children Ganesh and Skanda, and all of their numerous animals: Shiva's bull Nandi, Parvati's lion, Ganesh's mouse Mushaka, and Skanda's peacock.

As in all examples of multiplicity, Hindu authors and artists highlight rather than obscure the significance of this opposition. Emphasizing both the householder tradition that focuses on fertility, family life, and the maintenance of the ancestors, as well as the renouncer tradition that rejects domestic life in favor of the spiritual, Shiva embodies the tension within and reciprocity between these two fundamentally opposed lifestyles.

This tension is reinforced by a number of other stories of Shiva depicted in posters and icons often seen in Hindu homes and temples and, frequently, in art museums throughout the world. For example, the famous tenth-century bronze statues sponsored by the Chola kingdom in south India depict Shiva as the King of Dance (Naṭrāj). An image with many meanings, Shiva's Tandava dance creates the world as it destroys the demonic obstacles depicted underneath his feet, while it also highlights the significance of the performative arts in South Asia.[3]

In the creation story of the Churning of the Cosmic Ocean (*samudra manthana*), the gods and demons compete for the vessel of immortality (*amrita*). One of fourteen objects generated from their tug-of-war contest that resembles the churning of the Vedic ritual fire, this vessel (*kumbha*) is celebrated at the Kumbha Mela, one of the largest festivals in the entire world. Before one of these fourteen items, the black Halāhala poison, could completely destroy both gods and demons, Shiva drinks it, causing his throat to turn black and earning him the moniker of Nīlakaṇṭh (Black-Throat).

As the Destroyer of the Triple City, Shiva invokes all the gods into his chariot and bow and arrow and, along with his band of ghouls, destroys the demons who attempted to attain immortality. Finally, and in a story similar to the beheadings of Ganesh and Daksha, Shiva castrates himself in response to a variety of challenges by the Seven Sages in the Himalayan Pine Forest. More than old myths that are occasionally remembered and retold, these stories continue to be ritualized in grueling pilgrimages to the mountain headwaters of Himalayan rivers and in temple veneration of the combined linga-yoni that represent the joining of the male and female principles of creation (Figure 2.3).

Shiva's identity as a cultural outsider begins in several hymns of the Rig Veda that describe the deity Rudra "the Howler" as both a violent warrior as well as a gentle healer (TS 2.33). The *Shrī Rudra* passage of the *Taittirīya Saṁhitā* (TS) of the Yajur Veda praises Rudra as a protector amidst descriptions of the construction of the brick altars for the Vedic fire ritual. Greeted with a *namaste* as the author seeks the deity's blessings, Rudra, though clearly terrifying, is described throughout as both *aghora* "not dreadful" and as *shiva* "gentle." It is this second description that becomes personified in the classical and equally

Figure 2.3 The combined linga-yoni at the entrance of shrine of the goddess Kali. Bhaktapur, Nepal

complex deity of the same name. The first three lines of this section's long first verse read as follows:

> Namaste, Rudra, to your wrath, and your arrow I also honor. Namaste to your bow, and your two arms I also honor. With your most gentle arrow and bow and with your gentle missile, have mercy upon us, O Rudra. That body of yours, Rudra, is gentle, not dreadful, and has an auspicious appearance. With that body, most potent to heal, O haunter of the mountains, please look upon us.
>
> (TS 4.5.1)

A few verses later, the text includes a long *nāmāvalī* for Rudra, one of the earliest such lists of names that lauds a deity for their distinctive physical and behavioral characteristics.

> Namaste to Bhava and to Rudra. Namaste to Sharva the warrior and to Pashupati the lord of cattle. Namaste to the black-throated one, and to the white-throated. Namaste to the wearer of braids, and to him of shaven hair.
>
> (TS 4.5.5)

Many of the names in these passages, seen also in the Vedic hymn to the wandering gang of vrātyas, will become standard in later stories of Shiva. He is black-throated because of the deadly poison that he drank at the churning of the cosmic ocean; his unkempt hair reflects a renouncer's lack of attention to their own physical appearance; and the rest houses and cremation grounds at the Pashupatinath Temple in Kathmandu represent one of the most popular gathering spots for renouncers – often called *aghora* – during the Shivratri festival in early spring (Figure 2.4).

The text concludes with a long request for Rudra to be merciful:

> Your gentle form, Rudra, is gentle and healing. With the auspicious and healing form of Rudra, show mercy on us for life. This thought we offer up to the strong Rudra, him with plaited hair, the destroyer of warriors: "Let our bipeds and quadrupeds be healthy, and let all in this village be prosperous and free from ill. Be merciful to us, O Rudra, and give us delight; with honor let us worship you, destroyer of warriors. The health

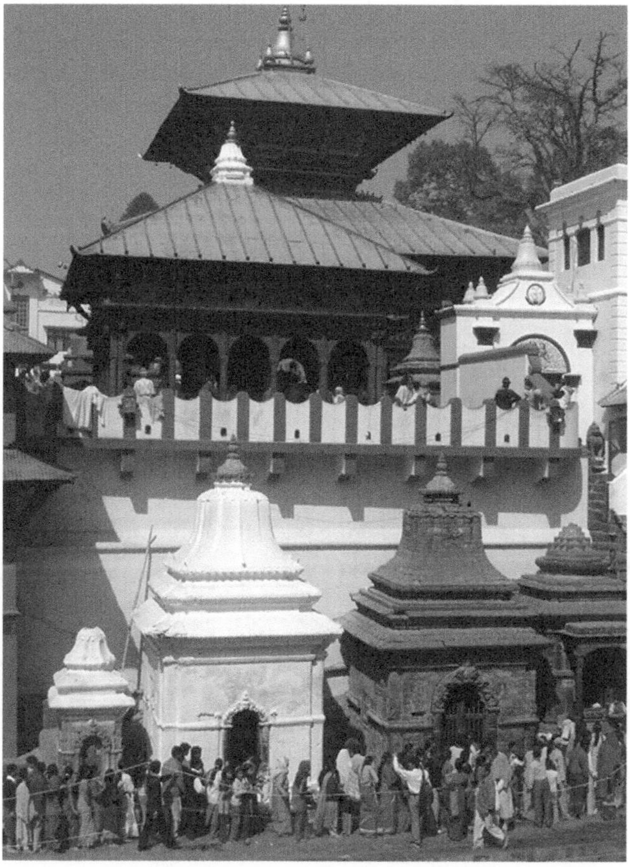

Figure 2.4 Men and women line up to enter the Pashupatinath temple during the Shiv Ratri festival. Kathmandu, Nepal

> and wealth that father Manu won by sacrifice: May we attain that, Rudra, under your leadership."
>
> (TS 4.5.10)

This early form of Shiva already begins to combine multiple physical and behavioral traits. More than just a renouncer who lives in the cremation grounds or atop the mountains outside of society, he also has the power to bless animals and to give life, health, and prosperity.

The fierce Vedic Rudra appears throughout the later Hindu tradition not only as Shiva but also in the form of the equally fierce Bhairav. The "ideal of transgressive sacrality," as one author refers to him, Bhairav crosses the boundary between gentle and haunting (Erndl 1989: 247). A deity of the cremation ground who appears as early as the fifth century CE and is displayed in masks and full-bodied forms throughout South Asia, Bhairav appears both as an assistant of goddesses and as a solitary deity in his own right.

Take a moment to look at the image of Bhairav in Figure 2.5 and think about what you see. This approximately one-foot-tall statue of Pachali Bhairav sits in a niche on the back side of his temple in the village of Pharping in the southern part of Nepal's Kathmandu Valley. Similar to literally hundreds of other images of Bhairav installed in shrines and temples throughout South Asia, his appearance might lead us to ask questions that are inevitably filtered through Western categories: "Is he good or evil? Is he a god or a demon? Will he bring damnation or salvation?" Embracing the concept of

Figure 2.5 Pachali Bhairav in the back niche of his temple. Pharping, Nepal

multiplicity and simply answering "Yes!" to each of these questions, we come to see Bhairav much like the Vodou *lwa* Ogou who is "defined by contradiction" and who "contains his own paradoxes of personality, which are teased out in possession-performance and in song" (97).

Connected to the temple in Pharping where he is regarded as an early local king, Pachali Bhairav is also celebrated at another temple some twenty miles north in Kathmandu. Located near the cremation grounds on the banks where the Vishnumati and Bagmati Rivers meet, his shrine serves as the starting point of his autumnal festival that overlaps with the ten-day festival to the equally fierce goddess Durga. Along with his brother Ganesh and the royal goddess Taleju, Bhairav possesses local elders of the community who walk in a grand procession while carrying icons of all three deities. Following another Bhairav who takes the common form of a festival beer pot, the three gods and the local community walk north through the city and end their procession at the city's central royal palace where a buffalo is sacrificed in full view of the public and of the living goddess Kumari, embodied in the form of a young girl.

Bhairav can also be worshipped more privately and sedately. The text of the *Shrī Bhairav Chālīsā* ("The Forty Verses of the Glorious Bhairav") is one of many such short texts devoted to one of many deities. Cheaply available at temple shops and written in an accessible mix of classical Sanskrit and conversational Hindi, the text opens with an acknowledgment of Bhairav's complexity:

shrī bhairav saṅkaṭ haraṇ maṅgal karaṇ kṛpāl |
shyām varaṇ vikarāl vapu lochan lāl viśāl ||

The glorious Bhairav removes all harm and mercifully provides us with blessings. His body bears a horrible black complexion, while his red eyes are large and beautiful.

The rhyming scheme of this passage (*saṅkaṭ haraṇ* | *maṅgal karaṇ*) reflects a common thread throughout this text that regularly juxtaposes his fierce destructiveness with his protective goodness. Elsewhere, this text refers to Bhairav as the "king of ghosts" (*bhūtoṁ ke rājā*), the "protector of the city of Varanasi" (*kāśī kā kotvāl*), and "the lord who is dear to his devotees" (*nāth bhaktan ke ati ho pyāre*).[4] Whether in recordings of this recitation on social media or in local festivals in Nepal, the fierce Bhairav is represented as a deity to whom people pray for protection from obstacles rather than as a demon they fear.

Bhairav's association with death reflects a key trait for renouncers who follow the lead of Shiva. Living in cremation grounds, covering themselves in ash, and performing their own funeral as a transitional rite of passage, renouncers embody the boundary-crossing nature of Shiva, Rudra, and Bhairav. At the same time, socially, they perform the dangerous work that separates themselves from the standard social, economic, and sexual life of the householder, as they seek to acquire the *tapas* (ascetic heat-energy) that fuels their practice. In this next section, we will see how the classical texts of the Upanishads establish the philosophical core that supports the culture of Hindu renunciation, as these texts begin to establish Shiva as "the eternal spirit which the Hindus usually call Brahman."

The Upanishads

Hinduism has long negotiated its place in India with the many other religions practiced there: Christianity in the south, Islam and Sikhism in the north, and Judaism and Zoroastrianism in the west. Like these other religions, Hinduism is always changing and developing, as it adapts to and incorporates material from its religious neighbors.[5]

Among the many forms of Shiva – fierce warrior, gentle healer, and family man – it is his identity as a renouncer residing on the outskirts of society that most informs the next historical phase of Hinduism. Appearing in the texts of the Upanishads and related most closely to the person of Shiva, the concepts and practices of renunciation represent a significant element also at the core of the contemporary traditions of Buddhism and Jainism.

Unlike the many traditions mentioned above whose historical roots lie outside of India (Christianity) or that are relatively recent (Sikhism), the three traditions of Hinduism, Buddhism, and Jainism grew up together in the fifth century BCE in a north Indian urban environment, around the city of Varanasi on the Ganges River. Here, authors and thinkers reformulated the authority of Vedic ritual and its rural background, as they engaged in conversation with, selectively borrowed from, and translated and critiqued the doctrines, practices, and lifestyles of the others. Engaging also with other religious and philosophical positions that did not survive, they laid the foundations for the complex Hindu, Buddhist, and Jain traditions that would soon diverge from one another, even though they would continue to share and debate their respective versions of yoga, tantra, and devotion.

The complex relationships among Hinduism, Buddhism, and Jainism can be seen in many ways. They share a core terminology. Within their shared languages are the key terms of *dāna* (donation), the ritual gifts given to temple icons via their officiating priests; the site of the *āshrama* (monastery) where monks lived and worked; and the *ahiṃsā* (non-violence) central especially to the Jain tradition advocated by Mahatma Gandhi who protested the violent tactics of the British Empire in twentieth-century India. Hindu thinkers also had to reckon with the term *dharma* (religious ethics, message, and practice), which Buddhists came to use to represent their entire tradition – "the Dharma" – a concept that will sit at the core of the following chapter.[6]

The historical relationships between these South Asian religions can also be seen in their material cultures. The contemporary Newar religion of Nepal's Kathmandu Valley displays a hybrid culture through its displays of Hindu and Buddhist icons, temples, and festivals literally side by side in the city streets, obscuring the religious distinctions that we in the West too strictly insist upon.

Moreover, the picturesque cave temples of Ellora carved from volcanic hills of western India display this same intercultural dynamic. Beginning with a series of Buddhist monastic complexes with large icons of the Buddha as their meditational focus, the caves conclude near the end of the first millennium with the construction of a set of equally impressive Jain temples. At Ellora's very center is the magnificent monolithic Mount Kailash, a massive Hindu temple that replicates the Himalayan mountain where Shiva and Parvati reside. The fulcrum of the Ellora complex, Mount Kailash presents Hinduism not as the oldest religion of South Asia but as one part of its ongoing and ever-changing religious history. And it does this through the complex figure of Shiva who appears as both a transcendent renouncer and a domestic householder who achieves *moksha*, the goal of the Upanishads, through the proper techniques of *yoga* and *sannyāsa* (renunciation).

A core of approximately a dozen Upanishads were composed beginning in the seventh century BCE, thus some two centuries before the life of the Buddha. Concluding the Vedic canon, these texts are written in the form of dialogues between teachers and students and detail a number of *upanishad*s, the secret teachings after which the texts are named and that describe the ultimate connections among the interrelated components of the universe. These connections frequently center on the *ātman*, a term variously used to name one's physical body and the animating breath(s) within it. A proper understanding of these connections results in the journey of one's *ātman* – ultimately, one's eternal soul – through the cycle of reincarnation, the innovative understanding of life after death that the Upanishads introduce.

The Upanishads' reformulation of Vedic authority might be summarized with the word *karma*. Considering the root meaning of the term *karma* (cognate with the English word "creation" and most basically translated as "action"), the texts translate the proper performance of precise ritual action to the proper knowledge of that ritual. Detailed in the Chandogya Upanishad, the Doctrine of the Five Fires uses the imagery of Vedic ritual to teach this lesson. As with many older Vedic elements, the five Vedic fires are here reinterpreted as the world, rainclouds, earth, man, and woman, while the author re-identifies the constituent parts of each. For the first fire, the world, for example,

> Its firewood is the sun; its smoke is the sunbeams; its flame is the day; its embers are the moon; and its sparks are the constellations. In that very fire gods offer faith, and from that offering springs King Soma.
>
> (5.4)

Immediately after this reinterpretation of the Vedic ritual, the text details the three possible paths of the atman, based on one's proper ethical behavior (also *karma*). Some become tiny creatures who are endlessly reborn; some embark upon the temporary path to the ancestors, some of whom have a pleasant rebirth while others enter a foul womb; and still others follow the permanent path to the gods (5.10). This path to the gods is presented as the best option as it concludes with the atman's identity with the universal Brahman.

We encountered the term *brahman* in our discussion of Vedic ritual in the previous chapter, where the term names the priest who oversees the speech of the priests throughout the entire ritual: "Thus, the *brahman* oversees the *brahmins* who speak *brahman*." The use of the term *brahman* in the Upanishads continues these applications by abstractly personifying the verbal power of the Vedic priest as the universal impersonal principle by whom the entire world operates.

The Chandogya Upanishad uses a series of analogies to make more concrete this abstract principle. In a dialogue that is meant to establish the limits of ancient Vedic ritual, Uddalaka challenges his son Shvetaketu, who just returned from twelve years studying with his teacher, to show him how little he actually learned. Among a range of metaphors that includes many rivers merging into the ocean, the collective nectar gathered by bees, and the empty space inside the seed that grows into the great banyan tree, Uddalaka illustrates the *ātman* as the essence that resides at a person's core. He concludes each of these examples by telling his son, with one of the great *mahāvākya* ("great sayings") of the Upanishads: *tat tvam asi* – "You are that."[7]

The brief Mandukya Upanishad introduces a concise variant of multiplicity that connects a series of relevant philosophical concepts. It begins with the twin assertion that the universal brahman and the meditational syllable AUM are each the entire world and the identity of atman and brahman. The text then analyzes the three constituent parts of the syllable ॐ AUM (A, U, and M) as it uses a 3+1=4 formula seen throughout the tradition, where a set of four components is analyzed into two parts: the first three represent parts of a composite and standard whole with the fourth introducing an element that transcends and troubles that composite whole. (In the next chapter, we will see this troubled formula in two related elements of dharma.) The fourth and final component of the syllable is "the soundless and auspicious (*shiva*) aspect" beyond the spoken syllable. Unpronounceable, this silent component is "not comprehended through the senses or by the mind" and points to the transcendent ideal of *moksha*. The Mandukya then equates the AUM syllable both with the three times (past, present, and future) and the time beyond as well as with the four states of consciousness. Beyond waking, sleeping, and dreaming, the Mandukya asserts a mysterious fourth state beyond that is "the real and true Self," knowledge of which allows practitioners to "enter the Self via the self."

The knowledge of this mysterious fourth element provides both a continuity with and a break from the earlier Vedic tradition. Whereas Vedic ritual texts stressed the ritual drinking of soma as the primary strategy for achieving immortality – "We drank *soma* and we became immortal" *apāṁ somaṁ amṛtā abhūma* (RV 8.48.3) – the Upanishads repeatedly emphasize instead the proper knowledge of atman and brahman.[8]

Among the many Upanishads that discuss this proper knowledge as the path to immortality, the Kena Upanishad asks the question, "By Whom (*kena*?) are the world and its people able to properly function?" It answers this question by naming brahman: "It is the Ear of the ear, the Mind of the mind, the Speech of speech, the Breath of breath, and the Eye of the eye." Describing the path and goal of the renouncers who understand their identity with *brahman*, this verse concludes with: "The wise ones, having renounced and gone forth from the world, become Immortals" (*atimuchya dhīrāḥ pretyasmāllokāt amṛtā bhavanti*) (1.2).[9] Using words that grammatically resonate with the Sanskrit *moksha* (*muchya*, spiritual liberation), *dharma* (*dhīrāḥ*, to meditate), and *preta* (*pretya*, ghostly spirits), this introductory passage describes the difficult spiritual path that renouncers travel in order to achieve complete transcendence of the physical world.

The Kena continues by asserting only the contingent, temporary, and dependent power of the Vedic pantheon. It particularly addresses Agni, Vayu, and Indra, the three gods who represent the three components of the Vedic universe: earth, sky, and middle realm, respectively. The text narrates how the three gods fail a test administered by an unknown force to burn, blow away, and possibly destroy a single blade of grass – the third episode involving Indra is interrupted before his test is accepted. Immediately after Indra's failure, the text introduces, surprisingly but appropriately, the figure of Umā (Pārvatī). Daughter of the mountain and wife of Shiva, Umā addresses Indra directly, reminding him that it is only through brahman that he possesses any divine power whatsoever.

The teacher in the text's framing narrative concludes the text with an assertion of its secret *upanishad*, which resembles the Doctrine of the Five Fires:

> Of the *upanishad*, austerities (*tapas*), self-restraint, and sacrificial rites (*karma*) are the foundation, the Vedas are the limbs, and truth is the abode. Whoever knows this (*ya evam veda*) *upanishad* shakes off all sins and becomes firmly established in the infinite and the highest Heaven, yea, the highest Heaven.
>
> (4.8–9)

Schools of renunciation and devotion

The model of education often referred to in the Upanishads is that of the *guru–shishya* relationship, where a single male student (*shishya*) lives with his married male teacher (*guru*). Upon completing his studies of at least one of the four Vedic texts, the student then continues on to himself become either a householder or a renouncer. In some cases, students establish their own *sampradāya*, a tradition or school of thought over which they now serve as guru. Although sectarian affiliation is hardly a requirement for Hindu practice, Hindu communities have long organized themselves into these *sampradaya* schools. Influenced by the non-dualism (*advaita*) of the Upanishads, Shaiva renouncers have long practiced within schools that have as their goal the attainment of complete identity with the divine other.

Among the many Shaiva *sampradaya* within which ascetics have lived and worked, several are worthy of closer attention. Established by their guru Gorakhnāth in the thirteenth century, the Kānphaṭa or Nāth yogis once had a strong presence throughout South Asia. Physically defined by their pierced ears (*kān phaṭa*), Nāth yogis attend the Shivratri festival, especially in Kathmandu, Nepal. This festival is celebrated at the Pashupatinath Temple on the banks of the Bagmati River and refers to "the Great Night of Shiva." As the story goes, this festival recalls a tribal hunter from Varanasi who, traveling deep into the jungle, climbed a bel tree fearing for his life. Sleeping in the tree overnight, he pleased Shiva by fasting all night and by dropping leaves and shedding tears that fell onto a Shiva linga below. Although his linga was venerated by accident, Shiva still accepted the hunter's actions as those of deep devotion.

Some of the most well-known Shaiva schools derive their names from characteristics or names of Shiva: the Kāpālika, from the skullcap bowl that renouncers and fierce forms of Shiva carry as a begging bowl; Pāshupata, from Shiva as "lord of beasts"; and Aghori, referring to his "not dreadful" epithet throughout Shaiva literature.

Like most yogis, those who attend Kathmandu's Shivratri festival take on certain physical characteristics in emulation of Shiva: their hair is worn in dreadlocks piled atop their heads; they wear strings of rudraksha beads around their necks; they wear the Shaiva sectarian mark of three horizontal lines across their forehead; and they smoke marijuana from their chillum pipe in order to attain mystical union and immortality as part of Shiva's gang. Their emulation of Shiva inspires many (young male) householders to temporarily become a part of Shiva's gang, communing with his human representatives, most directly by sharing a smoke from their chillum. Finally, the location of the festival within sight of the cremation grounds at the Pashupatinath Temple reinforces the tendency of some renouncers to take their initiation and reside in the cremation grounds, especially at the Manikarnika Ghat on the Ganges River in Varanasi.

The strictly non-dual school of Advaita Vedanta, with the eighth-century philosopher Adi Shankaracharya (Shankara) as its founding guru, has had a major influence on Hinduism as a whole. The Dashanami sampradaya founded by Shankara represents a powerful organization with monasteries (*maṭh*) throughout India whose troupes of resident naked ascetics (*nāga akhāṛā*) represent some of the most prominent and photogenic figures at the Kumbha Mela festival. Shankara's commentaries on the Upanishads have also come to shape the ways that these texts are commonly read, namely that all Upanishads support the identity of atman and brahman. We must keep in mind, however, that the lessons and goals of the Upanishads, having been written over the course of centuries by authors from different Vedic schools located across India, are various.

The easiest place to see this diversity of perspectives is in the theistic viewpoints of several later Upanishads. These texts clearly show the influence of Shaiva devotional schools that advocate an emotional longing for a divinity who personifies the universal nature of the abstract brahman. Whereas several Upanishads use the general term *deva* ("a god") to refer to the singular universal brahman, the Shvetāshvatara Upanishad in particular clearly develops early Shaiva devotional tendencies. Using the name Maheshvara, a common epithet of Shiva, we are to venerate brahman as "the Great Lord (Maheshvara) among lords, the supreme god among gods, the highest master among masters, the god beyond the highest, and the lord of the world" (6.7).

This text concludes by asserting that one should show complete *bhakti* (devotion) to the god, as one should also show to their guru (6.23). This attitude of devotion to a semi-personified brahman who bears the names of Shiva shows the complexity of the larger Hindu tradition by blurring the lines between the paths of Action, Knowledge, and Devotion. Even beyond the schools of ascetics who seek refuge in Shiva the renouncer, other Shaiva schools are more significantly devotional in nature, their rich literary history ensuring their survival into the present day. Echoing philosophical themes from the Upanishads and the ascetic dissatisfaction with the world, poets and ritualists within these schools speak of divinity in devotional and dualistic (*dvaita*) terms that highlight a fundamental separation between the deity and the devotee who desires to be one with Shiva.

The Shaiva Siddhanta school draws on the literature of the sixty-three Nāyaṉmār devotees of Tamil south India. Marking the beginning of this tradition is Kāraikkāl Ammaiyār (550 CE), a female saint whose devotional poetry describes Shiva in many ways we have already seen: he is the Bearer of the Ganges River, the cosmic Dancer, the Drinker of Poison, and Destroyer of the Triple City. Following her miraculous reception of a sweet mango from Shiva that so frightened her husband to the point that he abandoned her, she sought to renounce all connections to her broken domestic world and to join Shiva and his gang. Drawing on his many names and stories, she fixates on Shiva and addresses him as the

> lord who eternally dances
> in that wide cremation ground,
> attended by ghouls singing with powerful voices
> and goblins worshipping your ankleted feet.
> (Pechilis 2012: 62) ("Garland" v. 15)

Despite the occasional disgust she expresses towards the ghouls "who gorge gleefully on the corpses to their hearts' content" (Pechilis: 71, v. 2), she approaches her lord in the cremation ground and revels in her successful transformation:

> Should I attain a blessed view
> of his highest form,

I would not wish for anything else
even if I was entitled;
the lord with the third eye
has granted me some knowledge
and I have joined his loyal band of ghouls (*pēy*).[10]
(Pechilis 2014: 66) ("Wonder" v. 86)

Although not counted among the Nāyaṉmārs who are frequently depicted in statues in south Indian temples, the ninth-century poet Manikkavachakar remains a popular Shaiva devotional poet. His 400-verse *Tirukkovaiyar* was instrumental in establishing this early Shaiva devotional theme. The poet names Shiva as the patron of his poems, with each composed as a tribute to Shiva along with his beloved wife-goddess, Umā, as they travel throughout the many south Indian landscapes named and described throughout. Blurring the boundaries between poetry of romantic love and theistic devotion, as such poets often do, Manikkavachakar writes of the object of his affection:

I will make her understand that the bright spear-like eyes cause me to suffer
like devotees who are denied the chance to contemplate
the lord who dances
with red matted locks
lit by a lovely slice of the moon.
(Comeau 2020a: 27)

Another school is the Vīrashaiva ("strict followers of Shiva") whose poets wrote nearby to the Nāyaṉmārs in the contemporary south Indian state of Karnataka. Also known as the Lingayats for the mark of Shiva that they wear around their necks, Vīrashaivas began writing their devotional poetry to Shiva in the tenth century. The many poets of this school used a variety of names for Shiva to describe the many facets of his character. Basavaṇṇa refers to him as "Lord of the Sangam," echoing the significance of the confluence of two or more rivers; for most Hindus, the most significant sangam is the one at Allahabad/Prayagraj where the Ganges and Yamuna rivers meet together with the mythical Sarasvati River and where the Kumbha Mela festival is celebrated. The female Mahādēviyakka refers to Shiva as the "Lord White as Jasmine." And Allama Prabhu calls Shiva the "Lord of Caves," highlighting the importance of interior secrecy and the transformation of the self.

This focus on the internal runs throughout the work of the Virashaiva poets. Protesting against the superficiality of external rituals and symbolism, they desire instead the immediacy of Shiva, which they express through the common devotional language of separation and intimacy. For example, Basavaṇṇa asks:

Why why did you bring me to birth
wretch in this world,
exile from the other?
(Ramanujan 1973: 71)

In another poem, he describes his intimacy with Shiva like that of a mother with her child:

> As a mother runs
> close behind her child
> with his hand on a cobra
> or a fire,
> the lord of the meeting rivers
> stays with me
> every step of the way
> and looks after me.
> (Ramanujan 1973: 71)

Written, read, and performed as a means of protest by the lower classes against upper-caste and upper-class orthodoxy, this poetry still maintains its connection with the long tradition of non-dualism beginning in the Upanishads. For Mahādēviyakka, for example, Shiva is

> Like
> treasure hidden in the ground
> taste in the fruit
> gold in the rock
> oil in the seed
> (Ramanujan 1973: 115)

For comparison, the Shvetāshvatara Upanishad refers to Shiva/brahman as "the one god hidden in all beings," using the Sanskrit word *gūḍha* (hidden) that also translates as "cave" (6.11). Reading this devotional poetry allows us to think differently about the Path of Knowledge and practices of renunciation. More than just revering the single male renouncer who seeks non-dual union with Shiva, Hindus have incorporated traditional Shaiva concepts into other distinct and interlocking variations that appeal to many different individuals and communities.

Women, too, practice asceticism, though not always in ways identical to men. Among a supportive female community, their renunciation is often "communal and positive, rather than individualistic and negative" (DeNapoli 2013: 100). A path often started after the death of their husband, their devotional asceticism represents an alternative to the householder life of wife and mother and culminates in the goal of "meeting god."

One particular female renunciate movement, the Brahma Kumari or Om Shanti movement, was founded by the guru Dada Lekhraj in the early twentieth century. Providing a particular religious opportunity for South Asian women to experience renunciation, women in the movement dress all in white like widows or like corpses destined for the cremation ground, they remain celibate, and they abstain from eating meat, garlic, and onions. Brahma Kumari members practice forms of yoga and meditation in order to gain a proper understanding of the fundamental difference between the individual soul and the physical body and material world in which they reside.

In acquiring this wisdom, members avoid the millenarian collapse of the world predicted in Dada Lekhraj's apocalyptic visions of the end times. Instead, as pure souls independent of their bodies, they achieve unity with a form of Shiva who speaks through the guru. Supporting the theological doctrine of the end times, the acts of renunciation practiced by the movement's women – especially of sexual chastity by its permanent "surrendered" members – provide them with a degree of independence rarely afforded to women in mainstream society. Although this autonomy in the form of radical separation from the outside world has sometimes resulted in hostility towards the movement, even coming from within one's own family, the relatively small Om Shanti sect continues to expand beyond India as it has become part of the contemporary global guru culture that we shall see more of in Chapter 8.[11]

Yoga

The Upanishads also introduce the concept of yoga, key to the practices of renouncers who follow the path of Shiva. As we saw above, the Kena Upanishad asks a series of questions – "By Whom (*kena*) do the world and its people continue to function properly?" – whose collective answer we already know: it is only through *brahman* that our senses fully operate. The text's opening verse, however, uses forms of the word *yoga* at the end of each half-verse to remind its readers of their tenuous relationship to their own physical bodies and to represent a process by which practitioners bypass their ordinary sensory and mental perception of the world.

Connecting themselves to yogic practices and to their final liberation that ultimately results from these practices, the newly liberated and isolated consciousness (*kaivalyam*) achieves final *samadhi* (concentration), a yogic form of the final stage of *moksha*. In light of this description, Geoffrey Samuel defines yoga as a set of "disciplined and systematic techniques for the training and control of the human mind-body complex [...] for the reshaping of human consciousness towards some kind of higher goal" (2008: 2).[12]

Among the Upanishads, it is the Shvetāshvatara Upanishad that most clearly emphasizes yogic practice. Its third chapter begins with the standard statement on proper knowledge leading to immortality: "They who know this become immortal" (*ya etad vidur amṛtāste bhavanti*) (3.1). The remainder of that chapter focuses on the multiple forms of Shiva, identified as brahman who "dwells as the inner Self of every living being ... [and] takes them back into Himself at the end of time" (3.2). He is the Vedic Purusha who created heaven and earth and who also, being the size of a thumb, resides within the heart of each person (3.3). He is also Rudra whose "blessed form is auspicious (*shiva*), not terrifying, and not sinister-looking" (3.5).[13] The conclusion of the chapter reiterates its introduction and the ultimate goal of the yogi: "They who know Him become immortal" (*ya etad vidur amṛtāste bhavanti*) (3.13).

But it is Chapter Two immediately beforehand that most clearly describes the early philosophical foundations of yoga. Like the Rig Veda whose opening verses each begin with a reference to the central concept of Agni the fire god, the verses of this chapter each begin with a form of the word *yoga*: inspired by the Vedic god Savitri whose very duty is to inspire meditation, our minds truly come into being when we yoke our minds to the gods and to brahman. The remainder of the chapter describes elements common to contemporary yoga practice: keeping the body straight, restraining the senses, attending to the breath, and keeping the mind under control (a "wagon yoked to unruly horses" (2.9) (Olivelle 2008: 256)). By doing so, the solitary yogi, having perceived the true nature of the self and ultimately the true nature of brahman, becomes free from all sorrows (2.14–15).

The famous Gāyatrī mantra from Rig Veda 3.62.10 invokes Savitri, with both Gayatri and Savitri often depicted as forms of Sarasvati, the goddess (of) Speech.

The principles of various yoga systems are contained in a variety of texts, but the one that has become the most famous classical source for contemporary yoga is Patanjali's *Yoga Sutras*. Written near the turn of the Common Era, the *Yoga Sutras* are aligned with the Samkhya system of philosophy that establishes a dualism between one's true Spirit and the illusory Matter that only appears to exist here. Beginning with the verse *yogaś-citta-vṛtti-nirodhaḥ* – "Yoga is the cessation of the turnings of thought" (1.2) – the *Yoga Sutras* assist one in realizing this distinction. The benefits of continued yogic practice include such worldly powers as flight, invisibility, and mind reading. Ultimately, however, one seeks to obtain *samādhi* (pure contemplation) as the final step of the eight-limbed Ashtanga Yoga described in the text and that releases one from this world of suffering.

Written in 195 short *sūtra* aphorisms, and with only four verbs in the entire text (!), interpretation is required. Commented upon, translated, ignored for centuries, revived, interpreted, and reinterpreted again, the *Yoga Sutras* have lived a number of lives. Later Indian interpretations of yoga focus less on final samadhi as they view yoga through a theistic and particularly devotional lens. In fact, authors of the final commentaries on the text in the 16th century drew upon the vibrant Hindu devotional tradition by asserting union with *brahman*, Shiva, or another deity as yoga's ultimate goal (White 2012).

Modern yoga

In the past several decades, yoga has grown into a global billion-dollar industry. In addition to the explosion of yoga studios with teachers trained in one of several Indian traditions, yoga is practiced everywhere from the local YMCA to public sessions at downtown art museums to "goat yoga" at rural farms to where this chapter began – American public schools.[14] Modern yoga, as it is often called, participates in a complex dynamic with its South Asian homeland: some teachers and students desire to use its original Hindu religious and Sanskrit-language roots in order to tap into its exotic nature, while others might shed this language in order to appeal to a more general and secular audience.

The overwhelming focus of modern yoga practice is its use of physical postures (*āsana*), leading to its frequent description as "postural yoga." These postures and the breathing techniques that typically accompany them are intended to improve one's focus, physical fitness, and mental well-being. These forms of postural yoga are often connected to the larger yoga industry with its plethora of commodities: specialized clothing and accessories tailored towards its largely white middle-class consumers in the West. Despite its widespread popularity and the various ways that teachers and practitioners reinforce its exotic and Oriental roots, Andrea Jain, a scholar of the yoga tradition, has argued, "there is no direct, unbroken lineage between the South Asian premodern yoga systems and modern postural yoga" (2015: 3).

The global reach of yoga was recognized in the inaugural International Day of Yoga in 2015. Encouraged by Narendra Modi, the Prime Minister of India, and recognized by the United Nations, the International Day of Yoga has brought to the fore a number of related sensitive issues. More than an annual public celebration of yoga as a physical practice, this event has also become a political celebration of Indian culture and an economic appeal to the Indian and global middle class that practices yoga.

While the 2015 event set several world records for yoga participation in the Indian capital city of New Delhi, its celebration in Vancouver, for example, was not as successful. The proposed mass yoga session there was canceled a week before the event due to negative responses to its corporate sponsorship (including by a major gas company), its overlap with National Aboriginal Day, and as it would have shut down one of the city's main bridges for much of the day where the session would have occurred. The common objection to this event was a certain myopia about the gulf between the ultimate goal of classical yoga (*samadhi* contemplation and the detachment from this world of suffering) and the corporate money, middle-class whiteness, consumerism, and global politics that were supporting it.[15]

The International Day of Yoga is itself part of a larger backlash against the global consumerism that underlies modern yoga. With the emphasis of modern yoga squarely on the physical and mental benefits it provides, efforts have been made to re-emphasize yoga's Hindu religious roots. (In recent years, many Christian groups have also reinterpreted the physical postures of yoga to be analogous to prayer and praise within their own tradition.) This mix of religion, politics, and nationalism emerges at several points in the history of India, most notably amidst cultural contact with the British Empire, thus between "East and West." The Hindu American Foundation, for example, has been at the forefront of numerous such issues, here working on a campaign to "Take

Back Yoga" from its mass commercialization and commodification and to reassert its Indian roots and spiritual benefits beyond simply physical fitness.

The connections between yoga and spirituality that we see among these contemporary Hindu responses have their own roots in late nineteenth-century India. Once again in dialogue between India and the West, the monk Swami Vivekananda (more on him later) proposed a fourth yoga – Rāja Yoga (the royal yoga) – that he coupled with a "practical Vedanta," and the Indian nationalist Shri Aurobindo put forth his Integral Yoga as a means to divinize spirit and nature in a complex system of spiritual evolution.

With their thought based largely in the Upanishads, whose non-dual philosophy equates the individual atman with the universal brahman, these systems of practical yoga sought the social and political uplift of Hindus throughout India. Combining the wisdom of the Vedas, science and rationalism, and a sense of national pride, Vivekananda and Aurobindo laid the foundations for the systems of modern yoga developed and propagated in the West by B.K.S. Iyengar and Pattabhi Jois beginning in the early 1960s.[16]

Conclusion

It was in 2015, the same year as the International Day of Yoga, that the Supreme Court of California adjudicated the yoga case in the Encinitas school district. The Encinitas program was supported by the Jois Yoga Foundation whose headquarters are in Mysore, India, and where Jois himself trained and first taught. That Jois had received a traditional education in yoga – along with his classmate Iyengar, whose Western school of yoga has become equally popular – raised a red flag for the plaintiffs that the school program was religious and thus a violation of the constitution. In a "friend of the court" brief, Mark Singleton, a scholar of classical and modern yoga, asserted that yoga, "as it has developed in the United States in the past 150 years is a distinctly American cultural phenomenon. [...] Many of the elements which contributed to its current form are in no way inherently religious."

All parties in the case agreed that Hinduism was, of course, a religion and that the eight-limbed Ashtanga Yoga at the heart of the school district's program constituted a part of that religion. What was at issue, however, was the school district's particular application of Ashtanga Yoga. In previous conversations, the school district already removed any component that reflected its distinctly Indian cultural origin "or that could be arguably deemed religious." This included all Sanskrit language: the names of the physical postures (*āsana*) and hand gestures (*mudra*), the *namaste* greeting, and chanting the syllable *AUM*.

What remained in question was the content and religious nature of Ashtanga Yoga. Its first seven limbs presented few problems: *yama* (moral codes), *niyama* (observances), *āsana* (postures), *pranayama* (breath control), *pratyahara* (withdrawing the mind), *dharana* (concentration), and *dhyana* (meditation). Its eighth and final limb, *samadhi* (union with the divine), however, presented a sort of litmus test for the court.

Despite some content that connects to the first seven limbs – especially certain ethical teachings, breathing exercises, and, of course, the physical postures – the court recognized that "nowhere in the District's curriculum is there mention of *any* of the eight limbs of Ashtanga, and there is certainly no mention of the final limb (union with the divine)." The court supported the school's argument that, "as *implemented*, the District's yoga program is clearly *not* Ashtanga eight-limbed yoga," by noticing the absence of this eighth limb: the school never "instructed children that through yoga they would become one with God and that yoga could help end the karmic cycle of reincarnation." Acknowledging the many health-related purposes for which yoga is often practiced and for the secular nature of the district's yoga classes, the court ultimately rejected the claim that the school's yoga program advanced Hinduism and thus violated the establishment clause.

Building on prior legal cases that adjudicated the reading of the Bible in public schools, this case is instructive for the ways that it extends these arguments to a new and more religiously diverse America. Such cases in the past often dealt with underlying tensions between ethnic groups – with Irish and Italian Catholics, for example, whose papal authority structure and practices were seen as not standard or even anti-American. The 2015 yoga case was similarly about issues of immigration, ethnicity, and diversity, as much as it was about the specific practice of yoga.[17]

For our purposes, this case is equally instructive for the ways that it questioned the very nature of Hinduism, especially as practiced and perceived in the West. At the same time that the International Day of Yoga sought to celebrate the expansion of Indian culture beyond its borders, the Encinitas case reinforced, for some Americans, the difficulty of transmitting religions and cultures around the world. Although a system of practice nearly completely devoid of its Indian religious roots, yoga still represented an exotic cultural form whose constituent pieces could not be readily translated to a Western environment.

The many forms of Shiva seen throughout this chapter will continue to appear in later chapters. The next two chapters will, however, shift to forms of the god Vishnu. Rather than liberation from this world of suffering through the practice of difficult austerities, such as we see throughout Shaiva traditions, practices directed towards forms of Vishnu reinforce instead householdership and the daily life that the majority of Hindus live. Differing sharply from the narratives and practices related to Shiva, these domestic Vaishnava religious forms will reinforce the diversity of the global Hindu tradition and require new responses to the question "What *is* this thing called Hinduism?"

Notes

1 All quotations concerning the court case are taken directly from its transcript, Sedlock v. Baird, 235 Cal. App. 4th 874, accessed at www.lexisnexis.com/clients/CACourts.

2 In other versions of the story, Shiva's servant Nandin decapitates not just any elephant but Airāvata, the elephant vehicle of Indra (Doniger 1975: 262–269).

3 Jessica Frazier (2010) writes of how the study of Hindu aesthetics "can function as revelation" of reality itself, as these works of art transform the spectator as if they were being initiated into the devotion of, or as if they were even being possessed by, the divine.
4 This text includes its own *nāmāvalī* of 108 names of Bhairav, including such names as *śmasānavāsinī* (the resident of the cremation grounds), *śūlapāṇī* (he who carries a spear in his hand), and *bhūtādhyakṣa* (the leader of ghosts).
5 Many of these inter-religious connections are handled in Pechilis and Raj 2015.
6 The example of the core Jain tenet of fasting (*sallekhana*) is seen especially in the twentieth-century figure of Mahatma Gandhi. Although part of the austere lifestyle practiced by many Hindu renouncers, the narrative of the Buddha's enlightenment rejects this extreme form of renunciation, as it establishes itself as a "Middle Path."
7 Another famous *mahāvākya* that similarly universalizes multiplicity is *aham brahma asmi* ("I am brahman"). See Olivelle 2008 for accessible translations of the major Upanishads.
8 Thus, the Kaṭha Upanishad reads: "When one perceives this immense, all-pervading *ātman* as body-less within bodies, and as stable within unstable beings, then the wise one ceases to worry" (2.22 [trans. Olivelle 2008]).
9 This same conclusion is repeated verbatim in the following chapter as the result of "realising the *ātman* in every being" (2.5).
10 The Tamil term *pēy* is the same as the Sanskrit *preta* or *pretya*, which we encountered in Kena Upanishad 1.2 that addresses the wise ones who have "gone forth" from the world and become Immortals. For more demon devotees, see Craddock 2010.
11 McKendry-Smith 2022 and Babb 1986 (Chapters 4–6).
12 David Gordon White notes that later tantric texts, such as those we will handle in a later chapter, build upon the ideas and practices of yoga. Rather than attaining freedom from suffering, these texts guide the practitioner through visualizations and ultimately identity of one's body with powerful god/desses (2012: 12).
13 Later, however, the author pleads: "O Rudra, do not, in Your wrath, destroy our children and grandchildren. Do not destroy our lives; do not destroy our cows or horses; do not destroy our strong servants. For we invoke You always, with oblations, for our protection" (4.22).
14 The organization Yoga in Schools has as its mission "to empower students and teachers with yoga-inspired exercises to promote lifetime wellness"; their vision is "to make yoga available in all schools so that students and teachers develop body-mind awareness and the ability to nurture their own well-being" (https://yogainschools.org/index.php/about).
15 Ashraf 2015. My knowledge of this event in Vancouver, which came to be known as the "OM the bridge" controversy, comes from the 2023 "Yoga and Settler Colonialism" presentation by Rumya Putcha and Shreena Gandhi, hosted by Adheesh Sathaye as part of the Traditions of Yoga webinar series at the University of British Columbia in Vancouver.
16 Baier 2019.
17 In 2021, the state of Alabama reversed its legal ban on yoga in public schools.

References

Comeau, Leah Elizabeth. 2020a. *Material Devotion in a South Indian Poetic World*. London: Bloomsbury.

Frazier, Jessica. 2010. Arts and Aesthetics in Hindu Studies. *The Journal of Hindu Studies* 3 (1): 1–11.

Ramanujan, A. K. 1973. *Speaking of Śiva*. Harmondsworth: Penguin.

Key terms

Ashtanga Yoga
atman and brahman
samadhi
sampradāya
Festivals: Ganesh Chaturthi, Kumbha Mela, Shivratri
Forms of Shiva: Rudra and Bhairav
Poets: Kāraikkāl Ammaiyār, Mahādēviyakka, Manikkavachakar, Basavaṇṇa, Nāyaṉmārs
Schools: Advaita Vedanta, Shaiva Siddhanta, Virashaiva/Lingayat
Texts: Upanishads, Yoga Sutras, Shrī Bhairav Chālīsā

Persons

B.K.S. Iyengar
Pattabhi Jois
Swami Vivekananda

Study questions

1 How does the story of Ganesh and his beheading set up the fundamental Hindu tension between the ideal lives of the householder and the renouncer?
2 How do different Upanishads contribute different elements to the complex character of Shiva?
3 How does the place of the cremation grounds bring together ritual, philosophical, poetic, and practical components of Shiva's worship?
4 What tensions have arisen as yoga has come to be practiced in the West?

3 Ram and *dharma*

Preservation, power, and politics in the eternal city of Ayodhya

The story of Rāma, first written in the Sanskrit Ramayana by the sage Valmiki several centuries before the Common Era, begins with a dialogue between Valmiki himself and another sage, Narada. Narada asks Valmiki:

> Is there a man in the world today who is truly virtuous? Who is there who is mighty and yet knows both what is right [*dharma*] and how to act upon it? Who always speaks the truth and holds firmly to his vows? Who exemplifies proper conduct and is benevolent to all creatures? Who is learned, capable, and a pleasure to behold? Who is self-controlled, having subdued his anger? Who is both judicious and free from envy? Who, when his fury is aroused in battle, is feared even by the gods?
>
> (1.1.2–4 [Goldman 2021: 51])

Narada responds with one of the text's several *nakha-shikha*, descriptions of Rama from head to toe, or literally from his toenails to the top of his head.[1] Over fourteen verses, he details Rama's physical and moral characteristics, portraying him as the Maryāda Purushottama, the ultimate civilized human being. Despite scholarly debate over whether these first chapters are aware of Rama as a divine form of Vishnu, or whether this concept only develops at a later time, this opening passage describes him as "mighty as Vishnu" (1.18). Whether Rama is a proper avatar of Vishnu or not, Narada's *nakha-shikha* foregrounds three integral themes of his character that will become central for a study of Classical Hinduism.

First, Narada's description mirrors the *nāmāvalī*, the list of names that we saw with Shiva and Bhairav in the previous chapter. A way to sing the praises of any god or goddess, such lists will become a significant element in the developing Path of Devotion. One of the three central yogas of Classical Hinduism, Devotion incorporates elements of the previous Paths of Action and Knowledge – Vedic ritual, the philosophical unity of the Upanishads, and Shaiva renunciation – as it develops new systems of ethics, bodies of literature, and sets of ritual practices. Although Rama represents a significant figure in the Path of Devotion, with the veneration of his icons, the celebration of his festivals, and the chanting of his name, the following chapter on Krishna will detail this theme more specifically.

DOI: 10.4324/9781003475033-4

Second, Rama's physique – he has strong shoulders, large eyes, and he wields a huge bow – points in two simultaneous directions. As part of the Path of Devotion, this physical description reflects his icons and those of other gods and goddesses that begin to be worshipped in early medieval Indian temples and whose forms are recognizable throughout the Hindu world today. It also reflects his identity as a king who is "the protector of all living things" (1.12). With the basic act of *puja* modeled after the welcoming rituals traditionally offered to kings and queens, Vishnu and his wife Lakshmi – of whom Rama and his wife Sita are avatars – are depicted as king and queen in poster-art images, temple icons, and human actors in festivals. Ensuring the wealth, fertility, and stability of kingdom and cosmos, they display their strength through emblems of rulership (the crown and throne) and of military might (the scepter and weapons) in their royal court that doubles as the temple where they are venerated.

In the most recent example of Hindu kingship, Vishnu and Lakshmi were represented in the persons of the king and queen of Nepal, with queens and princesses often adding "Lakshmi" as a suffix to their names. Ruling the country from Kathmandu's palace in the center of the capital city until a Maoist rebellion and civil war toppled the throne in 2006, the king was seen as an earthly representation of Vishnu who annually received his right to rule from the blessing of the living goddess Kumari at the autumnal festival of the Vedic king Indra. Although Nepal is no longer ruled by a king and queen, images and rituals of royalty – communicated through forms of Shiva, Vishnu, the Goddess, as well as Buddhist deities – still permeate many of its major festivals.[2]

Finally, accompanying the descriptions of his physical strength are passages that describe Rama as someone who knows and protects *dharma* (1.12–14). Referring to the ethical foundation of Hindu life, these passages are as much political statements about the responsibilities of kings in early medieval India as they are theological statements about the role of Vishnu and his avatars in the world. These three themes of Classical Hinduism – devotion, royalty, and dharma – are regularly intertwined and will take us through the next two chapters as we look at Rama and Krishna, the two main avatars of Vishnu.

As the previous chapter used the term "Shaiva" to refer to those religious elements related to the god Shiva, this and the following chapter will use the common Sanskrit adjective "Vaishnava" to refer to texts, images, and practices related to the god Vishnu.

The *avatar* of Vishnu

The stories of all of the major Classical Hindu deities – forms of Shiva, Vishnu, and the Goddess – are told in the eighteen core Purāṇas ("the old stories"). Composed throughout the long era of Classical Hinduism, these texts comprise a large body of literature nearly impossible to summarize. Most generally, these texts compile stories of kings, sages, renouncers, and husbands, wives, and children, as its stories detail temple ritual practices, pilgrimages to sacred places throughout India, as well as some of the most popular Hindu stories ever told.

Many of the Puranas include stories of Vishnu's ten avatar ("descents"). Like Indra who defeated his demonic enemy Vṛtra when he threatened the entire cosmos, each of Vishnu's avatars, whether animal, quasi-human, or fully human, similarly dispatches a demonic enemy. Within the structure of Classical Hinduism, in each case the enemy threatens dharma, the political, cosmic, and moral order of the universe. Vishnu's first three avatar – the Fish, Tortoise, and Boar – reflect Indra's victorious acquisition of water in the Rig Veda, as they secure victory within the chaotic setting of the ocean. The next group includes avatars who encounter more human enemies whom they must vanquish in battle: Narasingh the Man-Lion, the three-stepping Trivikrama, the axe-wielding Parashuram, and the two main avatars of Rama and Krishna. The final subgroup of avatars includes Balram, the historical Buddha, and the future avatar Kalkin, who will usher in the end of the current age.[3]

Each of Vishnu's avatars represents a concrete exemplar whose story reinforces their power to restore dharma. Although stories of all of Vishnu's avatars are told in the Puranas, not all avatars are equally venerated. Some avatars possess primarily regional significance: Parashuram is remembered for having made southwest India habitable by reclaiming it from the sea; Narasingh is worshipped in south India as a figure who presides over transitional times and places; and Balram, sometimes referred to as Haldhar (the Plowman) for his association with agriculture and alcohol, accompanies his brother Krishna in his journeys along the Yamuna River in north India.

Simultaneously gods, kings, and warriors, only Rama and Krishna have a global significance, with each the focus of a long epic Sanskrit poem: the Ramayana and the Mahabharata, respectively. The complex stories that these two epics tell are simultaneously secular and religious, providing the basic cultural materials for the Hindu devotional tradition. Part of a larger Vaishnava tradition, these epics and their various tellings are found in many other languages and popular media throughout the global Hindu community.

One of the main shifts we encounter in moving from classical written Sanskrit to vernacular languages spoken in India is the dropping of the final short /a/ from grammatically masculine or neuter nouns. (Feminine-gendered terms such as the names of goddesses [Sarasvatī and Sītā] typically end in long vowels that are not dropped.) For example, referring to the manifestations of divinity on earth, the term *avatāra* is regularly pronounced and spelled *avatār* or even *avtār*. Similarly, the name of the god Rāma is spelled as in the Devanagari script and is regularly pronounced and spelled Rām throughout India: in common daily greetings between friends on the street ("Hey Rām!" or "Rām Rām!" or "Sītā-Rām!") and in group chants during public funeral processions ("Rām nām satya hai!" [God's name is truth!]). In this chapter, I will use "Rāma" when discussing the classical Sanskrit and "Rām" when discussing vernacular and contemporary references. This small distinction should provide no difficulty to readers.

Vishnu and his avatars are the subject of a prolific body of devotional literature and poetry. Beginning as early as the fifth century, and running parallel to the Nāyaṉmār poets of the Shaiva Siddhanta school discussed in the previous chapter, the Vaishnava Āḻvār poets helped to define a new non-Vedic form of Hindu devotion. Part of the larger Shri Vaishnava school in the Tamil south, Alvar poetry culminated in the theological systemization under Ramanuja in the eleventh century, whose "qualified non-dualism" (*vishishta advaita*) brought together traditional elements of Shaiva non-dualism and renunciation with Vaishnava dualism and devotion. This synthesis helped to moderate the Shri Vaishnava's multiple schools that debated the proper attitudes toward devotion: whereas the Vatakalai school advocates devotional activity that leads to one's salvation, the Tenkalai school supports a more passive approach that grants full responsibility to divine grace.

Nammāḻvār is considered the greatest of the twelve Alvar poets, those "immersed" in their devotion to Vishnu. His *Tiruvāymoḻi*, a collection of 1,102 verses, self-consciously innovates in its languages and genre by introducing itself in Sanskrit as "the ocean of Tamil Veda in the which the Upanishads of the thousand branches flow together" (Ramanujan 1981: xi). Amidst his many poems on Krishna, on Vishnu as the creator who churned the ocean, and on each avatar individually, Nammalvar writes of all of Vishnu's avatars together in a very short poem:

> Before I could say,
> "He became cowherd
> fish
> wild boar,"
> he became a million million.
> (Ramanujan 1981: 49)

Throughout the *Tiruppāvai* of Andal, the only female poet among the Alvars, she tells of her separation from and intimacy with Vishnu. Often placing herself as a *gopi* cowherdress within Krishna's rural narrative universe, she writes also of Vishnu's other avatars, including Vāman, (a.k.a. the three-stepping Trivikrama) who by measuring out the world with his three steps retakes physical control of the world from the demon Mahabali. In a rare example of devotional literature towards Vaman, Andal writes that as a result of such devotion,

> our land will be free from evil
> rains will fall three times a month
> and the *kayal* will leap agilely

amidst the thick, tall, red grain
the spotted bee will sleep
nestled in the *kuvaḷai* bloom.
and when we clasp their heavy udders
the great, generous cows
will fill our pots ceaselessly.
limitless wealth is certain to abound.
(Venkatesan 2010: 53)

Like that of Nammalvar's *Tiruvāymoḻi*, Andal's poetry is recited daily in homes and temples. More than just a poet, however, Andal is also considered to be a goddess. Her attention to natural fertility in the poem above alludes to Andal herself as a manifestation of Bhū Devī, the earth goddess, and of Shri, the feminine principle eternally connected with Vishnu in the theology of the Shri Vaishnava school. For many women, her poetry provides an opportunity to highlight the feminine principle of the universe and to find their own place within a religious culture that does not always directly attend to their needs.[4] The vow that results in the fertility described in this poem is the annual bathing ritual conducted during her winter festival where she is the presiding deity. During this festival, her temple images are processed through the streets and are bathed at multiple locations, replicating Andal's own ritual baths in honor of the vow.

Icons of Andal are venerated with flower garlands in temples throughout the southern Tamil country that connect her to larger patterns of Vaisnava worship.[5] Her narrative is rooted in these very garlands: as a young girl, she decorated herself with the garlands of marigolds initially destined for Vishnu. During its annual Brahmotsavam festival, priests convey these same garlands – along with her distinctive green-leaf parrot and other garments – from the icon of Andal at her temple at Srivilliputhur to the famous south Indian temple at Tirupati. Located on fourteen acres amidst the Tirumala hills, this temple is rooted in the Shri Vaishnava school and is dedicated to Venkateshwar, the Lord of Venkata, or Venkatadri, the Lord of the Venkata Hills.

The fame of this temple extends far beyond these hills. A major pilgrimage destination, many people come here to participate in its distinctive tradition of shaving one's head as a tangible sign of a spiritual debt that one has paid off. This wealthy temple also draws in local Muslims who see the goddess Shri as a manifestation of the Muslim girl Bibi Nancharamma (Mohammad 2014: 232). Venkateshwara temples have been built throughout the global Hindu community, often with icons of the goddesses Bhu Devi and Shri Devi flanking Vishnu. Among these many temples is the Shri Venkateshwara Temple in Pittsburgh; inaugurated in 1976, the Pittsburgh temple is one of the very first American temples ever built.

This study of Vishnu and his avatars allows us to clarify the limits of multiplicity in several ways. Rather than every god or goddess simply being a version of every other one, Vishnu and his multiple avatars represent a structural consistency with each other. The two epic traditions have at their core an easily distinguished yet complementary pair of forms of Vishnu. Identified with the Solar lineage and living in the second era within the recurring cycles of the Hindu universe, Rama is the main character of the Ramayana, while the Lunar deity Krishna lives during the subsequent third era and represents the driving force behind the Mahabharata. Given the very human ways that Rama and Krishna are written – more than the fish, tortoise, or boar avatar – their characters, each the center of a culturally rich devotional Vaishnava epic tradition, appeal to different sensibilities. Whereas his moral uprightness and kingly virtues create an aura of distant respect towards Rama, the playful attitude that Krishna displays, especially as a child, makes him more personal and relatable.

> The Classical Hindu system of time is based on a four-part cycle of long eras (*yugas*). Each subsequent *yuga*, named after the number thrown in a game of dice, is a lower roll and thus a less perfect era than the previous: the original and perfect Krita Yuga (a throw of 4), the second Treta Yuga (3), the third Dvāpara Yuga (2), and the current and morally debased Kali Yuga (a throw of 0).

The avatar of Vishnu also represents a structural opposition to Shiva. Whereas Shiva and his wife Parvati reside on Mount Kailash among the tallest mountain peaks on earth, Vishnu and his goddess-wife Lakshmi reside on the serpent Shesha on the ocean at the bottom of the universe. This difference in location signals a difference in function. Shiva is associated primarily with meditation, the renunciation of social order, and the acquisition of the heat-energy *tapas* that threatens the very order of things; in doing so, he encourages some to seek a life among the ghouls of the cremation grounds.

Vishnu, on the other hand, is responsible for the maintenance of *dharma* fulfilled by those householders who reside in the everyday world. Although some antagonism has existed between those who strictly follow Vishnu and Shiva, within contemporary Hinduism they represent a complementary pair that signals the balance that sits at the very core of Hinduism: between what is called *pravritti* and *nivritti*, the simultaneous and dynamic engagement with and disengagement from the world.

Classical Hinduism: Dharma

Derived from a Sanskrit root that means "to fix in place, to stabilize" and defined variably as "religion, law, or ethics," dharma refers to the social and cosmic order that humans and gods seek to maintain. Building on his relatively minor role in the Rig Veda, where he is repeatedly stated to be equivalent to the sacrifice (*viṣṇur vai yajñaḥ*), Vishnu takes on the role, in later Classical Hinduism, of the maintenance of dharma. Stepping out of the shadow of Indra with whom he had regularly been paired, Vishnu develops a set of consistent narratives that, again, like the Vedic story of Indra's defeat of the serpent Vṛtra, blends themes of fertility, royal power, and kingship. Along these lines, and as seen in the *nakha-shikha* of Rama above, Vishnu and his avatars work to stabilize the world and to restore dharma when it is threatened from the outside. In doing so, they provide a safe and stable place for humans to live.

One place on the ground where we see Vishnu's role in maintaining dharma is in the village of Ghatiyali in the western state of Rajasthan. Here, Vishnu appears as "Four-Arms," a name that indicates one facet of his standard appearance. He carries in his four arms two auspicious items, a lotus blossom or flower and a conch shell, and two weapons, a discus and a club. Centrally located next to institutions associated with modernity and technology, Four-Arms provides the space for religious festivals such as the Ram Lila and readings of the Ramayana, the witnessing of legal decisions, the ritual protection of animals, and a variety of rites preceding and following pilgrimage, marriage, and death. Surrounded by powerful caves and stones associated with moksha, renunciation, and the veneration of Shiva, Vishnu's central shrine is a "place for establishing consensus, for hearing about and benefiting from *dharma* [and] for conducting protective rites that crosscut lines of caste and neighborhood" (Gold 1988/1993: 43). A protector of biological, social, and divine harmony, Vishnu oversees, sustains, and protects the village from external impurities that threaten its internal harmony (Figure 3.1).

This notion of harmony as it relates to dharma draws upon three fundamental components of Classical Hinduism: the Human Goals, Social Classes, and Stages of Life. Each of these components uses the 3+1=4 formula that we introduced with the AUM syllable from the Mandukya Upanishad, whereby the fourth element transcends and troubles the composite whole. First, the concept of the four Human Goals (the four *purushārtha*) details the various elements that an individual must balance in order to live a well-rounded life. The first of these goals is dharma itself, the proper performance of religious and ethical duties. Artha relates to one's financial, political, and domestic responsibilities. And texts on kama detail the proper ways that one should enjoy oneself among the pleasures of the city. These three goals are especially relevant for the Householder, detailed below, with full texts describing each. (The dharmic *The Laws of Manu*, the *Arthashāstra* that details the life of the king, and the *Kāmasūtra* describing physical love are among the most famous of all of these texts in each of these three categories.)

Moksha, the fourth element, describes one's spiritual liberation or release at the end of a life of suffering, the goal of all the Indic religions of Hinduism, Buddhism, and Jainism. Moksha relates directly to the Renouncer who completely gives up domestic life, the structural opposite role of the Householder. As with the four components of the syllable AUM and the four states of consciousness in the Upanishads, the fourth element of moksha is separate from and transcends the other three Human Goals.

As the four Human Goals guide the life of the individual, the larger practice of dharma ensures the complex functioning of the universe. *The Laws of Manu*,

Figure 3.1 Four-armed Vishnu. Bhaktapur, Nepal

written in the first centuries of the Common Era, represents the most well-known text that describes dharma. Part of the larger Sanskrit genre of dharma texts – categorized as *smriti, shāstra,* or *sūtra* – *Manu* was, much like the Upanishads, written in the form of a dialogue between students, teachers, sages, and gods. Ultimately placed into the mouth of the "self-created" Svayambhu and beginning with an account of his creation of the world, *Manu* saw itself as more elevated and universal than other texts that detailed such skills as linguistics, weapons, or medicine. At once a book on individual manners and family etiquette, a legal text that assigns penalties for criminal violations, and an explication of the law of karma, rebirth, and final liberation, the text represents one of the foundations of Classical Hinduism.

Like all texts, *Manu* was not composed in a vacuum. Following the conversion to Buddhism of emperor Ashoka in the third century BCE, Buddhist monks and monasteries began to receive increased support and patronage. It was during this time that Buddhists began using the language of dharma, referring to Buddhism itself as "the Dharma." Much of what we refer to as Classical Hinduism arises from the competition for religious and material resources at this time. Thus, the text of *Manu*, the epic *Mahābhārata* that we will see in the following chapter, and, by extension, the larger concept of Hindu dharma came to exist in a dynamic relationship with rising Buddhist powers in early medieval India.

Describing more than simply a general way of being good in the world, *Manu* structured its discussion of dharma around other two related social and cultural components that have come to define the Hindu tradition: Social Class (*varṇa*) and Stage of Life (*āshrama*). The combined Sanskrit term *varṇāshrama dharma* indicates the intimate relationship between them and the ways that one adheres to both simultaneously. We will discuss the second component first and then move to a larger and more complex discussion of the thornier issue of the Social Classes.

Because the text of *Manu* presumes for the most part a uniform audience of brahmins from the highest Social Class, it organizes social life according to the other component of dharma, the four Stages of Life. These stages structure a person's life from childhood (though not quite from birth) to the end (though not quite to death). A person's social life begins as a Student; following initiation, the student lives with their teacher, exercising yogic control of their senses and studying Vedic texts and rituals. The Householder settles down to have a family and to live a life that most of us would consider "normal," while performing regular Vedic fire rituals and honoring their ancestors with water and rice ball *piṇḍas*. *Manu* argues that the Householder life is the best stage since all the others depend upon it (6.87–90). (In a fascinating example of symbolic and ritual multiplicity that blends life and death and that is still practiced today, the rice ball pindas that honor the deceased ancestors can also be consumed by the wife of the sacrificer-husband should she wish to become pregnant [3.262–3].) Seeing one's own gray hair, wrinkles, or grandchildren, the Forest Dweller moves to the wilderness away from the daily life of the home. There, they will restrict their diet, senses, and the other pleasures of the Householder life.

After paying one's debts to the rishis, ancestors, and gods through Vedic study, children, and sacrifice, one becomes a *sannyasi* Renouncer living alone away from civilization. Continuing and extending the life of the Forest Dweller, the Renouncer is marked by their "bowl, the foot of a tree, a ragged piece of cloth, a solitary life, and equanimity towards all" (6.44 [Olivelle 2005: 150]). Controlling breath, practicing meditation, and freeing themselves from all attachments, the Renouncer seeks moksha, the fourth Human Goal, and desires to attain the eternal *brahman*. Although some dharma texts allow for one to make a direct leap from Student to Renouncer bypassing the domestic bliss and worldly attachments of the Householder, *Manu* clearly describes this as a sequential process.

The third and final component of dharma is the set of four Social Classes (*varna*). From high to low, these are the Brahmin (priests), Kshatriya (kings and warriors), Vaishya (common workers), and the Shudra. Concerned with the religious and political situation of its time, *Manu* directs its attention mainly towards brahmins and kshatriyas and the sometimes tense dynamic between them: brahmins should devote themselves to Vedic learning and virtue, and kings should devote themselves to supporting brahmins and justice (41). It is possible that the anxiety the text shows towards low-caste people is culturally intertwined with the influx of foreigners to India at the time (the Greeks from the northwest, the Huns from Central Asia, and the Chinese from the East), and of the rise of heterodox sects such as Jainism and especially Buddhism from within India. Seeing these groups as political threats, Vedic brahmins structured an ethical system that identified these groups as cultural others while intensely defending their brahmanical privilege (39).

The fourth class of the Shudra is marked as different from the upper three "twice-born" classes, similar to how the other fourth elements – the Renouncer in the Stages of Life, and moksha among the Human Goals – were marked as transcending standard householder dharma. Subordinate to the upper three classes whose members may wear the sacred thread as a mark of their Vedic initiation, the primary task of Shudras is solely to serve those three upper classes. *Manu*'s opening passage of the creation of the world draws on the account of the Purusha in the Rig Veda, specifically evoking its creation of the classes from, respectively, his mouth, arms, thighs, and – for the lowest of the Shudra – his feet (1.31). It is for *Manu*'s dependence upon this rigid class structure that Shudras, members of the lowest class, annually burn copies of *Manu* (Dutt 2019: 111).

The set of Social Classes represents one component of what is often referred to as "the Indian caste system." The ultimate irony behind the concept of caste is that despite it being one of the things that most people in the West "know" about Hinduism, the term "caste" does not come from any Indian language but was rather imported by the Portuguese. Landing in western India in the seventeenth century and recognizing from their home country the hierarchical social system they saw in India, they used the Portuguese term *casta* to describe this Indian system.

Contributing to the Indian system of social stratification and hierarchy, versions of which are found literally everywhere in the world, the second component of the class system is *jāti*. Translated as "birth" (and related to the English word *genesis*), one's jati is represented by one's family name. Taken together, the four varna and the thousands of jati found throughout South Asia contribute to a complex set of relationships that operates in a variety of ways.

The caste system operates both horizontally and vertically. On a horizontal level, one can observe the functioning of an entire village or even a single festival in which different caste members produce particular goods and perform certain services. The Indra festival of Kathmandu, Nepal, for example, is celebrated as members of many of the city's castes perform their traditional duties:

Oil-pressers raise and lower the festival's central wooden post; high-caste brahmin Rajopadhyay priests lead the puja of the Vedic god Indra; Brass-workers install the mask of Bhairav that is sacred to the Farmers; Sweet-makers cook food for the king and for the living goddess Kumari, played by a girl of the Buddhist Shakya caste. That members of lower castes no longer play the festival music they traditionally did signals the growing awareness of the ever-present vertical dimension of caste.

Whereas the horizontal dimension allows for some semblance of equality and community, the vertical dimension of caste enforces inequality and discrimination through a set of strict hierarchies. These hierarchies are reproduced, governed, and disciplined by communities reinforcing traditional standards that restrict who one may eat with, marry, and worship with. Despite the modern Indian quota system that reserves seats in government schools and offices and thus ameliorates historically limited educational and employment opportunities, unequal treatment towards those of lower castes continues. Inequalities are felt especially among those who reside completely outside the caste system, thus below the Shudra in the four-varna system. Referred to as outcaste or Harijan ("children of God," as Gandhi referred to them), they regularly refer to themselves by the term Dalit, "the oppressed." Not restricted to rural villages, systems of inequality extend to Indian cities and are even carried to global Hindu communities in the West.[6]

Scholars continue to write about the complex presence of caste as a system that divides and conquers, both in recent history and in contemporary times. Rupa Viswanath writes about the complex economic, agricultural, and religious conditions that came together to both facilitate and complicate the situation of Pariah outcaste workers in nineteenth-century British colonial India. Urban historian Juned Shaikh writes about the ways that caste was integral, at the turn of the previous century, to the construction of the modern city of Bombay (now Mumbai) as it reinforced the oppression of Dalits even within the context of a global capitalist economy. In her book *Fierce Gods*, anthropologist Diane Mines narrates a caste conflict that arose when a low-caste villager in south India took a pinch of devotional ash from the flame inside a local goddess temple, thus transgressing the village's understood social and spatial boundaries. And Yashica Datt, a journalist based in New York City, herself a Dalit whose family is from near the Indian capital of New Delhi, has written a powerful memoir entitled *Coming Out as Dalit*, in which she details the various strategies that she and her family have deployed in order to "pass" as upper-caste and thus to avoid the discrimination Dalits typically experience.[7]

Although caste oppression presents a reality for many in India even today, we must remember that hierarchy is embedded in systems of social and cultural power wherever we might live. In her award-winning book, *Caste: The Origins of Our Discontents*, American historian Isabel Wilkerson compares the Indian caste system to the systems of oppression that culminated in the Holocaust against Jewish people in Nazi Germany and the American institution of slavery that led to the centuries-long system of prejudice against Africans and African-

Americans. In the American system, Wilkerson argues, race is the superficial language while caste is the underlying grammar.

All three of these systems of power, the most explicit and insidious examples of caste among myriad global systems of inequality, are structured along sets of guidelines that Wilkerson refers to as the eight pillars of caste. These pillars include a reference to a divine will that transcends and reinforces the appearance of the system as natural; the restriction of marriage and occupation by those in power to dehumanize others and to maintain the status quo; and the language of purity and pollution that communicates the inner (im)morality of those at either end of the hierarchy and that legitimizes arbitrary punishment against those at the bottom.

That such systems of inequality are historical, artificial, and universal is an obvious fact but one that is easy to conceal and forget. One such example of the historicity of the Hindu caste system can be seen in the re-working of the Nepalese system by the Rana family in 1854. Coming from outside the royal Shah family and rising to power in Kathmandu via a bloody coup, the Ranas reorganized caste in order to place themselves – kshatriya warriors by birth – in the highest category alongside brahmins and renouncers.

These three themes of Classical Hinduism – devotion, royalty, and dharma – and the three specific components of dharma including caste will play a significant role in the text of the epic Ramayana and the complex figure of Rama.

The Rāmāyaṇa

The *nakha-shikha* description of Rama with which the Ramayana begins introduces readers to the themes of devotion and dharma that permeate the epic. Holding Rama as the exemplar of those who know, practice, and protect dharma, the Ramayana presents Rama as one of the two most important avatars of Vishnu and as a figure worthy of devotion. Valmiki's Sanskrit Ramayana is the oldest telling of Rama's story and thus is commonly referred to as the Ādi Kāvya (the first poem). Many other influential tellings were composed in other regional languages throughout India and beyond, however. Challenged by some conservative Hindu thinkers in India, this diversity of the Ramayana tradition has long served for most Hindus as a flexible tradition whose multiple voices and diversity of media allow audiences to adapt the characters, stories, and relationships to a number of relevant social and cultural situations.

Whereas Valmiki's Sanskrit epic presents Rama as a very human king who undergoes trials of dharma, most subsequent tellings are more explicitly within the bhakti tradition.[8] Kamban's twelfth-century Tamil *Iramavataram*, composed during the height of the Chola empire that also produced the famous bronze images of Shiva as lord of the dance, is fully in the bhakti tradition while also drawing on the heroism typical of the earliest Tamil poetry.

The fourteenth-century Sanskrit *Adhyātma Rāmāyaṇa* approaches the traditional story from a non-dual perspective. Firmly establishing Rama and his wife Sita as Vishnu and Lakshmi, as the co-creators of the universe, and Rama ultimately as brahman, the text focuses on devotion to Rama as the means to final liberation.

Tulsidas's sixteenth-century Hindi *Rāmcharitmānas* – "The Ocean of the Deeds of Rāma" – continues these devotional themes in what is arguably the most influential telling in contemporary India. The *Mānas*, as it is often called, provides the foundation for the famous Ram Lila festival celebrated throughout north India but especially in the town of Ramnagar ("the city of Ram") across the Ganges River from Varanasi. Here, the thirty-day festival recreates the entire epic in multiple locations throughout the town. Amidst the festival's many ritual actors playing every conceivable epic role – brahmin priests, queens and princes, large crowds, and even monkeys and bears – the "Great King" of Varanasi, the Maharaja, makes his royal presence felt. He rides the royal elephant, performs puja, and attends the Bharat Milap, the meeting of Ram with his brother Bharat after his return to the capital of Ayodhya after fourteen years in exile. In these festive moments, the crowd addresses him as a form of Shiva with shouts of "Har Har Mahadev!", appropriate in a city so clearly associated with the god whose renouncers populate the city and its cremation grounds.

An epic in seven books, the Ramayana contains innumerable characters, locations, and themes, but its main story can be summed up as follows. In the city of Ayodhya in north India, the child Rama is born into the royal lineage of his father, King Dasharath. Rama's mother Kaushalya is the official queen but is one of three co-wives who each has children of their own. Some years later, after receiving all of the necessary training, Rama, the eldest of the four sons and exemplar of dharma, is selected to be crown prince. On the day of his coronation, the junior wife Kaikeyi reminds the king of a boon that he promised to her many years ago when she saved his life on the battlefield. Banished to the forest for fourteen years, and with Kaikeyi's son Bharata to occupy the throne – which he rejects out of deference to Rama whose sandals he installs on the throne instead – Rama lives a simple life in the forest with his wife Sita and his brother Lakshman.

The seven books (*kāṇḍa*) in sequence are: Bala Kanda (Rama's birth and childhood), Ayodhya Kanda (Rama's time in the capital city of Ayodhya), Aranya Kanda (Rama and Sita in the forest), Kishkindha Kanda (Rama and Lakshman in the Kishkindha hills), Sundara Kanda (the "beautiful" book of Hanuman), Yuddha Kanda (the battle between Rama and Ravana), and Uttara Kanda (the final book).

All goes well enough until they encounter Shurpanakha in the Dandaka forest. Although in some tellings she first transforms herself into an exceptionally beautiful woman, she is a *rākshasī* demoness who desires to make Rama her husband. And she is different from Rama in every possible way: he is handsome, she is ugly; he is fit and trim, she is misshapen and potbellied; his voice is sweet, hers is sinister (*bhairava*); he behaves well, and she is an ill-mannered old hag. Expressing faithfulness to his wife, Rama sarcastically suggests that the demoness might rather be interested in his brother Lakshman, who continues where Rama left off, attempting to pass the hag back to his big brother. Not fully comprehending their rather cruel teasing, the rustic demoness again proposes to Rama as she threatens to kill and eat Sita. Having heard enough, Rama orders Lakshman to cut off her nose and ears as punishment for her threats both on Rama's marital dharma and on Sita's life.

This episode is key for three significant reasons, all of which take us deeper into both the epic and into Classical Hindu notions of dharma. First, the entire epic turns on this plot point. Immediately following her disfigurement at the hands of Rama and Lakshman, Shurpanakha turns to her brother, the ten-headed *rākshasa* Ravana. Seeking to avenge this violation of his sister, Ravana creates a golden deer to entice first Rama and then Lakshman away from the hut on an impromptu hunting foray deep into the forest. While they are away, Ravana approaches the lone Sita in the guise of a renouncer, kidnaps her, and flies off with her in his chariot to his distant kingdom of Lanka. The epic ends (spoiler alert!) with Rama's decapitation and killing of Ravana and his successful return to Ayodhya with Sita. The south Indian epic of Kampan makes the connection between these two events explicit, noting that the day that Rama and Lakshman cut off Shurpanakha's ears and nose "marked the beginning of the labor to be ended by cutting off the heads of Rāvaṇa" (2924) (Hart and Heifetz 1988: 105).[9]

The second reason that Shurpanakha's disfigurement is significant is that it highlights the theme of conflict in Rama's adherence to perfect dharma. In an episode later in the epic's fourth book, Rama and Lakshman encounter the monkey-king Sugriva. Reflecting Rama's own troubles, Sugriva's throne has been usurped and his wife taken by his brother, Vālin. Rama fulfills his promise to recover both by killing Valin, thus earning the undying devotion and service of Hanuman, lauded as Rama's messenger who will help Rama recover his own kingdom and wife. The only hitch in this episode is that Rama kills Valin while he is already engaged in one-on-one battle with his brother, essentially by shooting him in the back. As he lies on the ground, Valin addresses Rama in a deathbed speech in which he questions all of the qualities for which we are to praise Rama. He says:

> Rāma is well-born, virtuous, powerful, compassionate, and energetic. He has observed vows, knows pity, is devoted to the welfare of the people, knows when to act, and is firm in his vows [*dṛḍha-vrata*]. [...] I did not know that your judgment was destroyed and that you were a vicious evildoer [*a-dharmic*] hiding under a banner of righteousness [*dharma*], like a well overgrown with grass.
>
> (4.17.14–15, 18 [Goldman and Sutherland Goldman 2021: 369])

Rama responds by doubling down on the connections between royalty and dharma, holding his brother Bharata up as an exemplar. Ruling Ayodhya in Rama's absence, Bharata is the knower of dharma, artha, and kama, the three domestic Human Goals. The knowledge of these three reinforces Bharata's royal obligation to spread dharma and to hold transgressors of dharma responsible. Maintaining that dharma is subtle (*sūkṣma*) and difficult to understand, Rama specifically accuses Valin of incest since he should have cared for his younger brother's wife as a daughter-in-law rather than as a wife. Rama punished him – executed him, we might say – because he had abandoned dharma. (And anyways, Rama tells Valin, since he is a monkey, he may be hunted under any conditions.)

More questions of dharma arise in the epic's final book. Throughout the epic, Rama is regularly described as upholding the three main components of dharma: the four Stages of Life, the four Social Classes, and the four Human Goals. The Ramayana already plays around with these components, however, as it portrays Rama and Lakshman, who are *kshatriya* warriors by birth, as *sannyasi* renouncers who enter the forest and appear to seek some form of *moksha*. The text highlights the theme of the four Social Classes specifically in the episode of his killing of Shambuka. Ruling a perfect kingdom where nobody dies before their time, Rama is confronted by a brahmin whose young son has died. They attribute this glitch in Rama's kingdom to a *shudra* of the lowest caste who dared to engage in yoga, a religious act reserved only for brahmins. Rama swiftly fixes this mistake by killing Shambuka with the powerful weapon he had previously used to defeat Ravana. As he restores order – here in the form of caste dharma – the brahmin's son immediately revives.

One final example calls into question the issue of Rama's relationship to dharma within the political context of what is sometimes called Rāmrāj, the political power that Rama wields over the kingdom of Ayodhya. In a startling twist to the end of the epic, before returning home to Ayodhya, Rama questions Sita's faithfulness to him. He suddenly tells her that he has fulfilled his royal duty by dispelling the world of its demonic enemies, and she, having lived in the house of another man, the rakshasa Ravana, is now free to go wherever she pleases. Shocked by his rejection, she reminds Rama of her miraculous birth directly from the earth – hence her name Sītā – and commands Rama's brother Lakshman to build her a funeral pyre. Referring to Rama as "he who knows all dharma" (*sarva-dharma-jña*), Sita calls the fire god Agni to witness her innocence of any wrongdoing. Passing the dramatic *agni parīkshā*, the trial by fire, Sita proves her loyalty to Rama: her husband, the king of Ayodhya, and an avatar of Vishnu.

Years later, however, Rama hears the citizens of Ayodhya wondering aloud how he could have taken Sita back after she had lived in Ravana's house. Feeling a conflict between his attention to the Human Goal of artha (his rule of the kingdom) and of kama (the love he feels towards his wife), he exiles Sita from Ayodhya, banishing her to the forest as his family had done to him so many years before. Pregnant with twin sons, Lav and Kush, the heirs to Rama's throne in Ayodhya, Sita finds shelter in the ashram of none other than the sage Valmiki, the author of the Ramayana.

Hearing his sons chanting the Ramayana as he is wandering through the forest, Rama stops and notices Sita. With the best of intentions, Rama – here referred to as "he who knows the dharma" (*dharma-vit*) (7.88.2) – deigns to give Sita one more chance to display her innocence and to once again prove herself "pure" (*shuddha*). In anticipation of her potentially monumental declaration, all the world's beings gather. While maintaining her innocence, Sita does not stoop to publicizing her purity once again to the world. Rather than subject herself to one more trial by fire, she calls upon Mother Earth (Mādhavī Devī) to take her back to the earth whence she was born.[10] As all the world's beings watch on in amazed silence, Mother Earth suddenly appears; splitting open the ground, she places Sita on a throne borne by nāga serpents and together – silently, miraculously, and finally – they enter the underworld.

All of these actions – the disfiguring of Shurpanakha, the slaying of the low-caste renouncer Shambuka and of the monkey-king Valin, and the two-fold banishment of Sita – represent Rama's questionable applications of dharma. Warranting various and extensive explanations throughout the Hindu narrative tradition, these three episodes highlight the serious and difficult questions that authors and audience members struggled with as they contemplated the complexities of Hindu dharma. Rather than viewing these stories as flagrant transgressions of dharma, we should see them instead as parts of a body of great world literature that highlights questions more than answers, ethical quandaries rather than statements of orthodox theology, and the perpetually subtle and difficult nature of dharma.

The contemporary Ramayana

The third reason that these stories of troubled dharma are important is because they extend the Ramayana narrative into the twenty-first century. With the classical tellings of the Ramayana as their template, contemporary Indian authors have continued to refashion these stories as they wrestle with the role of dharma in the present day. One of the most famous twentieth-century tellings was that presented on Indian television over 78 weeks from 1987 to 1988. Basing his show on previous "mythologicals" from the early Bollywood film industry, from the text of Tulsidas's *Mānas*, and from Ram Lila festival performances, series creator Ramanand Sagar brought entire cities to a standstill as captivated audiences watched kings, queens, heroes, and gods enact the classical story in the relatively new and scarce medium of television (Lutgendorf 2006).

Sagar concluded his TV text with an image displayed in poster-art images and temples throughout the Hindu world: the tableau of Ram and his family back together on the throne in Ayodhya (Figure 3.2). This image thematically resembles that of Shiva with Parvati and a re-capitated Ganesh: while displaying their ultimate victory, it highlights and simultaneously covers over domestic problems that all viewers already know exist. And Indian viewers demanded that Sagar tell this difficult part of the story. His creation of a follow-up 39-episode series called *Lav Kush* the following year told those stories from the final book of the epic, where Ram exiles his wife, Valmiki vouches for Sita's innocence, and Mother Earth mercifully provides Sita with moksha from her world of suffering.

Figure 3.2 Ram and Sita return to Ayodhya, greeted by Lakshman and Hanuman

The TV Ramayana was created and shown at a tenuous time in the history of modern India. With a growing sense of Indian nationalism in the 1980s following decades of secular rule by the Congress party, and while India was in the process of remaking its socialist-leaning economy with reforms that would introduce its citizens and corporations to participation in capitalist global markets, conservative political forces used a rhetoric of Ramraj to institute a strictly Hindu-inspired government in India, opposed to one perceived to be secular, Western, or Islamic. Watched by millions of people in India at that time, the series generated a devotional fervor that standardized images that were simultaneously religious and political – the dharmic kingdom of Ram – that Hindu politicians continue to use to this day.

The flashpoint for this ideological conflict came only just five years later at the Babri Masjid in the city of Ayodhya. Built by the Muslim Mughal ruler Babur in the early 1600s, this mosque came to be seen as the place where Ram himself was born. After decades of conflict, on December 6, 1992, conservative political forces led the charge of thousands of radical Hindu volunteers to completely dismantle the monument. This event led to weeks-long communal riots between Hindus and Muslims throughout India, especially in the city of Bombay, and the deaths of hundreds, mostly Muslims. Taking hold of the country when and how it did, the TV epic served as a "catalyst in sparking a Hindu awakening across India, and bringing Hindu nationalism to the forefront of public and political spheres" (Verma 2019).[11]

Their ultimate goal is to build – or as some would say, "rebuild" – the temple to Ram, a nationalist promise similar to the Zionist and American Christian fantasy of rebuilding the Jewish temple in Jerusalem. India's Supreme Court ruled in 2010 that Muslims have ownership over one-third of the temple site, with two Hindu plaintiffs each possessing the other two-thirds; the court subsequently ruled in 2019, however, that Hindus may proceed in building a new temple to Ram on the site, while Muslims may rebuild their mosque on an adjacent plot. In 2020, amidst several political decisions that marginalized Muslims in India, Prime Minister Narendra Modi laid a ceremonial cornerstone for the forthcoming construction of the Hindu temple.

The Ramayana tradition has had much more sedate effects on the Indian public, however. Building on and playing off of the many Sanskrit, medieval, and devotional Ramayanas, contemporary authors have continued to tell new stories, gravitating towards those characters who exemplify the intersection of the tradition's subtle notions of dharma with modern notions of social justice. Sympathizing with these characters, writers and playwrights have variously attended to contemporary issues of caste in Shambuka's story, of gender and power with Shurpanakha, and of colonialism and domination with Ravana.

It is Sita, however, who has especially drawn the attention of female authors who see her as a model for the difficulties they encounter in their own lives. Within the context of the simple life that Gandhi advocated in the 1930s and 1940s, the author Kumudini published "letters" written by Sita as she adapted to life in the palace in Ayodhya and later as she anticipated an austere life in the forest. In a letter to her mother, she writes of the uselessness of the royal finery she once needed in the court of Ayodhya: "Now all I need is bark cloth. Nothing else is suitable to wear, if you consider how much it rains in the forest [...] Now I need not ponder the color of saris. I feel great peace of mind" (Richman 2008: 49).

A local women's song multiplies the tests that Sita must endure to prove her domestic value. She must reach into a hole in the ground and obtain a snake that she will coil and use as padding for the burdens she carries on her head (Richman 2008: 56). And in a short story published in 2003, "Volga" imagines the meeting between Sita and Shurpanakha, two women wronged by Ram; having grown accustomed to the jungle, Shurpanakha tends a beautiful garden and Sita, once she has finished raising Ram's sons, says that she will "take refuge with my Mother Earth" (Richman 2008: 98).[12]

Finally, the Ramayana, and especially Tulsidas's sixteenth-century Hindi-language *Mānas*, has provided guidance for generations of Indians who worked as indentured servants in sugar plantations as part of the British imperial economy. Sent off to east and south Africa and to Fiji, Guyana, and Trinidad in the Caribbean in the late nineteenth century, Hindus carried the text with them as they began their first journeys westward. Reflecting their own arduous journeys and struggles, Ram's exile and his battle against a powerful foreign foe became part of a counter-colonial narrative that annually culminated in the famous burning of Ravana at the end of the Ram Lila festival.

Conclusion: devotion in the Ramayana tradition

This chapter has considered the complex issue of Hindu dharma through the Ramayana textual tradition and its primary figure of Rama, one of the two main avatars of Vishnu. The *nakha-shikha* description of Rama at the beginning of this chapter introduced us also to the theme of devotion, which suffuses the Ramayana tradition in innumerable ways. For example, members of the Rāmānandī Sampradaya, more ascetic than the strictly devotional Shri Vaishnava school, repeatedly chant the name of Ram in the presence of icons of the Ram Parivar ("the Ram family"), present in temples throughout the Hindu world, while also considering him a formless manifestation of the ultimate brahman.

But the epic's absolute exemplar of devotion is Hanuman. Having met Ram during his conflict with Valin, Hanuman is a monkey warrior who vows to become Ram's devoted messenger and assistant. In Tulsidas's epic, he and his monkey army build a bridge to Lanka to rescue Sita; after devotionally writing Ram's name on each one, the stones float and the army is able to cross over (Figure 3.3). Upon returning to Ayodhya and receiving a pearl necklace as a gift of thanks from Sita, Hanuman bites into each pearl searching for the divine essence of each; when questioned about his curious process, Hanuman rips open his chest to display images of Ram and Sita, explaining that his own value is completely dependent upon the presence of the divine on his heart. And the *Hanumān Chālīsā*, the forty verses of Hanuman, is regularly chanted – usually weekly on Tuesdays – in temples throughout the global Hindu world.

Outside of the text, Hanuman is ever-present in icons that dot the South Asian landscape. In some smaller images, he appears in iconic, quasi-iconic, or even fully aniconic forms that mask his simian identity. Daubed or even fully covered in red powder sometimes rendering his face a nearly perfect red sphere, Hanuman serves as a guardian at temples for other gods and goddesses, especially for Ram. One of his most prominent appearances as a guardian is immediately outside the main door to the old palace in Kathmandu where Nepal's king and queen – themselves manifestations of Vishnu and Lakshmi – once ruled. This entire area with its temples, resting porches, and tourist shops is called Hanuman Dhoka (Hanuman's Gate).

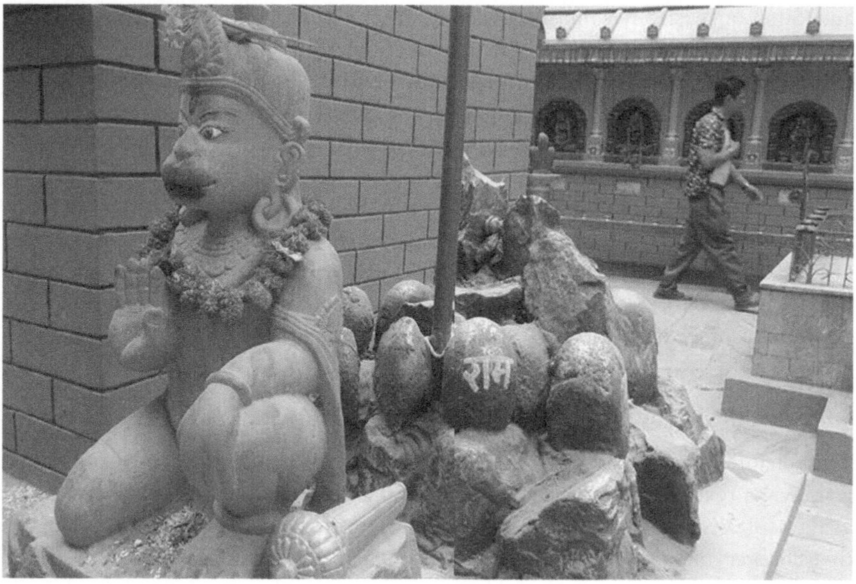

Figure 3.3 Hanuman guarding the shrine of the mother goddess Chvasa Ajima, with Ram stones nearby. Kathmandu, Nepal

In the past few decades, however, Hanuman has become an even greater focus of Hindu devotion.

Admiring Hanuman for his *shakti* and *bhakti*, simultaneously his independent power and his selfless devotion to Ram, many middle-class Hindus see Hanuman as speaking to their own situation in a rapidly urbanizing and sometimes excessively bureaucratic India. Drawing upon Hanuman's own middle status between upper and lower classes of deities, the Indian middle class has increasingly come to venerate Hanuman as a powerful go-between. Appearing in ever larger statues, Hanuman continues his role as Ram's messenger through an accessible form of devotion. Long a focus of devotional activity, Hanuman has come to occupy a more central place than ever could have been predicted, sometimes outshining Ram himself.

In the following chapter, we will continue the theme of devotion – and, to a lesser extent, of dharma – as we shift our focus to Krishna. The second major avatar of Vishnu, Krishna receives systematic and elaborate forms of devotion and introduces us to a universe that, though entirely different in its particular details from that of Ram, should also begin to feel quite familiar.

Notes

1 The monkey-god Hanuman provides another *nakha-shikha* of Rama to his kidnapped wife, Sītā (5.33.8–19).

2 See Mocko 2016 for Kathmandu's for the changing roles of royalty in Kathmandu's festival season.
3 This list adds up to eleven, since in different texts and among different communities, Balram occasionally replaces the Buddha. Focused solely on Krishna, the twelfth-century *Gītā Govinda* equates Krishna with Vishnu, listing Haldhar and the Buddha as the eighth and ninth avatars.
4 In one specific example, in the large south India city of Madras, the Goda Mandali (circle of Goda/Andal) provides a setting for women to sing and dance the poetry of Andal (Naryanan 2007: 186).
5 See Comeau 2020b for a description of the local markets where such garlands of marigolds are strung together and purchased.
6 See Pariyar 2018.
7 Viswanath 2014; Shaikh 2021; Mines 2005; Dutt 2019.
8 Like Ramanujan, I discuss other "tellings" of the epic rather than other "versions" so as to avoid the preconception that there is a single original text from which all others are derived (2004: 134).
9 Joyce Flueckiger (2020) writes of large cement images of Ravana that take center stage during Ram Lila celebrations in the central Indian state of Chattisgarh. Philip Lutgendorf (1994) writes of similar, though even larger, monumental images of Hanuman being installed throughout north India. For more on Hanuman, see Lutgendorf 2007.
10 In the first book of the epic, the authors use the same language to describe the infant Sita emerging from the earth (*bhūtalād utthitā*) (1.65.14–15).
11 Anand Patwardhan's 1991 documentary *Ram Ke Naam* (*In the Name of God*), filmed largely on the ground in Ayodhya, examines the rhetoric and activity on the part of both conservative forces seeking the destruction of the mosque and secular forces seeking understanding between all sides.
12 Nina Paley's 2008 animated film *Sita Sings the Blues* (fully accessible on the Internet) touches on similar themes as she considers the Ramayana as a way to work through her own breakup.

References

Dutt, Yashica. 2019. *Coming Out as Dalit: A Memoir*. New Delhi: Aleph.
Goldman, Robert P. and Sally J. Sutherland Goldman. 2021. *The Rāmāyaṇa of Vālmīki: The Complete English Translation*. Princeton, NJ: Princeton University Press.
Ramanujan, A. K. 2004. Three Hundred Rāmāyaṇas: Five Examples and Three Thoughts on Translation. In *The Collected Essays of A. K. Ramanujan*. Oxford: Oxford University Press, 131–160.

Key terms

avatar
Alvar poets
Andal
dharma
the four Human Goals
the four Social Classes
the four Stages of Life
Texts: The Laws of Manu, Ramayana, Tiruvāymoḻi of Nammāḻvār, Tiruppāvai of Andal, Hanumān Chālīsā

Persons

Ramananand Sagar
Yashica Datt
Isabel Wilkerson

Study questions

1. How do multiple social and ethical principles and categories come together to construct the complex notion of Hindu dharma? How is this dharma practiced and challenged in the contemporary Hindu world?
2. From the Ramayana, how do the figures of Rama, Sita, and Hanuman exemplify key notions of dharma?
3. How do the poetry and practice of regional versions of the Ramayana display changing values across South Asia?

4 Krishna and *bhakti*

Devotion, play, and performance in the twelve forests of Braj

The tenth-century *Bhāgavata Purāṇa*, one of the most famous texts detailing devotion to Krishna, tells his story of lifting Mount Govardhan. One day in autumn, Krishna approached the people of the land of Braj as they were celebrating the festival to the Vedic god Indra. Listening to the villagers explain that they were essentially praying for rain, Krishna told them that they should take all of the material items to be used for Indra's festival and redirect them to a festival for cows, brahmins, Mount Govardhan, and ultimately for Krishna himself. Angered by this change in plans, accompanied by the storm gods, and riding his elephant, Indra sent down torrents of rain to interrupt their new festival. Seeing his villagers under assault, Krishna lifted up the mountain and held it over the village like an umbrella, protecting them from Indra's rage.[1]

Among the many stories of Krishna from his childhood and adulthood, this one stands out for its many facets of Hindu devotion. Lodged within a series of stories in which Krishna defeats various forms of demonic evil – a calf, a donkey, various serpents, and ultimately the wicked King Kamsa – this story narrates a seismic shift in the Hindu tradition, though one that had certainly taken place centuries earlier. No longer beholden to the ancient system of Vedic ritual that depended upon the rote performance of correct rituals guided by high-caste priests, the rural villagers of Braj could now meet their spiritual needs immediately as they experienced the natural world around them directly (Figure 4.1).

The place of Braj provides not just a setting for many of Krishna's stories, but is also a place of pilgrimage due to its direct physical connection to Krishna. In much the same way that the Judeo-Christian "holy land" in and around Israel continues to be a place of pilgrimage for many from around the world as it represents the setting of the Bible, Krishna's land of Braj has long been a pilgrimage destination for those who seek to touch the soil, trees, and ponds where many of Krishna's stories occurred. Located in north India between Agra, the city of the Taj Mahal, and India's capital city of New Delhi, the rural Braj region contains places that are simultaneously geographical and mythological: Mount Govardhan, the town of Mathura, and the village of Vrindaban amidst the area's twelve forests.

DOI: 10.4324/9781003475033-5

Figure 4.1 Krishna among many deities at the shrine of the mother goddess Chvasa Ajima. Kathmandu, Nepal

Drawing on the themes of dharma and devotion from the previous chapter on Ram, this chapter will examine the many ways that devotion to Krishna, the other primary avatar of Vishnu, has become widespread throughout the world. After detailing some of the general practices and contours of devotion, we will return to the specific narratives and practices that more specifically comprise devotion to Krishna. One of the main themes of this chapter will be on the intense sensory engagement that devotion entails, the resulting intimacy generated between deity and devotee, and the various depictions of these relationships in South Asian artistic traditions.

Classical Hinduism: the Path of Devotion

The term Devotion is a translation of the Sanskrit term *bhakti*. A term that means "to share, to participate," *bhakti* indicates the communal manner in which individual bhaktas (devotees), families, neighborhoods, and global Hindu communities celebrate the deeds and power of gods and goddesses. As a more complete definition, we might consider *bhakti* to be a cultural system whose adherents display an emotional attachment to sacred objects and to the divine beings they refer to through poetry, narrative, and ritual practice.

Although the Path of Devotion is the most common form of practice found throughout the Hindu world today, we must also note its many distinctions from the religious forms that preceded it. Different from the philosophical non-dualism that we saw in the Upanishads and Shaiva traditions, through which one attains absolute one-ness with the supreme, Vaishnava dualism retains a distinct separation between forms of Vishnu and the bhaktas who venerate them. This dualism provides a model for *bhakti* traditions and defines the ritual life of Classical Hindu worship.

The Vaishnava Path of Devotion also differs from the Shaiva yogic traditions in terms of their relative engagement with the senses. Whereas Shaiva traditions often prize the yogic restraint of one's senses from engagement, attraction, and attachment to the outside world, practices of *bhakti* directly engage the senses on multiple levels. By inviting participants to activate the physical, visual, and auditory as integral components of worship, devotional traditions allow worshippers to immerse themselves in the total experience of these forms of Vishnu.

In some ways, and despite their many formal differences, bhakti resembles Vedic ritual more than it does Shaiva traditions. Retaining the basic notion that when we maintain proper relations with the gods, they will bestow upon us blessings of health, wealth, and fertility, Vedic ritual and Vaishnava bhakti are oriented much more towards the householder than to the renouncer.

It should be noted, however, that themes that appear to be uniquely associated with Vaishnava forms of *bhakti* have come to be associated with nearly all other deities as well. Thus, standard acts of householder devotion – described below under the heading of "Temple rituals" – are also regularly shown to forms of Shiva. This is sometimes referred to as Vaishnavization, a historical process by which communities practice more orthodox forms of worship, ethics, and lifestyle as they seek to fit themselves into a more recognizable, standardized, and middle-class model.

Two widespread and related examples of Vaishnavization involve shifts away from meat eating and animal sacrifice. Throughout Himalayan regions of South Asia, the tantric worship of fierce Shaiva and Shākta deities (Bhairav and Kali, for respective examples) is often performed with the beheading of an animal; a celebratory feast among the family or community follows. Forms of

Vishnu, however, will never receive such offerings. They instead receive offerings of grains, dairy, fruits, and vegetables, though offerings of coconuts and pumpkins readily allude to the heads of the animals offered in sacrifice and remind us of the power inherent in such offerings.

The process of Vaishnavization reminds us that despite the continued presence of extraordinarily diverse Hindu cultures, some elements of homogenization have taken root. Vaishnava styles of devotion have become some of the most influential religious expressions especially in Hindu communities outside of India.

Icons

The focal point of Hindu devotional worship is an icon (*mūrti*) or group of icons venerated in homes, temples (*mandir*), and city-wide festivals. More than just a statue made of stone, brass, clay, or another material, murti are worshipped as the deities themselves.[2] Icons become gods and goddess through a two-step process: their physical construction is followed by their religious consecration. The *Brihat Samhita*, a royal text from the sixth century, describes both parts of this process. For its construction, the icon should possess ideal dimensions that can be replicated by multiple artists: "The nose, forehead, chin, and neck are four digits long; so are the ears. The jaws and chin are two digits broad" (58.5). Rather than ensuring absolute uniformity across all images, however, the text describes unique features of each. For example, Vishnu is to be made with four arms, in whose hands he carries the conch shell, discus, and club, and with whose fourth hand he makes the sign of peace. Ultimately, the text states, "An image should be made in such a way that its ornaments, dress, decorations, and form conform to the traditions and practices of a particular place," with the result that "such an image, possessed of these good features, brings good fortune" (58.29).

The second process, which fully transforms the icon into a deity, is variously named as a consecration (*adhivāsya*), installation (*samsthāpya*), waking up (*jāgaraṇa*), or, in other texts and in local traditions, establishing the breath (*prāṇ pratiṣṭhā*). As the final part of the construction process, the icon's eyes are carved and the breath (*prāṇ*) of the deity installed (*pratiṣṭhā*) into the icon.[3] As described on the website of the Pluralism Project, the Sri Lakshmi Mandir in Ashland, Massachusetts, recently proceeded with its consecration of the goddess Lakshmi as such: "The Divine presence is invoked in prayer at the fire altar outside, and the power of the Deity is transferred ritually through silver or gold threads that have been strung from the fire altar to the image."[4] The *Brihat Samhita* describes the final celebration as the deity is processed into the temple by brahmins and worshipped by the larger community with flowers, colored cloths, and musical instruments.[5]

Never a part of Vedic ritual, temple icons came to prominence around the turn of the Common Era. Initially carved out of stone in the same workshops as Buddhist and Jain icons in Mathura in north India, icons came to replace the Vedic fire as the central object of Hindu worship. The permanence of icons and temples also reflects a drastic change in the Indian economy of that time. No longer a nomadic people ruled by local chiefs who seasonally wandered in search of greener pastures, average citizens in early medieval India were city-dwellers under the rule of a king who worked to become a universal monarch. The texts of this era, especially the two epics, Ramayana and Mahabharata, reflect this new urban focus with stories of urban kings whose reign is interrupted by a lengthy sojourn to the jungle. Their victorious return to a capital city reinforces this new urban economy, with the underlying epic culture reflecting these earliest forms of devotional Hinduism.

Icons of deities and the temples where they are installed and worshipped visually reflect the kings and palaces that came to sit at the center of the capital city. The religious rites performed to the icons of deities in their temples echo the rule of these powerful urban kings. Entrances into and processions around the capital city mark their sphere of influence, and puja rites inside the temple reflect the proper ways of greeting, welcoming, and serving powerful kings. And it was Vishnu who first instantiated the Hindu king, replacing the Buddha as the central royal-religious figure in the first centuries of the Common Era.

The centrality of Hindu icons stands at odds with dominant forms of religion in the West and remains sometimes difficult to process. Steeped in the culture of the Abrahamic traditions – Judaism, Christianity, and Islam – that expressly forbid the veneration of images, Western travelers, missionaries, and writers have often approached these icons with some trepidation. Walking along the banks of the Ganges River in the city of Varanasi in 1897, the famous American author Mark Twain expressed some degree of horror at the number and appearance of the many icons (or "idols," as he says) that he encountered there. He writes:

> In fact, none of the idols in Benares are handsome or attractive. And what a swarm of them there is! The town is a vast museum of idols – and all of them crude, misshapen, and ugly. They flock through one's dreams at night, a wild mob of nightmares. When you get tired of them in the temples and take a trip on the river, you find idol giants flashily painted, stretched out side by side on the shore.
>
> (Twain 1989: 504)[6]

From the same time period, the British missionary Lucy Guinness likewise refers to images of the monkey-god Hanuman as "disgustingly ugly." Drawing on a biblical demonological metaphor to refer to all of the gods, she states: "their name is legion, their legends infamous and monstrous." Finally, the Scottish missionary John Stoddard, referring to these same images as "hideous," "obscene," and "too disgusting to be illustrated," refers to their source, the religion of Hinduism, as "the most repulsive exhibition of idolatry, fanaticism, and filth that one can well imagine" (Beal 2014: 108–110).

Like the families who challenged the presence of yoga in American schools described earlier, Mark Twain and these others appear simply overwhelmed by the foreign and exotic nature of these images with which they are radically unfamiliar. Moreover, encountering these images strikes them as not simply unusual but also as a violation of the first of the biblical commandments against idolatry. More than the fact that Hindus simply do not view their images this way, the ritual attention directed to these icons, especially to those of Krishna, render them not only spiritually powerful but also visually stunning and aesthetically beautiful.

Temple rituals

The temple icon facilitates the central act of Hindu worship, *pūjā*. Based around an exchange of physical substances between devotee and deity, puja can be performed within a private family home, a small roadside shrine, a grand temple, or as part of a public urban festival. Focusing on the icon of the deity, the devotee presents an offering in the form of food, clothing, money, oil lamps, or a *bhajan* song – a word linguistically related to *bhakti* – displaying their dual and unequal relationship to the deity. The deity then completes this exchange by returning to the devotee their *prasād* (grace) as an item of fruit, flowers, sweets, and/or the distinctive red *tika* mark placed upon the devotee's forehead. While a priest typically moderates this exchange in the setting of a temple, this same worship at a family home or small shrine might be carried out by devotees themselves or with the assistance of family or friends.[7]

As one example, at the weekly Tuesday puja worship service to Hanuman at the Ganesh temple in the Flushing neighborhood of Queens, New York, participants recited the *Hanuman Chālīsā*, a forty-verse series of mantras taken from the Ramayana. After praising him for all of his good qualities, they received at the conclusion of the service the god's *prasad* grace in the form of, appropriately, a single banana. The exchange of such a simple relevant gift – one that becomes a physical part of the body of each participating devotee who consumes it – reflects Hanuman's superior position to his devotees, their praise and thanks for his continued acts of power in their lives, and the grace that he regularly shows them.

One of the most central and basic exchanges that often defines the act of puja is that of darshan. Reinforcing the hierarchy between deity and devotee as we have seen with the exchange of puja and prasad and with the namaste gesture, the exchange of darshan – difficult to translate into English – is that of a non-physical substance: the sacred sight, vision, or glance of the deity. When the devotee stands in front of and locks eyes with the icon of a deity – often accompanied by the namaste greeting and a puja offering – the devotee *receives* the darshan of the deity who *gives* it. In other words, the substance of *darshan* travels from high to low, just like the exchange of physical puja offerings and the leftover prasad blessing that follows.

The types and attitudes of bhakti can be seen and felt in many Krishna temples throughout the Hindu world. Similar in importance to the south Indian Venkateshwar temple highlighted in the previous chapter is the north Indian Govindadeva temple to Krishna in the city of Jaipur in the northwestern desert state of Rajasthan. Built in the 1730s as part of the palace of Jai Singh II and his new city of Jaipur (which translates both to "the city of victory" and "the city of Jai [Singh]"), the temple houses an image of Krishna as Govindadeva, the lord of cows. Jaipur was not the original home of this icon, however; married to an image of the gopi cowherdress, Rādhā, in the pilgrimage town of Vrindaban in 1633, Govindadeva and Radha were moved together to Jaipur amidst shifting patterns of politics and patronage.[8]

This temple is typically referred to as the Govinddevji Mandir, with the honorific suffix -ji appended to one of the many names of Krishna. Added to the end of the name of any person or deity (Shiv-ji or Lakshmi-ji), this suffix (-jyū in Nepali) conveys a sense of respect, like Sir or Madam.

The temple in which the icon is installed is part of the royal palace complex: it is the Palace of the Sun (Surya Mahal) that sits opposite the king's royal residence, the Palace of the Moon (Chandra Mahal). The temple's proximity to the king imbues the icon with a complex historical, geographical, and religious significance, reiterating the sense of royalty often contained in the narratives of Hindu gods and goddesses. The icons of Radha and Krishna provide a dual focal point for devotees to express their devotion. Dressed in sets of clothing that are donated and changed throughout the day and festival calendar, Radha and Krishna are venerated in many ways: songs and recitations of their many names; elaborate festival displays of jewelry, water fountains, flowers, and feasts, especially for Krishna's summer birthday; the duplication of Radha-Krishna in photographs and icons available for sale in the shops within and outside of the temple complex; and even online worship through the display of the icons on the temple website.

The devotion shown to these and other icons of (Radha and) Krishna allows devotees to display what the Vaishnava tradition refers to as the five *bhāva*s (the five attitudes towards God):

1 *shānta*, with peaceful love;
2 *dāsya*, as a servant;

3 *sakhya*, as a friend;
4 *vātsalya*, as a mother towards her child;
5 *madhurya*, as a woman towards her lover.

These five attitudes are displayed in a variety of relationships throughout the stories of Krishna that will be detailed throughout the second half of this chapter. Divided into three sections, each detailing one phase of Krishna's life – as child, lover, and universal deity – the next sections will narrate stories of Krishna's life contained in some of the most popular texts in all of Hinduism. Placing them within their larger devotional context, we will be able to see the many ways that these five attitudes provide devotees with an emotional foundation that has long influenced Hindu devotional practice.

Krishna as child: *lila* (in the *Bhāgavata Purāṇa*)

Especially in the 1960s, some American communities sought alternatives to a Christian religious culture from which they felt increasingly disconnected. Adopting some facets of Hinduism and Buddhism, some even began to regard Jesus as a peaceful yogi or even an avatar of Vishnu alongside Krishna and the others.[9] Despite the vast cultural and geographical distances that separate the stories of Jesus from those of Krishna, the many similarities between these two figures encouraged certain pockets of religious Americans to further this brand of interreligious dialogue: their names (Christ and Krishna), their ultimate purpose of saving the world from the current decline of goodness, and even the details of their respective birth stories – their lowly birth, their attempted assassination by a powerful king, and their families' movements from one place to another to safeguard their newborn.

Krishna's complete narrative cycle is contained in a variety of epic stories, philosophical dialogues, and devotional texts and songs. Composed at different moments in history, in different languages, and with different sectarian ideologies, these sources all attribute to Krishna a consistent set of themes and qualities. Variously incorporating the five devotional attitudes, the stories of Krishna's life construct a complete picture of a person whose divinity encompasses virtually every facet of the Hindu tradition.

Krishna's divinity permeates his entire life cycle and is evident already in his birth story. Told primarily in the opening chapters of the *Bhagavata Purana* (BhP) one of the most recent of the eighteen main Puranas, Krishna's birth story is directly tied to the fortunes of his uncle, King Kamsa. Always described as "wicked," Kamsa's identity as a demon reborn on earth makes him one manifestation of evil that each of Vishnu's avatars must defeat in order to save the world.

> An increasingly popular and global venue for the *Bhagavata Purana* is the Bhagavata Saptaha, a seven-day recitation and commentary offered by a guru on the life of Vishnu and his avatars, especially of Krishna.

Prophesied to die by his sister Devaki's eighth child, Kamsa imprisoned Devaki and her husband Vasudeva (BhP 1.10). During their unjust prison sentence, Devaki gave birth to six children all of whom Kamsa summarily killed. Her seventh child, kept safe by being transferred to the womb of the goddess Rohini, grows up as Krishna's older brother Haldhar or Samkarshana (he who pulls the plow and/or he who was drawn out). With the intervention of the goddess Yogamaya, and in order to keep safe the eighth child Krishna, Vasudeva exits the prison, places the newborn in a basket on his head, and wades through the swollen Yamuna River to the house of the couple Nanda and Yashoda.[10] The latter having just given birth to a daughter, Vasudeva switches the two newborns, his son for her daughter, and wades back through the river to his prison.

When Kamsa sees the birth of the eighth child who was to threaten his life, he grabs the girl by her ankles and dashes her against a stone. At the moment of her death, Kamsa immediately sees the true identity of the girl: she is at once the goddess Yogamaya, the natural force who put to sleep the guards of the prison, the female child who was in Yashoda's womb, and the goddess who now shows herself to Kamsa. Hearing her tell him that she will smash his body with her own hands and drink his blood, Kamsa realized that his murderous task had been thwarted and that the survival of Krishna would result in his own death.

Krishna's childhood, even to a certain extent his eventual killing of Kamsa later in the core tenth book of the *Bhagavata Purana*, draws on *vātsalya*, the attitude of a mother towards her child. In the story of the demoness Pūtanā, we feel the horror that Krishna's mother Yashoda must have felt as the demoness attempts to kill her child by feeding him with a poisoned breast and the relief she feels as Krishna defeats her by literally sucking her dry. We feel her frustration as Krishna and his friends eat the mudpies they make from the monsoon-soaked dirt of the fields or, in a moment of innocent naughtiness, steal the family's homemade butter from the clay pots kept high above the ground floor of their house. But his divinity is always close to the surface of these stories, especially when Yashoda pries her boy's mouth open to extract his delicious mudpies and she sees, for an instant before she is made to forget, the entire universe in his mouth.

These events of Krishna's childhood are defined by the term *līlā*. Referring both to Krishna's "playfulness" as a child and the roles that devotees can "play" in games, festivals, and devotional settings, lila provides many opportunities to intimately experience the life of Krishna. In the spring festival of Holi, children recreate the playfulness of Krishna by hurling colored water at one another, though village settings might include cow urine and other less pleasant substances. Role reversals along caste, class, and gender lines create a "festival of love" whose egalitarian ethos temporarily eradicates hierarchy while the festival's conclusion re-draws those very same conservative lines (Marriott 2006).

Rather than saying that people "celebrate Holi," Hindi-language speakers will say that they "play Holi" (*Holi khelne*). The general license that Holi affords to playfully interact with friends, family, and complete strangers has made the festival a staple of Bollywood film songs.

In the Gai Jatra ("Cow Festival") of the Kathmandu Valley, children dress in all white as cows who lead the recently deceased across the Vaitarini River to the other side, as even younger children dress as Krishna in his role as a village *gopa* (cow protector). And Krishna's summer birthday (Krishna Janmashtami) is celebrated with contests that recreate Krishna's identity as the *makhan chor* (butter thief). Forming massive human pyramids above the city streets, children compete to break the *dahi handi* (butter pot) amidst large public celebrations. More sedate celebrations of Krishna's birthday, such as that celebrated in the ISKCON temple in Brooklyn, New York, includes the anointing with water of portable festival images of Radha-Krishna and the rocking of his cradle, amidst music and the repeated chanting of his names.

In one of her devotional poems, Andal writes of this incident from the perspective of one of the gopis:

> You escaped Kamsa's savage net
> in the midst of that deep dark night
> only to torture the hearts of hapless maidens
> stranded here.
> Yaśodā lets you stray, bold and unpunished.
> O you who suckled the milk
> from the breast of the deceitful demoness
> Shameless one
> Please return our clothes to us.
> (Venkatesan 11)[11]

Being exposed to Krishna to whom they are also devoted, the gopis self-consciously see Krishna in the complex ways a woman sees her lover. This story of Krishna's *lila* introduces us to the theme of *kāma* (desire) that permeates the second phase of his life.

Unlike the Islamic calendar that is purely lunar and the Western calendar that is purely solar (except for the lunar Easter holiday), the Hindu calendar is luni-solar. Festivals are thus celebrated according to a calendar whose months begin and end with the full moon and are divided into two equal halves; the dark half begins with the waning full moon, and the bright half begins with the waxing new moon. The annual calendar then resets every solar new year (April 14). For example, Krishna's birthday (*Krishna Janmashtami*) is celebrated on the eighth day (*ashtami*) of the dark half of the month of Bhadra; occurring in the late summer, this day can fall anywhere between approximately August 11 and September 6.

Krishna as lover: *kāma* (in the *Gītā Govinda*)

After the gopis emerge from the river, Krishna encourages them to return with him to the land of Braj. Making a brief detour to lift Mount Govardhan, Krishna appears to them, playing his flute and "capturing the hearts of the beautiful-eyed women" (10.29.3).[12] His music was so seductive, it even aroused Kāma, desire personified in a very Cupid-like figure who pierces the hearts of lovers with his flowery arrows. With Kāma himself aroused, the women of Braj did not stand a chance. Fully immersed in their devotion to Krishna, the women, with their clothes and jewelry in disarray, drop everything they are doing – cooking dinner, putting on their makeup, and even feeding their children and taking care of their husbands – as they run to be near Krishna.

Their hope is immediately dashed, however, as Krishna suddenly vanished. Krishna was simply testing them, as he checked their pride at the intimate divine attention they anticipated. Their desire hardly quenched, the gopis searched for Krishna asking the trees where he might be. In his absence, they kept Krishna in mind by enacting his stories: several gopis defeated demons played by other gopis, one lifted up Mount Govardhan, while another stepped on the head of the poisonous serpent Kāliya. Arriving at the banks of the Yamuna River and disoriented by their separation, the gopis sang about Krishna and longed for his return.

Similar to Shiva's Tandava dance that creates the world as it destroys the demonic obstacles depicted underneath his feet, Krishna uses dance to defeat the serpent Kaliya. In the original story to which this gopi-centered story refers, Krishna defeats the water serpent who was poisoning the lake where Krishna and his friends swam and played. Some environmental groups in contemporary India have begun using this story as a metaphor for cleaning up waterways polluted by garbage and industrial runoff (Haberman 2006: 150–159).

And finally Krishna returns. Receiving attention from all of the gopis as they bask in his presence, Krishna explains that he disappeared as an act of service to them, so that they would break the enduring shackles of the household and further their devotion to him. What follows is the climax of this five-chapter scene, known throughout India as the Rās Līlā, "the Circle Dance" or "the Dance of Love." Depicted in images and contemporary dances, the Ras Lila places Krishna in the center of a circle of dancing gopis (the *gopī-maṇḍala*) as he multiples himself in order to share intimacy with each.[13]

This passage points up a sense of the multiplicity of dharma within the bhakti tradition. Although Krishna says that he wants the women to break their householder shackles, he also tells them before the Ras Lila begins, "The highest dharma of a woman is to serve her husband faithfully, to ensure the well-being of her relatives, and to nourish her children" (10.29.24 [Bryant 127]). Highlighted by the experiences of their senses that were "alive with pleasure from the contact of his limbs," the women experience a conflict between multiple types of dharma (10.33.17

[Bryant 141]). Just as Ram had to negotiate his dharma to his kingdom with that to his wife, so also the women in this intensely devotional passage must negotiate the dharma of renouncers who have no care for the things of this world with that of householders in general and of women in particular (*strī-dharma*). Thus, rather than liberating women as the text sometimes implies, the Ras Lila further places women within a singular domestic model, much like the Holi festival supports hierarchy by showing the absurdity of its total elimination.[14]

The gopis' devotion to Krishna is directly related to their separation from him. This concept of *viraha bhakti* (devotion in separation) is not unique to this passage but shoots through much of the bhakti tradition. We saw this earlier in the literature of the early devotional poetess Ammaiyār who wished for "a blessed view of [Shiva's] highest form" as she approached the cremation grounds wishing to be transformed into a ghoul. Devotional separation is further addressed and comes to be reversed in the twelfth century *Gītā Govinda*, a Sanskrit poem written by Jayadev. Retelling the narrative of the Ras Lila and picking up on one passage that details Krishna's dalliance with one particular gopi, the *Gītā Govinda* doubles down on the eroticism that is occasionally more subdued in the *Bhagavata Purana.*

When people refer to Radha and Krishna together, they typically say "Radha-Krishna" similar to "Sita-Ram" as they do in other places in India.

The *Gītā Govinda* is a poem about the interminable waiting period between separation and devotion, as Krishna and his favorite gopi Radha anticipate their meeting in the forest (Figure 4.2). Although composed in Sanskrit, the poem is

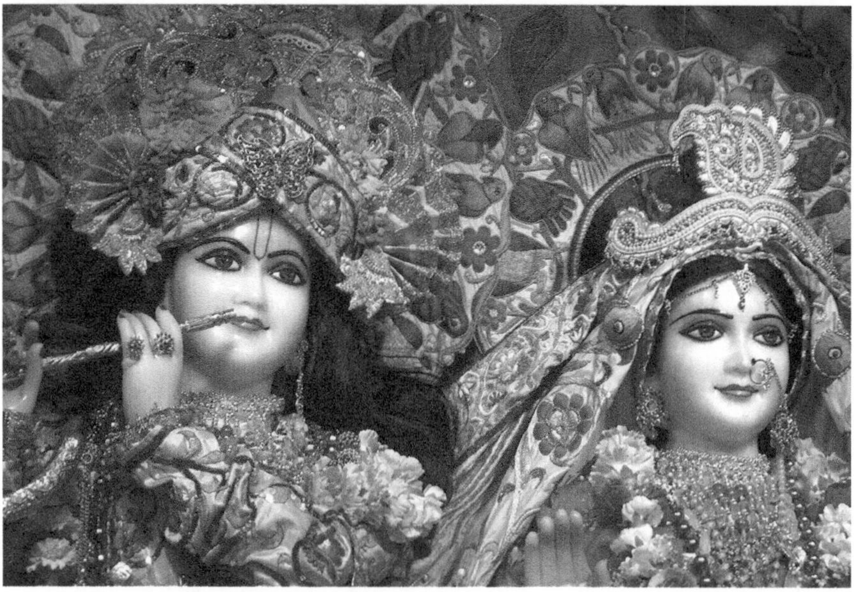

Figure 4.2 Temple image of Radha and Krishna

written for an audience that has already begun to read bhakti poetry in many regional vernacular languages throughout south and north India. This accessibility and the beauty of its language have led to its many types of performance, as the text has long been accompanied by local and regional melodies and rhythms. The content, as well, with its many refrains lends itself to memorization and repetition. One such refrain, repeated after every eight verses in the text's first chapter and evoking notions of devotion in separation, shows this well:

> In springtime, the sensual season so languorously
> long for forlorn lovers,
> Krishna strays and plays, my friend,
> dancing with young girls.
>
> (1.3.28–35)[15]

As Radha waits for Krishna, whom she suspects is out dallying with other gopis, Radha confides in her girlfriend and repeats the refrain: "I remember Krishna dancing in the Ras Lila, jesting in amorous prankish play" (2.1.2–9). But she is not the only one in anguish; Krishna, too, is concerned that *she* has forgotten *him*, and he pines for her: "Why is it that my sickness, this suffering of love in separation, keeps getting worse and worse?" (3.15). A series of dialogues follows between the two forlorn lovers, often with Radha's girlfriend as a go-between, in which they reconcile their confusion and miscommunication. The poem proceeds with a description of their love-making, erotically charged but never obscene, and concludes with Radha requesting Krishna to make her presentable once again – to fix her hair, makeup, and jewelry – as she departs from his forest abode.

The theme of devotional separation in the poetry of Ammaiyār, Andal, and the *Gītā Govinda* continues into the sixteenth century in the poetry of Mirabai. Mira (as she is sometimes referred to) wrote in a north Indian setting that fostered a group of authors known as the *sant* poets; often translated as "saints," this term literally means "those who ARE." Like Andal among the south Indian Alvars, Mirabai is the only female among them.

In dialogue with Islamic Sufi mystics, some *sant* poets, including Kabir and Guru Nanak, the founder of the Sikh tradition, viewed the divine abstractly.[16] Mirabai, however, much like Tulsidas who composed the Hindi telling of the Ramayana, operated within a more strictly Vaishnava devotional context. Often writing of Krishna as Giridhar, he who mercifully holds the mountain above his devotees, her devotion to Krishna liberated her from her *strī-dharma*, the strict gender roles that required her to uphold the virtues of the female householder. Surviving an assassination attempt by poison for transgressing dharma in this way, Mira, like Andal, declared her love for Krishna rather than for any human husband.

Krishna as lord of the universe: *avatar* (in the *Mahābhārata* and *Bhagavad Gītā*)

Differently divine throughout his life, Krishna's third and final phase marks a set of related shifts: from Radha's cowboy lover in the playful land of Braj to the more serene life of a warrior-king in the nearby city of Mathura. (His presiding over a kingdom in the far western capital city of Dvaraka only occasionally interrupts his otherwise continuous narrative set along the Yamuna River in the north.) This shift away from Krishna's childhood and youth and towards his royal office happens approximately midway through the *Bhagavata Purana*'s pivotal Book Ten (of its twelve books in total). But it is in the earlier epic Mahabharata where Krishna's royalty and divinity go more fully hand-in-hand, and he comes to be seen as an avatar of Vishnu and the universal form of God.

An epic of some 100,000 couplets in eighteen books, the Mahabharata remains one of the longest texts among the world's literatures. Like *The Laws of Manu*, as with many elements of Classical Hinduism, the Mahabharata developed over time before receiving its final form near the turn of the Common Era, so nearly a millennium before the *Bhagavata Purana*. Also like *Manu*, the epic marks a philosophical response to the growing royal patronage of Buddhism, Jainism, and other traditions. This dynamic becomes evident in the epic's long discussions of dharma, many of which explicitly account for notions of non-violence (*ahiṃsā*), presented here as the hallmark of Buddhism ("the Dharma"). Drawing on tales of war and heroism from the Rig Veda, the Mahabharata negotiates the non-violence advocated by Buddhist monks and kings with the unfortunate violence often required to maintain political power.

Like the Ramayana, the Mahabharata is performed in regional festivals, though neither as widespread nor as uniform as Ram's story. Localized and barely known outside of two regions in India – the Garhwal region in the Himalayan north and the town of Gingee in the Tamil south – these epic festivals take on distinctly local cultural flavors. Based on the epic plot familiar to all, these festivals focus on a diversity of related local traditions: the worship of weapons, the glorification of warrior heroes, and the power of goddesses. Adding characters and plot points unknown to the Sanskrit narrative, these local festivals are performed in support of local medieval kingdoms and contemporary social and cultural identities that locate epic tales among local people and places.

Also like Valmiki's Ramayana that was written in Sanskrit and achieved wide notoriety throughout the Hindu world, the story of the Mahabharata war greatly influenced regional literature. Composed by the sage Vyasa whose literary fame also includes the eighteen Puranas, it is included among the earliest Tamil devotional poetry, where Nammalvar writes of the central role of Krishna in "The Epic War":

> When our lord managed
> that spectacular Bhārata war,
> what noises!
> Noise of well-fed wrestlers
> falling in combat,
> the jitter
> of whole armies
> of regal men,
> and the noises of the gods

jostling in heaven
to watch the fun!
(Ramanujan 1981: 8)

The narrative core of the epic tells of a battle between two sets of rival cousins, the good Pandavas and the evil Kauravas. Losing a dice match, humiliated, and cheated out of their kingdom, the five Pandava brothers and their collective wife, Draupadi, are sent to the forest to live in exile for twelve years, much like how Rama is exiled from his capital of Ayodhya in his own epic. Only following a thirteenth year living incognito are the Pandavas able to return to regain their capital city. The Pandavas are victorious in their final battle against the Kauravas, a battle they only won with Krishna as their advisor and that can only be described as "apocalyptic" – virtually everyone on earth dies as a result of the universal war, leaving only a small remnant to tell the tale.

Introducing the epic's four war books (Books Six through Nine) is a long section called the *Bhagavad Gītā* (the Song of the Lord). One of the best-known of all Hindu texts, the *Gita* details a lecture on dharma given by Krishna to Arjuna, the mightiest of the five Pandava brothers. Reminding readers that amidst the chaos of the global civil war that the epic narrates one must still perform one's dharma, the *Gita*'s first verse situates the dialogue both on the battlefield of Kurukshetra near India's current capital city of Delhi as well as on the battlefield of dharma that we must all constantly negotiate (*dharma-kshetre kuru-kshetre*).

While the *Gita* is regarded as very auspicious, the Mahabharata as a whole is regarded as dark and inauspicious, much like the very names of Kurukshetra and of the burning grounds of Manikarnika Ghat in Varanasi. As a result, copies of the Mahabharata are traditionally not kept inside one's home.

As he approaches the battlefield with Krishna as his advisor and charioteer, Arjuna requests that Krishna position their chariot between the two warring sides where he sees friends, relatives, and teachers arrayed against one another in a battle that he feels ultimately nobody can win (Figure 4.3). Dejected at the thought of the impending civil war, Arjuna expresses his frustration, his pity, and his utter lack of will to fight:[17]

My limbs sink,
my mouth is parched,
my body trembles,
the hair bristles on my flesh.
The magic bow slips
from my hand, my skin burns,
I cannot stand still,

my mind reels.
I see omens of chaos,
Krishna; I see no good
in killing my kinsmen
in battle.

(1.29–31)

The remainder of the text represents more of a philosophical argument than a song, in which Krishna attempts to convince Arjuna to perform his proper caste duty as a Kshatriya warrior and to fight. Between Chapters Four and Eight, three of which detail the yogas of Action, Knowledge, and Devotion (Chapters Three, Four, and Twelve), Krishna develops an argument about the true nature of the universe, as he builds upon established Hindu concepts.

Drawing on the dualistic Samkhya system of philosophy that also underlies Patanjali's Yoga Sutras, Krishna distinguishes in Chapter Two one's true Spirit from illusory Matter. Alluding to the Purusha ("the Person") with its roots in the creation hymn of the Rig Veda, Krishna differentiates the physical bodies of Arjuna and those of his enemies from their core selves:

Figure 4.3 The Gita Mandir (Temple of the Gita) celebrates Krishna's role as Arjuna's advisor and charioteer in the *Bhagavad Gita*. Mathura, India

It cannot be cut or burned;
it cannot be wet or withered;
it is enduring, all-pervasive,
fixed, immovable, and timeless.
Death is certain for anyone born,
and birth is certain for the dead;
since the cycle is inevitable,
you have no cause to grieve!
(2.24, 27)

Krishna continues this theme of the irrelevance of the physical body – and thus the irrelevance of the death of that body – throughout the text. Beginning in Chapter Four ("the Yoga of Knowledge") and leading up to Chapter Eight Krishna establishes himself as the universal impersonal principle *brahman*. Echoing various non-dualistic passages from the Upanishads, Krishna tells Arjuna:

I am the taste in the water, Arjuna,
the light in the moon and sun,
OM resonant in all sacred lore,
the sound in space, valor in men.
(7.7)

Just as in the Upanishads, the ultimate goal of disciplined people is to attain immortality from which they will never return.

This goal is achieved by understanding brahman, by being disciplined in yoga (the *Gita* uses related terms such as *yukta* relentlessly), and by actively performing one's dharma. The *Gita* has maintained a long and nearly uninterrupted history among Hindu communities largely because of its flexibility: placing the householder and renouncer traditions in a dynamic relationship to one another, the text requires one to act in the world while also "relinquishing attachment and dedicating action to *brahman*" (5.10). Embodied in "stable wisdom" (*sthita-prajña*), devotees perform *nish-kāma karma*, action without the desire for the results of that action.

This flexibility has allowed communities from across the Hindu spectrum to variously interpret and apply Krishna's message for their own communities. The text has been used for both non-violent and revolutionary activity against the British imperial government in the late nineteenth and early twentieth centuries (including both Mohandas Gandhi and Nathuram Godse, the man who assassinated Gandhi); as a spiritual synthesis of integral yoga for a global society (Aurobindo Ghose); and as a practical strategy for increasing corporate productivity in the twenty-first century.

The final and unique element of the *Gita*'s message builds on the Vaishnava tradition described in this and the previous chapter. More than the solitary creator Purusha and the abstract *brahman*, Krishna is also an avatar of Vishnu within the larger path (or yoga) of devotion. Although the *Gita* does not use the term *avatar*, the structure and function of the concept is made particularly clear in a famous two-verse passage:

> yadā yadā hi dharmasya glānir bhavati bhārata I
> abhyutthānam adharmasya tadātmānam sṛjāmy aham II
> paritrāṇāya sādhunām vināshāya ca duṣkṛtām I
> dharma-samsthāpanārthāya sambhavāmi yuge yuge II
>
> O Arjuna, whenever there is a decline in *dharma*, and whenever there is a rise in *a-dharma*, I will then take physical form.
> To save the pious, to destroy evil, and to reestablish *dharma*, I will appear age after age.
>
> (4.7–8)

Laying the groundwork for subsequent Vaishnava theologies, Krishna states here that when the earth is weighed down by wickedness, he will emit his personal essence – his *ātman* – into the world in order to restore goodness and moral order (*dharma*).

The *Gita* displays Krishna's status as an avatar in two ways, both at the direct request of Arjuna. First in Chapter Ten, Krishna describes himself in a way that is linguistically consistent and at the same time somewhat overwhelming. Using a distinctive series of multiplicities, Krishna illustrates his power by describing himself as the greatest example of any category one can well imagine: of rivers he is the Ganges; of bodies of water he is the ocean, the destination of all (female) rivers; of trees he is the multi-rooted *ashvattha* fig tree, under which sages such as the Buddha attained enlightenment; of human beings he is the king; of warriors he is Rama. He also uses deities themselves to illustrate this point: "I am Vishnu striding among the sun gods [...], I am Indra, king of the gods [...], I am Shiva among the howling storm gods [...], and I am Krishna among my mighty kinsmen."

Next in Chapter Eleven, Krishna displays himself to Arjuna in a classic example of a hierophany. Long a staple from the field of Religious Studies, a hierophany is a sudden, shocking, and often overwhelming appearance of the sacred within time and space. Similar to the biblical God's appearance to Moses in the burning bush, Krishna must also mediate his universal appearance (*vishva-rūpa*) with some sort of divine eye (*divyam chakshu*) so as not to harm Arjuna's mortal form.

Repeatedly describing Krishna as *an-eka* – "not one" or "multiple" – Arjuna narrates his vision to the readers of the text. Appearing much like the creator in the Purusha hymn in the Rig Veda, Krishna possesses multiple heads, eyes, and feet seeing and moving in all directions and with multiple ornaments, weapons, and marvelous appearances that reinforce his appearance as a divine king. Watching Krishna destroy all of their enemies while admitting that he did not understand Krishna's divine identity, Arjuna requests that Krishna retract this terrible vision and return to his familiar, human, and gentle form.[18]

In the moments after this apocalyptic vision of mass destruction, Krishna provides the lesson that will carry the reader throughout the remainder of the text and throughout the Hindu devotional tradition. Krishna asserts that it is "only by *bhakti* that one can know, see, and enter into" him (11.54). And finally beginning in Chapter Twelve, Krishna analyzes his lecture on Action and Knowledge through the technique of devotion. With a mutual adoration set within a framework of devotion, Arjuna does indeed fight and with Krishna acting as his charioteer is guaranteed victory.

Conclusion

The *Bhagavad Gita*'s yoga of devotion constructs a new way of relating to one's self, to divinity, and to the universe as a whole. This new yoga will become and has remained immensely powerful and pervasive in both Hindu philosophy and practice. But it hardly occurs in a vacuum. The *Gita* details nascent devotional forms – especially that of the avatar and of the temple worship of divine forms – that are fleshed out in later text and practice.

Another facet of the Hindu tradition that furthers the strength of bhakti is the veneration of goddesses. The next two chapters will show a spectrum of the identity of and practice towards numerous Hindu goddesses. While the veneration of many of these goddesses is rooted in the devotional tradition, this worship will, like all Hindu practice, intersect with a variety of social factors, especially the roles of women in local South Asian societies.

Notes

1 Several centuries before this text and amidst her praise of various forms of Vishnu, the Alvar poetess Andal wrote, "You lifted the mountain as an umbrella; We praise your virtue" (Venkatesan 2010: 74).
2 Temple icons go by other Sanskrit names as well: *vigraha* and *pratimā*. Like the linga of Shiva, Vishnu can also be depicted an-iconically, in the form of a *shāligrām*, a black fossilized stone found mainly in the rivers of Himalayan Nepal.
3 When an icon needs to be repainted, refurbished, or otherwise repaired, the deity can be removed from the original icon, temporarily placed in a pot, and ritually returned once the repairs have been completed.
4 https://pluralism.org/murti-the-image-of-god.
5 Temples themselves are similarly consecrated and regularly reconsecrated. The Ganesh temple in Queens, New York, recently underwent its fifth reconsecration that focused on the anointing (*abhishekam*) of its central pot (*kumbha*).
6 See Chapter 8, "Other Gods" of Beal 2014. For a related Buddhist example, George Crane, in his 2000 book *Bones of the Master*, cites his own secular Jewish upbringing as a source of his hesitation at approaching an icon of the Buddha that his Buddhist monk and friend, Tsung Tsai, daily venerates in his home.
7 As part of the religious landscape of India, Sufi Muslims display and inhale clouds of *lobān*, a type of incense, as part of prayers and healing practices at shrines to the saints (Bellamy 2011).
8 Packert 2010.
9 Prothero 2003 (Chapter 8), refers to the American Hindu Jesus as the "Oriental Christ."

10 This particular image of Vasudeva with Krishna in a basket over his head has been reproduced in many devotional images.
11 In one of her devotional poems, Andal writes of this incident from the perspective of one of the gopis:

> "You escaped Kamsa's savage net
> in the midst of that deep dark night
> only to torture the hearts of hapless maidens
> stranded here.
> Yaśodā lets you stray, bold and unpunished.
> O you who suckled the milk
> from the breast of the deceitful demoness
> Shameless one
> Please return our clothes to us." (Venkatesan 2010: 11).

12 All translations of the *Bhagavata Purana* are from Bryant 2003.
13 The Vaishnava tradition expands upon this notion of feminine devotion to Krishna in another striking way: before entering the forests of Vrindaban and directly approaching Krishna, Shiva must bathe in the Yamuna River and ultimately transform himself into a gopi in order to attain the enlightenment he seeks (Haberman 1994: 22).
14 Coleman 2010 presents this argument in detail, noting in particular how Krishna, just as Ram in many passages, is referred to as "the knower of dharma" (*dharma-vid*).
15 All translations of the *Gītā Govinda* are from Siegel 2009.
16 We will spend more time with the sant poets in Chapter 8 of this book as we study their legacy in contemporary India.
17 Translations of the *Bhagavad Gītā* are from Miller 2004.
18 Robert Oppenheimer, the director of the Manhattan Project that produced the first nuclear bomb in 1940s America was also an amateur Sanskritist. Watching the first nuclear mushroom cloud that he helped produce, he famously recalled the following verse from the *Gita*: "If the radiance of a thousand suns / Were to burst at once into the sky, / That would be like the splendor / Of the Mighty One [...]. I am become Death / The shatterer of worlds" (11.12, 32 [Davis 2015: 173]).

References

Bryant, Edwin F. 2003. *Krishna: The Beautiful Legend of God: Śrīmad Bhāgavata Purāṇa Book X: With Chapters 1, 6, and 29–31 from Book XI*. London: Penguin.

Miller, Barbara Stoler. 2004. *The Bhagavad-Gita: Krishna's Counsel in Time of War*. New York: Bantam Books.

Siegel, Lee. 2009. *Gītagovinda: Love Songs of Rādhā and Kṛṣṇa*. New York: New York University Press/JJC Foundation.

Key terms

bhakti
darshan
kāma
mandir
murti
Mount Govardhan
Rās Līlā, "the Circle Dance" or "the Dance of Love"

the five bhāvas
Texts: Bhāgavata Purāṇa, Mahābhārata, Bhagavad Gītā, Gītā Govinda

Study questions

1 How does the Path of Devotion (*bhakti*) differ from the Paths of Action and Knowledge?
2 How do the different forms of Krishna encourage different relationships with his worshippers?
3 How does the apocalyptic nature of the Mahabharata relate to the devotional aspects of the Bhagavad Gita?

5 Lakshmi and *shri*

Glory, femininity, and domesticity among Hindu women

In nineteenth-century India, at the same time that Lokmanya Tilak was reviving the Ganesh festival in western India as a response to British colonial rule, Bankim Chandra Chattopadhyay was working in the eastern state of Bengal. Chattopadhyay wrote stories that reflected his concern about the relationships between Hindus and Muslims, between Bengal and the rest of India, and between India and the wider world. In 1882, he published the novel *Anandamath*, translated into English as *The Abbey of Bliss*, whose narrative center was a monastery (abbey) for Hindu youth. *Anandamath* quickly became a part of early independence movements: first for Bengal, which would soon be partitioned by the British into East and West Bengal, and then for all of India, in a series of movements that would conclude with independence from British rule in 1947. Its focus, however, is on the figure of Mother India (*Bhārat Mātā*), a goddess who resided at the heart of the abbey and who personified initially Bengal and eventually all of India.

Described in ways that hearken back to nature imagery in the Rig Veda, the goddess brought a sense of natural calm and fertility to a nation undergoing political turmoil. Beginning with the refrain *Bande Mātaram* – "Hail to the Mother!" or "I praise the Mother!" – the novel identifies its main characters as children of Mother India, a personification and deification of the nation itself. *Anandamath* describes her as follows, identifying Mother India with two of the most prominent goddesses of the entire Hindu pantheon:

> Thou art Durga, Lady and Queen,
> With her hands that strike and her swords of sheen,
> Thou art Lakshmi lotus-throned,
> And the Muse a hundred-toned.
>
> (Hay 1988: 134)

The novel attributes to the goddess a strictly dual identity: she is Durga the warrior who protects and defends her children with her weapons of steel, and she is Lakshmi who dispenses wealth and benevolence from her lotus seat.[1]

This duality reflects a common pattern in Hindu conceptions of goddesses: some goddesses are categorized as peaceful (*saumya* or *shānta*) while others are

DOI: 10.4324/9781003475033-6

considered as fierce (*ugra*). In the south Indian case of the goddess Gangamma, for example, her multiple local manifestations are represented as a set of sisters, some who are *shānta* and others who are *ugra* (Flueckiger 2013: 8–10). Across the subcontinent in the Himalayan north, women depict the goddess Gaura Devi in local songs both as a daughter who seeks a husband and as a form of Durga who slays the buffalo demon. In simple terms, Hindu goddesses are frequently categorized as either mild or wild.

This mild/wild dichotomy has become a regular part of Western scholarship on Hindu goddesses. Goddesses are nurturing benefactresses or threatening seductresses; they possess cool fidelity and maternal beneficence or hot sexuality and possessive virulence; they are goddesses of the breast or of the tooth; and they are independently supreme or a wifely consort to their prominent and divine male husband. Approaching a dynamic between these two poles, one author discusses the oscillation between the two faces of Durga, "a Goddess wherein devastating martial prowess coincides with compassionate care" (Balkaran 2019: 322).

While such conceptions are helpful in understanding the many ways that Hindus categorize, depict, and venerate goddesses, these strict dualities mask the extraordinary flexibility of Hindu goddesses and of the cultural traditions within which they are worshipped. The following two chapters of this book will highlight this flexibility of the goddess in two general ways, using the two goddesses from *Anandamath* – Lakshmi and Durga – as representative examples.

First, borrowing from these productive but simplistic dual conceptions, I will categorize Hindu goddesses according to two simple Sanskrit terms regularly attributed to them.

The one, *shri*, represented by the goddess of wealth Lakshmi, refers to the Glory of the goddess. The characteristic of *shri* refers to her more gentle, domestic, and traditionally feminine character. For Lakshmi, her *shri* manifests in the various ways that she distributes health, wealth, and children to those women (and men) who are devoted to her. This beneficent quality manifests typically in forms of the goddess associated with forms of Vishnu.

The other, *shakti*, represented by Durga, refers to her Power and to the protective and sometimes destructive ways she operates in the universe. Fierce forms of the goddess often appear as independent manifestations or allies of Durga, but they can also be associated with or even married to Shiva.

Like Shiva, the "erotic ascetic" who resides in the high Himalaya both as a single renouncer and as a husband and father to his family, goddesses are also regularly depicted and conceived of in both ways. Whereas individual depictions tend to highlight their *shakti* – the stories, abilities, and powers that each possesses – their representations with a divine husband foreground their *shri*. These joint depictions of deities as part of a married couple reflect the role of the human married couple as the basic ritual unit in many domestic rites of passage.[2]

The second way I will highlight the flexibility of goddesses is to place them along a spectrum between *shri* and *shakti*. This spectrum presumes that no single goddess is either pure *shri* or pure *shakti* but rather contains at least a bit of each. This spectrum also incorporates and in some cases contests scholarship on goddesses that restricts them to an either/or duality.

One key example of this feminine ambiguity can be seen with Ram's wife Sita in the *Ramayana*. Kidnapped by Ravan and taken captive to his capital of Lanka, she contrasts his awful behavior with that of the righteous Ram (*dharma-ātman*), reminding Ravan of (and threatening him with) both her *shri* and her *shakti*. She tells Ravan:

> It is only because I have not been so ordered by Rāma and because I wish to preserve intact the power of my austerities (*tapas*) that I do not reduce you to ashes with my own blazing power (*tejas*), for that is what you deserve.
> (5.20.20 [Goldman and Sutherland Goldman 2021: 469])

In this threat, Sita combines social and cultural categories that are often kept separate. As a woman concerned with doing her wifely duties, she saves the demise of Ravan for her husband Ram, a warrior, king, and avatar of Vishnu who regularly relieves the earth of its burden of demonic evil. At the same time, however, she has accumulated through her performance of domestic duties the *tapas* and *tejas* that male renouncers typically earn through powerful yogic practices.

Although the novel *Anandamath* highlights these two characteristics – Durga is a warrior who violently protects while Lakshmi gently inspires – the veneration of goddesses on the ground presents a much more complex picture. The Hindu universe presents a large number of goddesses who take on a variety of physical forms, some hidden in local nooks and crannies throughout South Asia and others who have ventured across the sea and reside in neighborhoods very close to us. At the same time, however, and drawing on notions from the Upanishads of the ultimate unity of all things (*brahman*), many Hindus will also affirm that this multiplicity of physical, ritual, and ideal forms of the goddess only represents various facets of the single Great Goddess (Mahādevī).

The multiplicity of goddesses becomes especially relevant when we consider their relationships with human women. Many of the texts we have already seen in this book suggest a secondary or even subservient role for women: for example, when *The Laws of Manu* asserts women's lifelong dependence upon the men in their family, or when the *Ramayana* has Sita fulfill her wifely duty of following Ram into the forest. Local traditions, however, present a more complex role for women who operate as active agents for their own well-being alongside their husbands and families, and who are accompanied by or even fully embody the goddess.

In response to the provocative question "Is the goddess a feminist?", scholars have tentatively answered: It depends.[3] The following two chapters of this book will in many ways consider how to answer this question by accounting for the complex work that goddesses do. By using the terms *shri* and *shakti*, and by considering the broad spectrum along which Hindu goddesses might be situated, we will be able to see the co-existence of the two forms of Mother India –

Lakshmi and Durga – and the innumerable forms of the Great Goddess in between. Working simultaneously to reinforce and transcend women's domestic roles, goddesses function holistically to "provide psychological comfort, and [...] the presence of positive female imagery at the heart of a valued symbol system" (Gross 2000: 107).

Hindu goddesses

One way to consider the commonalities underlying Hindu goddesses is to see the various terms by which they are referred to. Aside from *shri* and *shakti*, the most common title used for goddesses is *devī*. The most general Sanskrit term that translates to "goddess," this grammatically feminine term serves as the counterpart to the masculine *deva*. Terms used since the Vedas, *deva* and *devī* translate as "the shining ones" (and are related to the English "divine"), and can refer to any god or goddess. Nepali Hindus will use the compound noun *devī-devatā* – "[all of the] goddesses and gods" – to refer to the general pantheon as a whole.

Other terms and concepts applied to goddesses refer to their (potential) motherhood, regardless of whether or not they have actually conceived children. The terms Mā, Mātā, and Amman can be appended as a prefix or suffix to the name of any goddess: Mā Lakshmi, Durgā Mātā, and Māriamman. Amidst the dynamic diversity of Hindu goddesses, this commonality has led some Hindus to assert that "all the mothers are one." The notion of even unmarried youthful goddesses as mothers again picks up on ancient Vedic notions that considered cows, waters, and the rays of the sun as natural elements of life-giving fertility that are inherently feminine (and plural).

Finally, two terms pick up on the goddess's maternal nature and refer to her creation of the physical world. The goddess is Prakriti, the female companion of the male Purusha who is the material cause of the world in the creation hymn to Purusha in Rig Veda 10.90. This structural relationship between the underlying male and female components of the universe is reinforced in the dualistic Samkhya system of philosophy that grounds the practice of yoga. Whereas Samkhya establishes a dualism that favors the spiritual and stable Purusha over the material and moving Prakriti, the goddess-focused tradition gives the place of primacy to the female principle. A text on Durgā that we will discuss in some depth in the following chapter describes the goddess as the creator and destroyer of the physical universe: "You are the primordial material (Prakriti) of everything, bringing into force the three qualities [that comprise the entire universe]. You are the dark night of periodic dissolution, the great night of final dissolution, and the terrible night of delusion" (DM 1.59).

Relatedly, the term Māyā also connotes ideas of creation or construction. Considered within the non-dual Advaita Vedanta school as an "illusion" that clouds our vision of what is real and true, the title Māyā, again within the goddess tradition, is much more positive. Similar in sound to Mātā, grammatically related to the English "measure," and alluding to Maya, the male and semi-divine architect of the Pandava palace in the *Mahabharata*, Māyā is a feminine principle that is intimately related to the production of the material (and maternal) world.

This introduction to the vocabulary of the goddess provides a foundation for understanding the place of individual (and groups of) goddesses. Throughout this and the following chapter, we will see how these themes of fertility, maternity, and the physical world will supplement the elements of *shri* and *shakti* that all goddesses possess. In addition to seeing how each goddess takes center stage at one or another point throughout the Hindu calendar, we will also ground the characteristics of each goddess within a larger South Asian culture.

Goddesses and nature

Hindu forms of divinity have long taken natural forms. Various trees, for example, manifest as different male and female deities. The massive and many-rooted banyan tree is typically seen either as a form of Shiva or as representing "multi-faceted unity" in the shrines of many gods and goddesses housed beneath its canopy, and the pipal (or *bodhi*) tree is the manifestation or residence of Vishnu (as well as a reminder of the Buddha's enlightenment). The neem tree, on the other hand, is regarded as the arboreal form of the goddess. Useful for its medicinal products that are a part of the traditional health science of ayurveda, the neem tree reflects the life-giving properties of the goddess, whether she is known as Durga, Kali, Yellama, or simply *Nima Mai* (Mother Neem). Although typically depicted by herself, her occasional ritual marriage to the male pipal tree reinforces her capacity to restore domestic bliss, bestow fertility, and strengthen relationships between the human and natural worlds. Such marriages between trees reflect not only marriages between male and female deities but also rites of passage when humans marry trees. For example, during their *ihi* rite Nepali girls marry the bel tree as the first of their three marriages – to the tree in their youth, to the sun at their first menstruation, and finally to their human husband.[4]

Among other divinized aspects of nature, rivers are the most widespread natural features of the environment regularly seen as Hindu goddesses. Worshipped as free-flowing rivers, such goddesses encounter as obstacles the dams that India's first Prime Minister Jawaharlal Nehru referred to as "the temples of a modern India" (Haberman 2006: 5). Eulogized in story and song, rivers have long been venerated throughout India in daily rituals and annual festivals in which worshippers offer grains of rice, fruit and coconuts, yellow and red colored powder, and even long *sari* cloths that fully cross the river as they would the women who normally wear them. In all such performances, rivers bestow the benefits of health, wealth, and fertility as all goddesses do.

Two of the most important river goddesses are Gaṅgā (Ganges) and Yamunā. Depicted as standing atop a crocodile and tortoise, respectively, these two rivers are sisters who run together for nearly one thousand miles through north India. One sign of the power of these goddesses is the presence of their gilded and larger-than-human-sized statues, standing atop their tortoise and crocodile, flanking the main gate of the royal palace in Patan, Nepal (Figure 5.1). Numerous pilgrimage places have grown up along their banks, stretching from their Himalayan glacial sources to their confluence (*sangam*) at the town of Prayagraj, past the cremation grounds at the city of Varanasi, and to their collective eastern delta in Bengal and Bangladesh.

The story of the descent of the Ganges River as told in the *Ramayana* and other texts combines many themes relevant to goddesses. With the desire to attain *moksha* liberation for his ancestors who had been incinerated by an angry sage, Ram's ancestor, Bhagirath, performed acts of asceticism in the high Himalaya. After one thousand years of standing on one leg in harsh conditions, he acquired enough *tapas* to bring the Ganges from heaven down to earth. (The Milky Way galaxy is referred to as the Ākāsh Gaṅgā, the Ganges River in the sky.) As the earth was unable to bear the full force of the cascading celestial river, Shiva offered his body – and specifically his dreadlocks – as the path for Ganges to follow to earth. Wending her way through Shiva's hair and to her final destination in the (masculine) ocean, the touch of her waters liberated Ram's ancestors, just as the Ganges River does at Varanasi and at countless cremation grounds along the way.

The Yamuna River is directly connected to the life of Krishna, especially to his stories in the *Bhagavata Purana*. With its source near that of her sister in the

Figure 5.1 Statues of the river goddesses Ganga and Yamuna flanking the main door to the city's royal palace. Patan, Nepal

Himalayan mountains, the Yamuna flows southward through India's capital at Delhi, Krishna's land of Braj, and the city of Agra directly north of the Taj Mahal, as it meets the Ganges at their confluence. Similarly connected to the ancestors, death, and rebirth, the name Yamuna is sometimes connected to Yama, the Vedic god of death, and his sister Yamī. This connection with death recalls both the cremation grounds that reside along the river as well as the purification from sin and death that the healing touch of the river's water offers, especially at famous *tirtha* pilgrimage sites.

The Ganges and Yamuna are connected to a third river and sister, the Sarasvatī River. Although long since dried up, the Sarasvati first appears in the Rig Veda as descending from the mountains to attend the Vedic sacrifices held on the plains of northwest India (RV 5.43.11). The embodiment of ritual speech (Vāch, "voice") and the only goddess present at the sacrifice, she mirrors the sacrificer's wife who is the only human woman who attends the ritual and who embodies the fertility present within the sacrifice. As one river goddess among many (RV 10.75), she continues to appear as a mythical river on her own and as a sister of Ganges and Yamuna who in yogic texts together represent the three channels of the human body.

As a goddess of speech, Sarasvati is often described as the wife of Brahmā who chants the four Vedas. She is regularly depicted with the *vīṇa* musical instrument, a *mālā* string of beads for reciting mantras, a Vedic text, and the swan associated with the immortal *ātman*, showing her to function as a goddess of religion, culture, and education. Amidst the series of *samskara* (rites of passage) that celebrates one's life from conception to cremation, she facilitates the rite of passage of *vidyārambha* – the beginning of children's education – and is annually celebrated towards the beginning of February with the Sarasvati Puja, marking the start of the spring season.

Rivers are significant natural and cultural features of the Hindu landscape outside of India as well. As the Ganges River is responsible for purifying souls of the recently deceased, especially at Varanasi's central Manikarnika Ghat, the Bagmati River in Kathmandu performs a similar task. Its name, Bagmati, continues the association of goddesses and speech, as *Bāg* is a version of *Vāk*. Running southward from Nepal to north India, it eventually enters the Ganges. Its most famous pilgrimage place is the Pashupati temple on Kathmandu's eastern border that is dedicated to Shiva. The main location of the Shivratri festival, it is home to two main areas: Surya Ghat, the common cremation area down-river, and Arya Ghat, the royal cremation grounds just up-river, whose most active time in recent history followed the assassination of the majority of Nepal's royal family in 2001.

As it is sometimes said that every river is the Ganges, this most famous of all Indian rivers also appears globally. The borough of Queens in New York City, and especially its Richmond Hill neighborhood, is home to a number of Hindu temples, many of them goddess temples organized by the Caribbean Hindu communities who live there. Hailing especially from the country of Guyana, these communities will consider the waters of nearby Jamaica Bay at Crossbay

Beach to *be* the Ganges: "We call it the Ganges," one pilgrim said as he finished his prayers. "She takes away your sickness, your pain, your suffering."[5]

But even water, as calm and nurturing and maternal as it is, can still be dangerous. In a study of the religious feelings and potential for an environmental ethic that emerges from whitewater kayaking, Whitney Sanford uses the Hindu devotional metaphor of drowning in the love of Krishna to highlight the risk and danger that kayakers regularly experience (Sanford 2007: 878). We can use this instructive analogy the other way around as well; the danger of kayaking highlights the danger inherent in the religious metaphors of water and flooding from around the world that reinforce the fine line between life and death.

Lakshmi

As with all goddesses, Lakshmi possesses both *shri* and *shakti*. Originating as one of the fourteen objects created in the churning of the ocean, Lakshmi, the goddess of wealth, sits far on the *shri* end of this continuum. Poster-art images typically depict her with four arms: her two upper hands hold auspicious lotus flowers; one lower hand holds a vessel (*ghaṭa*) topped by a coconut and neem leaves, an assemblage of items used especially in south Indian rituals and temple displays; with her other lower hand dispensing gold coins into a pot on the floor at her feet. Elephants often flank her as animals of good luck providing her with the name, Gaja Lakshmi (Lakshmi with the elephants), and a ledger sometimes appears next to her showing her relationship with business and the economic new year. As with such images of other gods and goddesses, she is often depicted in a palace setting showing her identity as a queen.[6]

The wife of Vishnu, she is regularly depicted rubbing the feet of her husband as they sit together on the serpent Shesha on the cosmic ocean at the bottom of the world. As we saw in previous chapters, the primary role of the avatars of Vishnu is to maintain dharma, a role that extends to his wife as well. The term *avatar*, however, is not typically used for divine manifestations outside of Vishnu, and the texts – especially those of the diverse Ramayana tradition – are somewhat ambivalent about Lakshmi's appearances on earth. Valmiki's Ramayana only explicitly identifies Sita with Lakshmi towards the very end, immediately after her trial by fire, as Brahmā also clarifies Rama's position as an avatar of Vishnu: "Sītā is Lakṣmī; you [Rāma] are the god Viṣṇu" (7.105. 25 [Goldman and Sutherland Goldman 2021: 710]).[7] In the *Adhyatma Ramayana*, it is not Lakshmi but Vishnu, through his powerful *yogamāyā*, who incarnates as Sita (1.2.28). Similarly, only occasionally in the *Gita Govinda* does Jayadev describe Radha in relationship to Lakshmi; in one passage, the poet describes Krishna as "wishing to gaze at his beloved Lakshmi" (189).

Regardless of how specific texts handle the details of Lakshmi's narrative appearances on earth, Hindus in general tend to see Lakshmi as co-incarnating with Vishnu. The women's literature referred to in the Ram chapter makes this structural relationship even more explicit as women authors relate to and divinize Sita. By doing so, these female authors prioritize their own domestic situations, equating them to the more "authoritative" roles of king, god, and husband held by Ram.

The joint appearances of Radha and Krishna and of Ram and Sita replicate on earth the divine couple residing at the foundation of the world, with the places where they lived and traveled becoming places of pilgrimage and worship. Even more than Ayodhya, the north Indian city where Ram and Sita lived, the Braj region along the Yamuna River has long been the epicenter of the worship of Radha and Krishna. Here, Radha comes before Krishna – enunciated in the common greeting, "Radha Krishna!" or simply "Radhe Radhe!" – and the river takes on the physical, emotional, and erotic qualities of Radha and becomes, for many devotees, her natural embodiment. As one devotional poem to the Yamuna River states, "You appear in the eternal love play as a river equal to the lover Radha" (Haberman 2006: 222).

The *Lakshmī Tantra*

Always connected with Vishnu, Lakshmi can, as goddesses sometimes do, become more important than her male counterpart. The tenth-century *Lakshmī Tantra* is a product of the Pāñcharātra sect, a devotional tradition dedicated to forms of Vishnu, whose purpose is to "establish the supremacy of Lakshmī as the basic philosophical principle and to centre ritual worship upon her" (Gupta 1972: xxxv). Framed within a dialogue between Lakshmi and Indra, the *Lakshmī Tantra* portrays Lakshmi not as one among many goddesses, but rather as the Great Goddess. Here, Lakshmi describes herself as the body, essential nature, and divine presence of Vishnu.

Much of the text describes her many attributes and functions, most of which reinforce her embodiment of the principle of shri. Its chapter on the physical forms of Vishnu and Lakshmi describes her in ways familiar from statues and poster-art images: "She has four arms, large eyes, a complexion like refined gold, and she holds a [citron fruit], a club, a shield and a vessel containing amṛta [the nectar of immortality]" (4.38 [Gupta 1972: 23]). She possesses five functions: delusion, creation, maintenance, destruction, and grace. Amidst a long list of her names, she explains why she goes by the name Shri: "Beholding these attributes of mine, those learned in the Vedas and Vedāntas, who know how to relate attributes to their possessor, extol me as Śrī [...]: eternal, manifested as all and ever existent" (4.53–54 [23]).

Her universal nature entails many different forms of multiplicity. For example, she possesses six attributes: absolute knowledge (*jñāna*), sovereignty (*aishvarya*), potency (*shakti*), strength (*bala*), splendor (*tejas*), and the typically male quality of virility (*vīrya*) (Gupta 1972: xxv). With these six attributes, she tells Indra: "I instantly manifest God's different (forms) of bhavat (the absolute existing principle) by appearing in the diverse states of Vyūha etc. in whatever manner is appropriate" (11.6 [58]). The vyuha are Vishnu's four manifestations, a precursor to the concept of the ten avatars; in this text, Lakshmi is responsible for creating all of these diverse physical forms[8] (Figure 5.2).

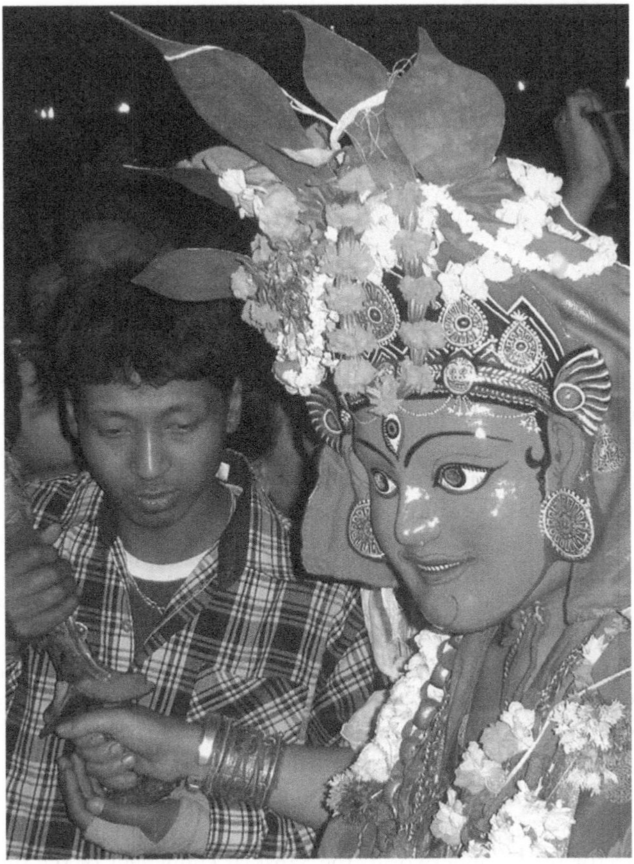

Figure 5.2 A young man keeps one hand on the sword of Mahalakshmi, one of the Mother Goddesses, as she dances possessed through the streets during a local spring festival. Kathmandu, Nepal

Establishing a correlation with Sarasvati, the goddess of speech and language, this text attributes to Lakshmi the quality of sound. Building on the connection between sounds, mantras, and yogic power, this tantric text focuses extensively on the letters of the Sanskrit alphabet and the resulting mantras that form a collective sonic embodiment of the goddess. These letters and sounds represent the very form of the world's creation, are to be visualized by practitioners as residing within a geometrical yantra figure, and are ritually placed on their bodies thus equating themselves with the sonic vibrations of the universe.[9] Hence, Lakshmi, "adorned with the garland of eternal akṣaras (sounds and letters of the alphabet)" refers to herself as "the mother of all mantras bestowing both prosperity and liberation" (18.36–37 [101]). Represented in letters and sounds, she is equivalent to Shabda-brahman, the ultimate impersonal sound of the entire universe.

Diwali

Lakshmi's major appearance is during Diwali, a festival that begins on the new moon day often in early November. Referring to the "row of lights" (Sanskrit *dīpāvalī*) that families, communities, and businesses light throughout its five days, this festival of lights in some places also commemorates Ram and Sita's victorious return to Ayodhya and everywhere annually celebrates Lakshmi's role as the goddess of wealth. Hindu communities worldwide celebrate in many and related ways.

One of the largest celebrations of Diwali in America is the Diwali Mela in Dallas, Texas, which attracts over 60,000 celebrants. For some twenty years, "The Dallas Festival of Lights – Diwali Mela [...] is a joyous occasion, commemorating the triumph of light over darkness and symbolizing unity, cultural diversity, and the spirit of togetherness."[10] In public festivals and private domestic celebrations, families celebrate Diwali with stories, songs, food, and lights.

In Nepal, this festival is referred to most often as Tihar, a Nepali variant of either "Diwali" or of the Hindi-language *tyauhar*, "the festival." Celebrating the beginning of the new year, as it does in many places, the festival transcends the land of the living (Shrestha 2006). One of its many names, Yama-panchaka, the five days dedicated to Yama the god of death, highlights its celebration of the family and its recently departed ancestors.

The festival's first three days are dedicated to the crow, the dog, and the cow, respectively. On these days, people leave offerings of food out for these animals and offer worship to them in the form of a tika blessing on their foreheads and a garland of marigold flowers around their necks. Common to all three of these animals is their association with death and the ancestors: crows communicate with the ancestors up in heaven; going back to Vedic times, Saramā is the canine protector of the underworld (the Sanskrit equivalent of the three-headed Greek Cerberus); and Vaitaraṇī the cow leads the ancestors across the Vaitaraṇī River away from civilization and to the other side.[11] These same three animals also appear together in *shrāddha* rituals for the dead when they are each fed a plate of food for three generations of ancestors (Gold 2000: 93).

The festival's third day celebrating the cow is the central day of Diwali and is also devoted to Lakshmi herself.[12] Amidst gambling, fireworks, shopping, and decorating, this middle day of the festival is the most festive. Walking through any downtown area in urban South Asia on this day, one can see hundreds of *rangoli*, colorful designs ornamented with marigold petals and rows of oil lamps. Displayed in front of every shop, these lamps – the *diwali* – attract Lakshmi, leading her directly into the shop whose new business ledger she blesses and where she provides her most direct contact with shop-owners, workers, and the prosperity that results from their labor (Figure 5.3).

These rangoli resemble geometric figures found throughout Hindu, Buddhist, and Jain art – especially the Buddhist mandala and the tantric yantra. Although Diwali sees a concentration of these images, as they provide a focus for

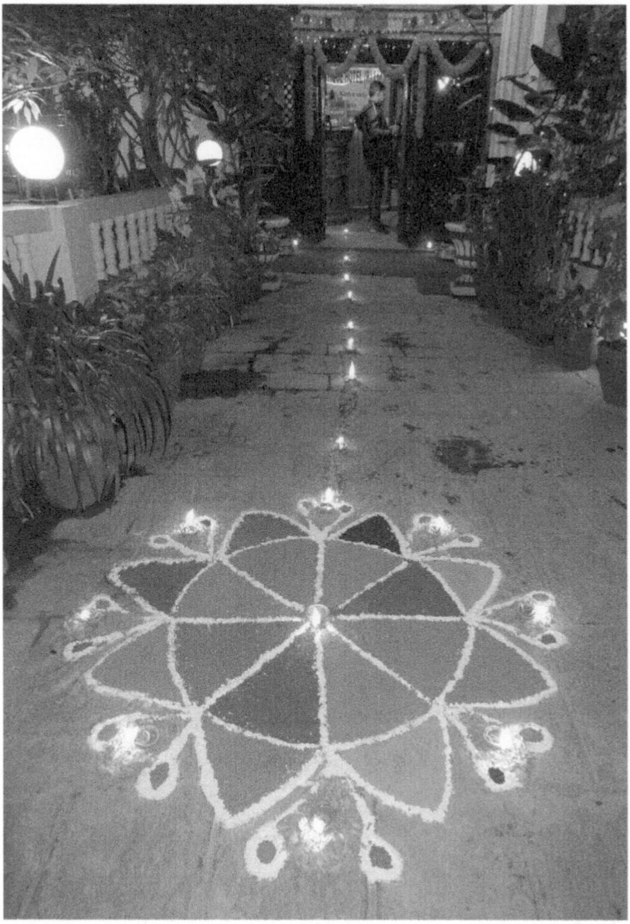

Figure 5.3 A rangoli invites Lakshmi into this hotel and guides her to protect and increase its wealth. Kathmandu, Nepal

celebrating the goddess, the physical world, and material generosity, similar designs are displayed throughout the Hindu calendar. Especially in the Tamil regions of south India, women design a *kōlam* anew each morning directly outside the front doors of homes, temples, and businesses to remember and embody Lakshmi, the earth goddess Bhūdevī, as well as the poetess Andal, regarded by Tamil women as the original kolam artist (Nagarjan 2018).

Newar folk images from Nepal similarly display Lakshmi as the goddess of wealth, though in a slightly different setting. Seated on a throne with her feet propped up on a tortoise (both a symbol of long life and the animal vehicle of the Yamuna River), she is flanked by a trader carrying a sack of gold, a female attendant holding up a mirror, and several *khyāḥ* – hairy beasts who are connected to the wealth of the earth and whose roots are in the high Himalaya; appearing in full regalia during several public festivals, their bawdy dances amuse both young and old alike. Along the bottom of some of these hand-colored images is the following couplet: (Figure 5.4).

> जय जय लक्ष्मी अन्त नजाउ
> स्थीर गरी बसी देउ घरमा आज
> *jay jay Lakshmi anta najāu.*
> *sthīra garī basī deu ghar mā āja*
>
> Glory Glory to Lakshmi! Please don't depart.
> Today, O goddess, please stay in our house!

Other popular Diwali images depict Lakshmi alongside Ganesh, as Hindu communities celebrate good fortune and new beginnings. Many of these images are further ornamented with the *swāstika* symbol. A Sanskrit term literally

Figure 5.4 Images of Lakshmi, depicted alongside Sarasvati and Ganesh or local images of wealth, for sale during the Diwali festival. Kathmandu, Nepal

meaning a "good sign," the swastika appears frequently throughout Hindu, Buddhist, and Jain religious spaces. Its relatively recent desecration by officials in Nazi Germany has had little effect on its auspicious role in South Asia. In fact, some global Hindu communities have been making efforts to restore the swastika and return it to its former glory.[13]

The fourth day of Diwali continues the celebration of domesticity and hospitality. For many Hindus, this day sees the celebration of Govardhan Puja, in memory of the day when Krishna held up the mountain to save his Braj-dwelling villagers from the storms of an angry Indra. This event is remembered by building and displaying mountains of food in homes and temples. In Kathmandu, the local Newar community instead celebrates Mha Puja. Literally translated as "the worship of the self," this puja gathers family members under one roof as they celebrate the family unit and perform puja to the house in which they live. Diwali concludes on the fifth day with *bhai puja*, the mutual acknowledgment of brothers and sisters. Similar to the late summer rite of *raksha bandhan*, brothers support their sisters with gifts of money and clothing, while sisters tie a rakhi thread around their brothers' wrists as a gesture of support and protection.

The global impact of the Diwali festival was made clear when, in 2022, the city of New York City made Diwali a public school holiday.[14] State assemblywoman Jenifer Rajkumar stated, "The time has come to recognize over 200,000 New Yorkers of the Hindu, Buddhist, Sikh and Jain faiths who celebrate Diwali, the Festival of Lights," and Mayor Eric Adams said, "When we take this period to acknowledge Diwali, we're acknowledging the light that is within us, the light that clearly can push away darkness."

Lakshmi and the goddess *vrat*

One regular act of gendered devotion is the *vrat*, the ritual vow. Occurring weekly, monthly, or annually as the case requires, vrats represent a type of asceticism that involves the restriction of pleasures and/or the willful addition of physical difficulties. One example of a male vrat occurs during the annual pilgrimage at the Sabarimala temple in the southwest Indian state of Kerala. Devoted to Ayyappan, the son of Shiva and of Vishnu in female form, millions of devotees prepare for forty-one days to make the forty-seven-mile pilgrimage to Ayyappan's forest shrine (Pati 2014: 215).[15] The strict asceticism of Ayyappan has resulted in the pilgrimage and the temple itself being restricted almost exclusively to men, in a controversy that has occasionally roiled contemporary Hindu religious and political groups.

Most vrats, however, provide active ways for women to worship the goddess. These vrats can be instrumental to bring about a certain result, protective to keep away negative influences, or of thanksgiving to express gratitude for positive results. A prominent form of Hindu devotion, the vrat represents a South Asian ritual form that crosses religious boundaries and that allows women to commune with powerful beings from different traditions: Jain, Sikh, Buddhist, Islamic, and Christian saints whose shrines dot the Indian landscape.[16]

In many of these cases, vrats bring women together – with song, ritual, and fasting and feasting – in veneration of a particular Hindu goddess (or god) and the help she (or he) provides them. In Tamil Nadu, for example, the summer vrat to ensure fertility from the Snake Goddess includes the procession of the goddess, cooking boiled rice and lentils (*pongal*), and even fire-walking (Allocco 2014).

The goddess Svasthani is celebrated with a vrat throughout Nepal's Kathmandu Valley every January. A goddess associated with Shiva and who contains clear aspects of both *shri* and *shakti*, Svasthani has until recently been represented not in a temple icon but only in the form of a book. The story recited each winter in her honor is – like Lakshmi and Sarasvati – a sonic form of the goddess who becomes present in homes throughout the region where her book is displayed and her story read (Birkenholtz 2018). Svasthani brings to pious families – especially to women – those benefits of health, wealth, and family typical of vrats and worship to Hindu goddesses.[17]

Lakshmi is also frequently the object of women's vrats. In the state of Rajasthan in northwest India, women perform a vrat to Mother Ten, a local form of Lakshmi. As the desert region begins to warm in early spring, women gather to tell stories of Mother Ten. Accompanied by the visual, sonic, and material elements that often accompany such ritual gatherings – singing songs, making colorful designs, and tying threads – women tell the stories of Mother Ten. In these stories, women tell stories about women, young and old, whose difficult circumstances reflect those of their own: their marriage and permanent move outside their birth home, the necessity of bearing children and solidifying their place in the home of their husband and mother-in-law, and their potential powerlessness in old age.

The stories of Mother Ten "seem simultaneously to celebrate the absolute power of the goddess over human welfare and to demonstrate mortal women's great aptitude for exercising their pragmatic wits" as they manipulate the men around them. These stories show women to be subject to various forms of abuse within a patriarchal structure, but also as agents who "seem to view these more as challenges to feminine ingenuity than as intolerable burdens" (Gold 2000: 97). As in the Diwali festival, Lakshmi blesses devoted women with the material, spiritual, and emotional resources required not to reject their lives as women but to provide the prosperity and security required within their extended family.

Varieties of regional Indian art regularly depict stories of goddesses, especially Madhubani art whose cultural roots are in Mithila, the homeland of Ram's wife, Sita. Artistic themes and styles are increasingly leaning feminist, as women artists in the region that straddles India and Nepal discover the skills and markets for their distinctive artistic styles. The Manjusha style of art frequently depicts the snake goddess, Manasā.

Goddesses and women

Vrats and vrat stories highlight the intimate relationships between women and goddesses. In doing so, they provide us with a way to avoid reiterating tired Western stereotypes of women living in other parts of the world as passive victims of male oppression. Instead, women are active agents who negotiate obstacles and opportunities within social and cultural structures to ensure success for themselves and their families.

At the same time, however, though women align themselves with goddesses, even taking on divine characteristics for themselves, their semi-divine roles and characteristics remain ambivalent. We might consider these complex roles and identities as one more example of Hindu multiplicity. Discussing the difficult relationships between "women in the material world" against "abstractions of the feminine as goddess figures," Mandakranta Bose argues, "Hindu thought forges links between goddesses and women, and invests women with mystical authority even as it locks them within subservient social roles" (Bose 2010: 10). This ambiguity between their mystical authority and social subservience can be traced back to Vedic times. The only woman present at the highest Vedic sacrifices, the sacrificer's wife embodies the ritual's themes of domesticity and hospitality. Although a required figure at the ritual, she also remains physically shielded from offerings of the sacred soma liquid (Jamison 1996).

Sanskrit texts have continued to establish these more subservient roles for women. One such text, the *Guide to the Religious Status and Duties of Women* (*Strī Dharma Paddhati*) was written in Sanskrit in the eighteenth century by the Tamil author Tryambaka. A "mixture of reality and utopia," the text prescribes the roles of the *pativratā*, the woman whose highest duty (*vrat*) is service to her husband (*pati*) (Leslie 1989: 3). Tryambaka writes the following about his gendered literary project:

> I have gathered together some of these sacred laws relating to women, those which have generally come to be considered the best and which are for the most part well known throughout sacred tradition. If virtuous women put them into practice, they will attain a good reputation, unequalled religious merit, immediate happiness in this world and heaven after death.
>
> (Leslie 1989: 32–33)

In his description of the pativrata, Tryambaka draws on conversations between gods and goddesses and heroes and heroines in many classical Sanskrit texts we have seen throughout the chapters of this book: the *Mahabharata*, many Puranas, and, of course, *The Laws of Manu*. From all of these texts, the duties of the pativrata might be summed up with the proclamation of Uma-Parvati, the wife of Shiva, of her wifely role to her divine husband: "[She] takes his vow as her own … [T]he good woman always regards her husband as a god … There is no goal, no deity like the husband" (281–282). Commenting on the author's earlier section on "the inherent nature of women," translator Julia Leslie writes:

"Tryambaka's concern, however, is not to present a coherent view of how women fit into the cosmic scheme of things, but to persuade women to conform" (255–256).

More than just another timeless (and tireless) example of the patriarchy tying women's lives to their husbands and families, this particular text represents an attempt at a cultural restoration of orthodoxy at a particular historical moment. Produced in south India in the eighteenth century, this text reflects perceived threats to Hindu dharma amidst Muslim, British, and Christian influence and incursion from the north. In this way, it is like *The Laws of Manu* that similarly reproduced a conservative interpretation of women's behavior at the turn of the Common Era in light of perceived threats from early Buddhism.

Few texts in the Hindu textual tradition communicate the multiplicity of women – their mystical authority and subservient social roles – better than *Manu*. One passage in particular clearly attributes to human women the qualities of goddesses:

> If they desire an abundance of good fortune, fathers, brothers, husbands, and brothers-in-law should revere (*pūjyā*) their women and provide them with adornments.
>
> Where women are revered (*pūjyante*), there the gods rejoice; but where they are not [revered] (*pūjyante*), no rite bears any fruit.
>
> Where female relatives grieve, that family soon comes to ruin; but where they do not grieve, it always prospers.
>
> When female relatives, not receiving due reverence (*a-pratipūjitāḥ*), curse any house, it comes to total ruin, as if struck down by witchcraft.
>
> If men want to become prosperous, therefore, they should always honor (*abhyarchyā*) the women on joyful occasions and festive days with gifts of adornments, clothes, and food.
>
> (*Manu* 3.55–59 [Olivelle 2005: 111])

With the same language used in the worship of goddesses (*pūjā*), this passage extends a woman's role from the performer of a devotional ritual to its object. And like goddesses, the women who are the proper object of these vrats glorify their domestic spaces (*shri*), while significant deviation from or the total ignoring of their worship leads to their powerful destruction (*shakti*) of those same spaces. In this way, women resemble Lakshmi who blesses house and family but must sometimes be coerced by her worshippers to do so.

The domestic worship of women of the household is rooted in a conservative system of ethics and etiquette, much like the *Strī Dharma Paddhati*. One of the most famous passages from *Manu* regards a woman's perpetual lack of independence:

> Even in their own homes, a female – whether she is a child, a young woman, or an old lady – should never carry out any task independently. As

> a child, she must remain under her father's control; as a young woman, under her husband's; and when her husband is dead, under her sons'. She must never seek to live independently.
>
> (*Manu* 5.147–148 [Olivelle 2005: 146])[18]

These verses from *Manu* constitute one of the most well-known passages in the West from any Hindu text. This is in part because it was the first text translated into English by officials in the British Empire, an imperial project that rested on constructing a Hindu Other against which it could contrast itself. More specifically, the British Empire required a weaker and barbarous Other that it could colonize. Arguing that a society does not treat its women properly – an argument the West frequently makes in its arguments against Islam – is an effective way to drum up support at home.

Despite the fame of this passage, it is hardly without difficulties in interpretation. We might first ask to what extent this passage *describes* the general plight of women in ancient India, rather than prescribing how women *should* act. Such a patriarchy can be found in many (pre-)modern societies, including our own. In one striking parallel, the American folk song "The Wagoner's Lad," sung by Buell Kazee in 1928 and included on the *Anthology of American Folk Music* in 1952, contains a very similar passage: "Oh, hard is the fortune of all womankind. They're always controlled, they're always confined. Controlled by their parents until they are wives, then slaves to their husbands the rest of their lives." We might also read this passage as conservative powerbrokers arguing that women shouldn't have the degree of economic independence that they actually do (Biernacki 2013: 648 n.15).

At least one corner of the tantric tradition, the subject of the following chapter, works to actually undermine this particular passage from *Manu*.[19] Challenging orthodoxy as tantra typically does, several of these texts show an awareness of *Manu*, playing off of it and satirically mimicking it. One such text reads:

> Having bowed down to a little girl, to an intoxicated young woman, or to an old woman, to a beautiful woman of the clan, or to a contemptible, vile woman, or to a greatly wicked woman, one should contemplate the fact that these [women] do not appreciate being criticised or hit; they do not appreciate dishonesty or that which is disagreeable. Consequently, in every way possible one should not behave this way [towards them].
>
> (Biernacki 2013: 654)

Echoing the Sanskrit sounds and language of *Manu*, this tantric passage offers a parody of the original. Shifting the main action from worshipping to bowing – literally, "offering namaskāra" (*namaskṛtya*) – this passage extends to *all* women – even the vile and wicked – the respectful action typically reserved for upper-caste males.

Conclusion

The domestic benefits Lakshmi and other goddesses provide highlight the sometimes fine lines between *shri* and *shakti*. In some Diwali stories, Lakshmi's blessings to one woman come at the expense of the other women and families throughout town. In essence, the pious woman makes a deal with the goddess in order to harness her power only for herself and her family.

More than simply displaying an arbitrary or capricious side to her character – highlighted in these stories with the presence also of the male personification of perpetual poverty or of Lakshmi's negative opposite, Alakshmi or Kulakshmi – these stories point to the complex nature of both goddesses and women.

The next chapter covers the goddess Durga. Extending our conversations on the many forms of the Hindu goddess, this chapter will shift its focus from *shri* to *shakti*, detailing the ability of women to harness the power of the goddess while further troubling the fine line between the religious techniques of devotion and tantra.

Notes

1 The novel's description of her as a hundred-toned Muse also draws on the imagery of the goddess Sarasvati whose association with the arts leads her to be regularly depicted with the stringed instrument *vīṇa*.
2 This social and ritual unit of the husband and wife is so basic to Hindu ritual that Shiva and Parvati are sometimes depicted together in one person, Ardhanarīshvara – literally, "the lord who is half female." Many *hijra* throughout India, members of the legal "third gender" who often work as singers, musicians, and sex workers and who present as women regardless of the sex assigned to them from birth, identify with this particular form of the god/dess.
3 Hiltebeitel and Erndl 2000. Other relevant volumes on the roles of Hindu women and goddesses include: Julie Leslie (ed.), *Roles and Rituals for Hindu Women* (1992); Tracy Pintchman (ed.), *Women's Lives, Women's Rituals in the Hindu Tradition* (2007); and Leah Comeau, *Material Devotion in a South Indian Poetic World* (2020).
4 See Haberman 2013 for more on trees in Hinduism.
5 Hindus Find a Ganges in Queens, to Park Rangers' Dismay. *New York Times*. Sam Dolnick. April 21, 2011.
6 The *Devi Sūkta* passage in the latter part of the Rig Veda represents one of the earliest hymns to the goddess where she explicitly refers to herself as Queen (*rāṣṭrī*) (10.125.3).
7 Similarly, the *Mahabharata* only rarely explicitly identifies Draupadi, the joint wife of the five Pandava brothers, as Shri or Lakshmi.
8 These four *vyūha* are Vāsudeva, Saṁkarshaṇa, Pradhyumna, and Aniruddha.
9 These letters are called matrika, the same word for the Mother Goddesses who are assistants of Durga.
10 www.dallasfestivaloflights.com.
11 In late summer, Nepalis celebrate the Gai Jatra – the "cow festival" – where children who have lost a family member in the past year dress up as cows and receive offerings of food that they transport to the recently deceased.
12 The Newars of Nepal's Kathmandu Valley consider the fourth day of the Diwali festival - here called Swanti - as the first day of the new year, according to their calendar, the Nepal Samvat (Nepal Era). In this calendar, the year 1146 corresponds to the year 2025

according to the Common Era in the Western calendar. Nepal also uses a national calendar, the Vikram Samvat, whose new year's day is April 14, the only solar festival in the calendar; this day is celebrated with a major pole-raising festival in the city of Bhaktapur, mirrored by the festival of the goddess Tunaldevi in the the Handigaon neighborhood of Kathmandu. In 2025 CE, the Vikram Era year is 2082.

13 https://apnews.com/article/religion-germany-race-and-ethnicity-europe-2c28b5892381cd4148dfde5bc4fbb004.

14 www.cnn.com/2022/10/20/us/diwali-nyc-public-school-holiday-trnd-reaj.

15 Vishnu's form is that of the seductive Mohini, whose first appearance is in the story of the Churning of the Ocean.

16 See Raj and Harman 2006 for examples of vrats from across all of these traditions.

17 Especially in Nepal, vrats cross religious lines, as Newar women celebrate the Buddhist goddess Tara for what she brings: "boons, good fortune, heaven, or even supernormal powers and the possibility of enlightenment itself" (Lewis 2000: 116).

18 This passage is repeated almost verbatim later in the same text: "Day and night men should keep their women from acting independently; for, attached as they are to sensual pleasures, men should keep them under their control. Her father guards her in her childhood, her husband guards her in her youth, and her sons guard her in her old age; a woman is not qualified to act independently" (*Manu* 9.2–3 [Olivelle 2005: 190]).

19 One tantric text, the *Mahānirvāṇa Tantra*, probably composed in eighteenth-century Calcutta by Hindu reformers who were negotiating British imperial power, clearly supports *Manu* (658).

References

Birkenholtz, Jessica Vantine. 2018. *Reciting the Goddess: Narratives of Place and the Making of Hinduism in Nepal*. New York: Oxford University Press.

Nagarajan, Vijaya. 2018. *Feeding a Thousand Souls: Women, Ritual, and Ecology in India: An Exploration of the Kolam*. New York: Oxford University Press.

Raj, Selva and William Harman (eds.). 2006. *Dealing with Deities: The Ritual Vow in South Asia*. Albany: State University of New York Press.

Key terms

Bankim Chandra Chattopadhyay
Diwali
shri
Texts: Lakshmī Tantra, Strī Dharma Paddhati, The Laws of Manu
vrat

Study questions

1 What are the many terms by which Hindu goddesses are known? What do these different terms – separately and together – tell us about how they are thought of and worshipped?

2 How are relationships between goddesses, nature, and especially rivers reinforced in Hindu thought and practice?

3 To what extent do Hindu women and goddesses overlap? How do the powers, rights, and responsibilities of one transfer over to the other?

6 Durga and *shakti*

Power, control, and sacrifice in the tantric world

Like the local devotional tracts detailed in previous chapters that extol the virtues of Bhairav and Hanuman, the forty-verse *Shrī Kālī Chālīsā* attends to the qualities of the equally fierce goddess Kālī. As part of its opening Kali puja, the text prescribes two types of worship: a standard devotional *pūjā* that consists of the worship of an icon of Kali with oil lamps (*āratī*), and the recitation of a protective tantric mantra of armor for the destruction of one's enemies. This combination of peaceful bhakti and fierce tantra within one short text reflects the spectrum of *shri* and *shakti* forms of the goddess and allows for a similar spectrum of practice by which devotees may approach her. Initially appearing as fundamentally different from other forms of Hinduism, tantra can be seen as applying gentle forms of devotional bhakti to transgressive rites and images that result in practitioners obtaining liberation from the world while still in their physical bodies.

Tantra typically operates within a Shaiva-Shākta orientation rather than a Vaishnava one – hence the regular presence of Bhairav in tantric texts and practices. As one exception, however, we saw in the previous chapter the example of the *Lakshmi Tantra*, a tantric text clearly within the Vaishnava fold. The example of the *Shrī Kālī Chālīsā* is a clearly Shaiva-Shākta text that declares its tantric nature in a number of different ways. On its very first page, it displays a powerful geometrical Kali *yantra* diagram that recalls the universal Shri Chakra or Shri Yantra. A geometrical form of the Goddess who creates and embodies the cosmos, the yantra is also embodied within tantric practitioners who visualize the image as residing within their own chakras (wheels) that comprise their spiritual body. The mantra that readers recite identifies Kali as a goddess who rides a human corpse rather than an animal, who wears a garland of human skulls rather than of marigold flowers, and who resides in the cremation grounds, rather than within a typical domestic household.

The devotional *arati* ritual with oil lamps that follows the recitation of the *Chalisa* only slightly moderates this intensity. Its opening verse addresses her in the most linguistically intimate way possible in the Hindi language: "Victory to you (*tū*) Kali – the Mother, Mother of the world – Durga who holds a skull cap." The intimacy of this first verse is made even more complex with the ways that it blends *shri* and *shakti*: in a theme that echoes throughout the *Chalisa*, and throughout the Hindu goddess tradition more broadly, the goddess who resides in the cremation grounds is also the Mother of the World (*jagadambe*).

DOI: 10.4324/9781003475033-7

The Hindi language possesses three forms of the second-person pronoun "you": the formal *āp*, the conversational *tum*, and the intimate *tū*. The last form, the most intimate, can be used between parents and children, among intimate partners, and between deities and devotees. Conversely, it can also be used as an insult directed towards human, animal, or divine enemies.

Residing at the other end of the spectrum from the lotus-throned Lakshmi, Kali represents one of the most extreme forms of Hindu shakti. An embodiment of the anger of Durga, Kali first appears in the text of the *Devī Māhātmya* – "The Glorification of the Goddess" – a text from approximately the seventh century. Drawing on the early Shaiva and Vaishnava devotional poetry from the Tamil south, this text tells three stories about the power of the goddess, the central one of which is one of the most famous stories in the entire Hindu tradition, Durga's slaying of the buffalo demon.

Kali's presence in the local *Shrī Kālī Chālīsā*, the pan-South Asian *Devī Māhātmya*, and the annual autumnal festival that celebrates the goddess reflect her widespread popularity alongside Durga throughout the contemporary Hindu world. Shifting away from the *shri* domestic glory seen in more peaceful goddesses, Durga, Kali, and other (groups of) fierce goddesses deploy their *shakti* tantric power to empower individuals, eradicate demonic evil, and restore equilibrium to an otherwise chaotic world. (Figure 6.1).

The tantric tradition

Our shift from *shri* to *shakti* in these two chapters on the goddess corresponds to a shift in religious modes from devotion to tantra. Whereas the Hindu devotional tradition entails a relationship of inequality where devotees pray to and worship deities, honoring and thanking them for the help they provide, tantra represents "strategies of embodiment" where humans can take on the powers of the divine for themselves. One scholar defines tantra as "an effort to gain access to and appropriate the energy or enlightened consciousness of the absolute godhead that courses through the universe" and as a "body of beliefs and practices which [...] seeks to ritually appropriate and channel that energy, within the human microcosm, in creative and emancipatory ways" (White 2000: 8, 9).

The tantric tradition created from scratch neither powerful goddesses nor the ability for individuals to appropriate their energy. Rather, shifts from *shri* to *shakti* gradually accumulate as communities accentuate and incorporate goddess-oriented tantra within a spectrum that includes Vedic, domestic, and devotional systems. Focusing on those elements available in these other ritual systems, tantric practitioners meditate on mystical geometric diagrams (*yantra*), chant secret and sometimes untranslatable syllables (*mantra*), and manipulate and consume impure taboo substances, as they seek to appropriate the powers

Figure 6.1 A young girl offers flowers to Kali during a spring goddess festival. Kathmandu, Nepal

of the universe for their own enjoyment (*bhukti*), for their attainment of powers (*siddhi*), and for their ultimate liberation (*mukti*).

We can speak of tantra – as we can speak about most aspects of the Hindu tradition – as operating on multiple levels separately and simultaneously. To fully understand the scope and practice of tantra, it might be helpful to think of tantra as represented on a grid. The left and right sides of the grid reflect a fairly strict South Asian cultural duality in which the impure left hand is used in the bathroom and the pure right is used in the kitchen and in transactions with people and the gods.[1] Dividing tantra into Left- and Right-handed Paths, gurus and their students confront and negotiate the traditional Hindu concepts of purity and pollution, as they directly engage with those impure and polluting substances that human society generally considers transgressive. The tantric tradition designates these substances within a set of five terms that in Sanskrit all begin with the letter /M/: wine, meat, fish, grain, and sex.[2] The ascetics we met in the chapter on Shiva, those who smoke marijuana in the cremation grounds during the Shivratri festival, are clearly on the Left-handed Path.

The Right-handed Path engages with those same five M-terms, but it variously translates and repurposes them so as to avoid their explicitly transgressive character. For example, the element of grain (*mudrā*) becomes detached from its character as a foodstuff – alongside meat, fish, and liquor – and becomes the set of hand gestures (*mudrā*) commonly seen in images of Hindu, Buddhist, Jain, and Sikh gods, goddesses, saints, and heroes. The Right-handed Path is especially associated with the tenth–eleventh-century Kashmiri Shaiva tantric Abhinavagupta, who left a prolific literature and a broad and deep lineage of important gurus that headed the many schools that branched from his system. For Abhinavagupta, the *mudrā* becomes the enlightened yogi's seal – the literal translation of the Sanskrit word – that names both the yogi's practices that lead to spiritual attainment and the spiritual attainment that results from those actions (Muller-Ortega 2000).

Many of these Kashmiri schools – for example, the Kaula, Trika, and Krama – are often referred to as "Shaiva-Shākta" for their focus on the union of Shiva and Devi. Although the intimacy and sexuality of this relationship is sometimes displayed rather publicly – the sexuality of Radha and Krishna in Jayadev's *Gita Govinda* and the erotic carvings on the temples at Khajuraho represent just two of the most famous examples – the ritual sexuality of tantrics initiated into a strict *guru–shishya* (teacher–student) relationship is performed with much greater secrecy. One tantric text describes the delicate multiplicity of tantric practitioners in this way: "They should be tantrics in private, Shaivas in outward appearance, but Vedic ritualists in their mundane observances, hiding the essence of their tradition, just like a coconut, behind these two layers" (quotation adapted from Sanderson 2015: 178). Less overtly sexual, this intimacy takes place most publicly, as will be evident throughout this chapter, in grand public royal rituals in which kings publicly display and declare their association with powerful goddesses.

On our tantric grid, we will refer to the lower and upper halves as the Esoteric and the Prosaic. The lower Esoteric level is represented by the Sanskrit textual tradition – for example, that of Abhinavagupta – that culminates in "emancipation." Here, qualified men and women who are initiated into a tantric *sampradaya* seek ultimate freedom from earthly snares and final union with the divine. The upper Prosaic level can be seen as operating within local South Asian communities, where everyday religious practices are punctuated by ritual acts that transgress orthodox ritual, emotional, and ethical boundaries.

This chapter will look at the interlocking facets of tantric practice that cross and integrate the several boundaries of this grid. Variously embedded in both the tantric textual tradition and in daily worship, practices of animal sacrifice, the ritual binding of powerful deities, and the embodiment of such deities in living persons – up to and including possession by deities, local spirits, and ancestors – represent forms of Shākta tantra that show the powerful presence of the goddess in Hindu religious life. A textual root of these practices can be found in the *Devī Māhātmya* (DM), the text in which the goddess Durga makes her primary appearance.

Durga slays the buffalo demon

Written from within the bhakti devotional tradition, the *Devī Māhātmya* (DM) provides a foundation for Hindu tantra.[3] The DM is framed within a dialogue between two men who are down on their luck: the king Suratha who has lost his kingdom and the merchant Samadhi who lost his wealth and family. The text's introductory story self-consciously presents a new facet of the Hindu tradition, as the sage Medhas teaches them about the new devotional tradition focused on a goddess. Medhas tells them about the goddess: "She is eternal, having the world as her form. She pervades all this (*idam sarvam*). And she emerges in various ways" (1.47).

The DM contains three stories, the central figure of which is Durga, though throughout the text she is referred to in nearly universal terms. All of the titles of the goddess listed in the previous chapter are applied here: Devi, Shri, Shakti, Mā, Prakriti, and Māyā. Referred to most often simply as Devi, popular and commentarial traditions refer to the goddess in three different forms in the text's three stories: Mahakali (Chapter 1), Mahalakshmi (Chapters 2–4), and Mahasarasvati (Chapters 5–13).

Especially during the October festival of Durga, Hindu temples display central images of these three goddesses together, and in some places processional icons of Kali are regularly dressed and ornamented as Sarasvati (Simmons et al. 2018: 234). The text reinforces the tripartite identity of the goddess, describing her in its first chapter as the creator, maintainer, and destroyer of the universe, roles often held by the three male gods Brahmā, Vishnu, and Shiva (1.56–57). As part of a long address to Devi in the opening chapter, the sage Medhas tells the king and merchant that She is: "the Great Knowledge (Mahāvidyā), the Great Illusion (Mahāmāyā), the Great Intelligence (Mahāmedhā), the Great Memory (Mahāsmṛtiḥ), the Great Delusion (Mahāmohā), the Great Goddess (Mahādevī), and the Great Demoness (Mahāsurī)" (1.58).

The first and shortest of the text's three stories tells how the Goddess of Sleep Yoganidrā exited the body of Vishnu as he was lying on the ocean at the bottom of the universe. By doing so, she allowed Vishnu to arise and defeat the twin enemies Madhu and Kaitabha.

The second story, that of Durga slaying the buffalo demon, has become one of the most famous stories in all of Hinduism (Figure 6.2). The story of the origin of Durga herself begins the story and plays on two common narrative tropes in Hindu literature: the yogic loophole and the conflict between the gods and demons. Not contained in the text of the DM but part of the larger Hindu narrative tradition, the yogic loophole is a long-standing strategy used by the demonic enemies of Vishnu.

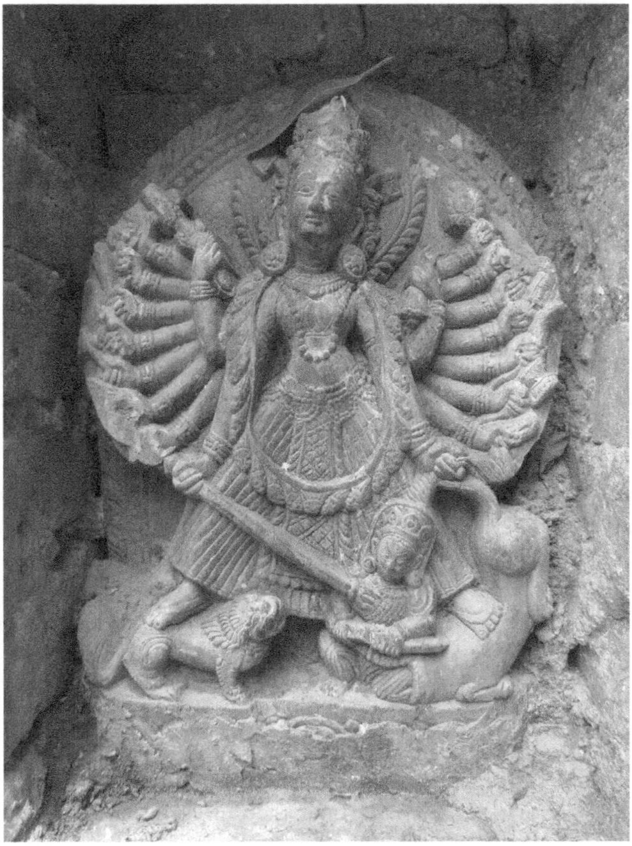

Figure 6.2 Durga slaying the buffalo demon. Pharphing, Nepal

This text's iteration of this trope begins when Mahisha, the buffalo demon, acquired a significant amount of *tapas* power from the large amount of yoga he performed. Seeking to cash in his *tapas*, he approached the god Brahmā in search of immortality, but was told: "All who are born must die. You cannot escape death." Not to be thwarted, Mahisha sought the next best thing, a wish not to be killed by man or god. Not considering for a second that he could be defeated by a woman, Mahisha inadvertently leaves open this loophole that will be his demise.

Like the Ramayana, the *Devi Mahatmya* possesses many different tellings, in both text and performance. In several tellings, the goddess represents both the violent martial enemy as well as the romantic marital object of the buffalo demon. Similarly, the telling of the yogic loophole described above is not contained in the Sanskrit text of the DM but is from, among other places, the *Amar Chitra Katha* comic book series (McLain 2009: 96).

Confident after winning his divine boon, Mahisha wages war against the gods. Stories of the conflict between gods and demons occur throughout the Hindu narrative tradition: Krishna versus Kamsa, Ram versus Ravana, and the universal battle in the story of the Churning of the Ocean. Building on the story of the yogic loophole, the story in the DM opens with the account of Mahisha's initial victory against the gods who, "expelled from heaven by the wicked Mahisha, wander on earth like mere mortals" (2.6).

Following their eviction from heaven, the gods sought safety in Brahmā. This practice of seeking refuge (Sanskrit *sharanam*) represents a technique related to Buddhist monasticism where men and women go for refuge to the Three Jewels – the Buddha, Dharma, and Sangha community – when vowing to become monks and nuns. Brahmā's own strategy for winning back heaven for the gods was, in a passage that foreshadows the text's third episode, his construction of Devi from parts of the male gods:

> By Brahmā her feet came into being; by the Sun her toes, by the Vasu storm gods her fingers, by Kubera the god of wealth her nose.
> By Prajapati her teeth were formed and by Fire her three eyes.
> The two *sandhyas* [sunrise and sunset] became her eyebrows, the wind god Vayu became her ears; the energies of the other gods also contributed to the form of the auspicious Devi.
>
> (2.15–17)

The episode ends by repeating the theme of headlessness that we saw with Bhairav and Ganesh in earlier chapters, as well as with an allusion to the soma drink of the Vedic priests, as Durga slays the Buffalo Demon:[4]

> Then the angry Devi, mother of the world, quaffed a superior beverage, and again and again she laughed, with reddened eyes …
> The Goddess said: "Roar, roar for a moment, you fool, while I drink this nectar! When you are slain here by me, it is the gods who soon will roar!"
> Having said this, she leapt upon the great demon, pinned his neck down with her foot, she pierced him with her spear, and cut off his head with a great sword.
> Then the whole demon army perished, and all the throngs of gods attained the highest bliss.
>
> (3.33, 36–37, 39b, 40)

The third and final story contains a number of interrelated episodes in which Durga vanquishes a series of demonic enemies. In preparation for the battle with the demons Chanda and Munda that opens the story, Kali suddenly and violently appears:

> From the knitted brows of Durga's forehead came forth Kali, with her dreadful face, carrying sword and noose.

> She carried a strange skull-topped staff, and wore a garland of human heads. She was shrouded in a tiger skin, and looked utterly gruesome with her emaciated skin.
>
> Her widely gaping mouth, terrifying with its lolling tongue, with sunken, reddened eyes and a mouth that filled the eight directions with roars.
>
> (7.5–7)

After her victory, Durga provides Kali with the epithet Chamunda, "she who defeated Chanda and Munda," a name that she is regularly known by still today.

The major episode of the third story is the battle with the demon Raktabija ("Blooddrop"), a demon who regenerates every time a drop of his blood touches the earth. In order to counter his massive army, Durga recruits the assistance of the Shaktis (the Powers of the Goddess) (Figures 6.3 and 6.4). Also called the Matrika (the Mothers) or the Matri-gana (the gang of Mother Goddesses), the Shaktis represent a group of powerful goddesses. Like Durga herself who was constructed of parts of the male gods, the Shaktis are personified female powers emitted from the male gods. Each Shakti bears the emblems, weapons, animal, and a feminine derivative of the name of her male counterpart. For example: "Like Indra, Aindrī bears the thunderbolt in her hand, she arrived seated atop the royal elephant, and she has one thousand eyes" (8.20).

Banding together to defeat the demon armies, each Matrika is given one verse to detail her attack. Again considering Indra's shakti Aindri as an example, "Daityas and dānavas were torn asunder by the thunderbolt of Aindrī. They fell by the hundreds, discharging torrents of blood upon the earth" (8.34). The climax of the episode occurs when the Matrikas then turn

Figure 6.3 During the Durga festival, a cloth painting hangs above the masks of the Mother Goddesses depicting Kali and Durga defeating the buffalo demon. Bhaktapur, Nepal

Figure 6.4 Mother goddesses (Kumari, Mahakali, and Barahi) dance through the city streets during the Durga Festival. Bhaktapur, Nepal

their attack to Raktabija, repeatedly assailing him with their weapons. But it is Durga and Kali who strike the fatal blows; a three-verse passage that concludes the chapter tells the bloody story from multiple perspectives: the goddess, the demon, the male gods, and the Matrika:

> Devī assailed Raktabīja with lance, thunderbolt, arrows, swords, and spears while Chāmuṇḍā drank his blood.
>
> The great demon Raktabīja fell to the ground, O king, battered by that array of weapons and drained of his blood.
>
> The gods attained immeasurable joy, O king, and the gang of Mothers born from them danced about, intoxicated by his blood.
>
> (8.59–62)

The text ends in a series of three steps. First, the female Shaktis who were emitted from the male gods are absorbed into Durga who stands as a unified embodiment of them all. With the diversity of female divinity within her, she speaks a verse that in form and content closely resembles the famous avatar passage spoken by Krishna in the *Bhagavad Gita* (4.7): "And so, whenever danger arises from demonic sources, I shall descend (*avatirya*) and bring about the complete destruction of enemies" (11.51).

Second, Devi utters what is known as a *phala-shruti*, a common statement of the "remembrance of the fruits," a statement of the benefits that result from reciting the text. Relevant to the introductory frame story of the sage, king, and merchant, Durga refers to her festival and states that those who recite and listen to the *Devi Mahatmya*

> will have no evil befall them, nor any misfortunes arising from wrong-doing. For them there will be neither poverty nor separation from loved ones, nor danger from enemies, robbers, or kings. Nor at any time will danger arise from weapons, fire, or flood [...] At the great annual *pūjā* performed in the autumn season, those who hear this poem of my glory and are filled with devotion will be freed by my grace from all afflictions and will be endowed with wealth, grain, and progeny. Of this there is no doubt.
>
> (12.4–5, 11–12)

Finally, the frame story of the sage, king, and merchant concludes with a devotional model for readers of the text.

> That they might obtain a vision of the Mother, the king and merchant settled on the riverbank and engaged in spiritual practice, chanting the supreme hymn to the Devī. They fashioned an earthen image of her on the riverbank, and the two of them worshiped the Devī with flowers, incense, fire, and offerings of water.
>
> (13.9–10)

As a result, the goddess appears before them and grants to the king a kingdom that will never slip from his grasp and to the merchant ultimate wisdom.

The stories and goddesses that the *Devī Māhātmya* introduces are key for the text's longevity and for the many goddess traditions present throughout the Hindu world. Using the rhetoric and practice of standard devotional traditions, the text provides a foundation for esoteric and prosaic *shākta* tantric systems and practices. The next section will look at the most famous example of a living goddess tradition, the autumnal festival to Devi that, mentioned in the *Devī Māhātmya*, concentrates its attention on Durga, Kali, and groups of fierce Mother Goddesses.

The Durga festival

The October festival of Durga precedes by one half-month the Diwali festival that has Lakshmi as its central goddess. Like Diwali, Durga's festival is referred to by a number of names that vary by location. Commonly referred to as Durga Puja, the festival's ten-day (Sanskrit *dasha*) duration provides many of these regional names: Dasain, Dasara, and Dusshera, as well as Navratri, the festival of nine nights.[5] The festival's final day is called Vijaya Dashami, the victorious tenth day when Durga slayed the buffalo demon.

Despite its regional diversity, many elements of the festival are commonly celebrated wherever we might be in the Hindu world. Among these common features is the presence of physical representations of the goddess. One of the most common images of Durga, in both poster art and temple icons, is that of Mahishasuramardini (Mahisha-asura-mardini, "She who slays the buffalo demon"). A quick Internet search will turn up many different versions of this image, most of them depicting her riding on either her tiger or lion as she is in the final act of beheading the demon, with his severed buffalo head lying on the ground beside him.[6]

Another common festival image is that of Kali standing atop Shiva. While not directly taken from the *Devi Mahatmya*, this image is often set against the backdrop of the battle between gods and demons that the text depicts. (Another setting of this image is the cremation grounds, often with vultures and jackals nearby.) This image is variously interpreted as Kali's dominance over Shiva or, with her tongue lolling out of her mouth, her shame at dominating her husband. Regardless, with the presence of Kali's many weapons and the garlands of skulls she wears, this image clearly communicates the intense *shakti* that she wields. As one author writes, "Kālī is the kind of figure who is capable of shaking one's comforting and naive assumptions about the world. In doing this, she allows a clearer perception of how things really are" (Kinsley 2004: 35).

In south Indian communities, the Dasara festival provides opportunities for families, and especially women, to keep *kolu* (pronounced and sometimes spelled *golu*). Translated as "dolls," these *kolu* images are collected throughout a woman's life and placed on tiered steps inside the living room of one's home to be visited by neighbor women throughout the festival. Depicting peaceful goddesses, local girls in cultural dress, and vessels that represent the goddess, *kolu* provide one of many ways that women celebrate the festival outside of orthodox and Sanskritic modes.

A second commonality of the festival is its ten-day duration, highlighted with different and special rituals on its first day and its final four days.[7] The first day is called Ghaṭasthāpana, "the establishment of the pot" of barley shoots. Largely a domestic ritual, the planting of barley seeds in a pot whose soil has been obtained from a riverbank at a sacred site reinforces the agricultural significance of this rite. Along with the harvest of the first rice paddy, the festival concludes ten days later as the barley shoots are harvested from the pot; sometimes called "the swords of Kali," they are worn as a decoration behind one's ear or in one's hair (Figure 6.5).

A final cross-cultural commonality of the festival is its emphasis on royal power. The series of rites during the festival's final four days reinforces this power through the worship of weapons, the concentration of rites at palaces, and attendance by powerful political figures. The palace of the medieval royal south Indian city of Mysore remains a prominent site where the festival reaffirms relationships between contemporary state officials, descendants of the local Wodeyar kingdom, and its connection to the medieval Hindu empire at Vijayanagar.

Figure 6.5 On the tenth day of the Durga festival, barley shoots are harvested from domestic pots and distributed to family and friends. Bhaktapur, Nepal

Probably the most famous celebration of the festival is the Durga Puja in the state of West Bengal, especially in its capital city of Kolkata. Similar to the display of *kolu* dolls in homes throughout south India, local youth clubs and organizations competitively construct, decorate, and display large *pandal* tableau of the goddess, frequently in her guise as the slayer of the buffalo demon or of Kali standing atop Shiva. Sometimes referred to as the world's largest street art festival, Kolkata's Durga Puja displays pandals that take on relevant contemporary themes as well. Recent pandals have displayed Durga as a nurse fighting the COVID-19 pandemic, leading migrant laborers to and from the city, and inside a replica of the Vatican's St. Peter's Basilica. At the end of the festival, all of these temporary displays of the goddess – and many smaller domestic ones – receive their *visarjan* as they are disposed of in the nearest body of water, the same fate that temporary images of Ganesh receive in his summer festival. For many in Kolkata, this visarjan occurs in the Hooghly River, the name of the local branch of the Ganges.

Prosaic tantra

Much more than the devotional celebrations of Kolkata's Durga Puja, the Dasain festival of Bhaktapur, Nepal, displays a wide spectrum of rites that are part of *shākta*-oriented prosaic tantra: animal sacrifice, binding the power of fierce deities, and human embodiment and deity possession.

Animal sacrifice is selectively forbidden throughout India and in most global Hindu communities outside of South Asia. In their place, eggs, coconuts, pumpkins, or gourds are frequently substituted. In Nepal, however, animal sacrifice remains an integral part of Durga's festival, during which animals from among the *pancha-bali*, "the five proper sacrifices," are regularly offered: chickens, ducks, goats, rams, and buffalo. The royal courts of Nepal annually sacrifice numerous buffalo who embody the demonic Mahisha, displaying headless carcasses in the public square as well as inside the most public courtyard of the royal palace. Goats are offered at the shrines of the Mother Goddesses outside of the city, and by families inside the city as they seek the goddess's blessings to recharge their tools – especially their cars, trucks, and motorcycles – for the coming year. And like many rites in which domestic celebrations mirror rites performed by and for the state, Vijaya Dashami represents the only day when animals are sacrificed inside the home, with a chicken or duck offered in front of the domestic pot of sprouted barley shoots.[8]

Seeking the goddess's protective blessing through animal sacrifice is often part of the tantric strategy of binding. Intended to temporarily or even completely harness the power of the goddess, binding can occur in any of three ways, sometimes all together: by chanting mantras, by dancing and performing other rituals, and by wearing threads. Just as the *Kali Chalisa* at the beginning of this chapter begins with mantras that provide the worshipper with a ritual form of defensive armor, other texts include mantras that provide the speaker with a set of verbal nails for binding deities and harnessing their power.

> The 1984 film *Indiana Jones and the Temple of Doom* depicts a farce of a Hindu ritual in India, a human sacrifice to Kali. Feeding off of the British fascination with and fictionalization of the criminal *thugee* cult in 1830s India, the film reinforces so many Western stereotypes of Hindu India, including a dinner scene that depicts the consumption of food that virtually nobody in India has ever eaten, that the Government of India forbade the film from being shot in India and banned it upon its release.

One of the most famous examples of ritual binding occurs in the origin story of the Tibetan Buddhist Samye monastery. The founding Guru Rinpoche was summoned from India by King Trisong Detsen in the eighth century to pacify the local spirits who, opposed to Buddhism, interrupted the construction of the monastery by tearing down in the night everything that was built during the day.[9] Guru Rinpoche entered into magical battle with these spirits, drawing on the ground a mandala of the Five Transcendent Buddhas. Meditating on that mandala for seven days, Guru Rinpoche subdued them, pinned them to the ground, and harnessed and redirected their power towards the protection of the monastery and of Tibetan Buddhism. This story is performed regularly throughout the Tibetan Buddhist world, including in Nepal's Kathmandu Valley, where large numbers of Tibetans in exile reside. On the Tibetan festivals of the new year Losar and Mani Rimdu, monks perform masked dances in which they portray the terrifying demons harnessed by Guru Rinpoche, in the form of dragons, birds, and buffalo.

One of the most memorable and powerful components of Nepal's Dasain festival is the Nava Durga (Nine Durgas) dance troupe, whose myths and rites are similarly connected to ritual binding. Wearing the masks and regalia of each of Durga's Shakti assistants from the *Devī Māhātmya*, the Nava Durga dancers immediately recall the story of Durga slaying the buffalo demon. But they also simultaneously embody the local Ajima grandmother goddesses who, living in the forests outside the city, would catch people who walked by, sacrifice them, and drink their blood.[10] Their reign of terror was only temporarily halted when they happened to catch a tantric priest who passed through the forest. Before they sacrificed him, he chanted a mantra that bound the goddesses making them unable to move, shrunk them, put them in a basket, and brought them home.

At his home, he hid the Nava Durga in a locked room where he worshipped them with tantric knowledge, offered them sacrifices, and made them dance. The goddesses allowed this relationship only as long as they remained hidden. One day, when the priest's wife opened the door and saw them dancing, thus breaking their agreement, the goddesses left the tantric's house. Recaptured along the way, the Nava Durga were brought to a temple in the center of the city occupied by members of the low Gatha caste who continue to embody and dance the goddesses during the festival today. It is through the actions of the tantric, his wife, and the Gatha that the Nava Durga goddesses, like the Tibetan Buddhist masked dancers who symbolically reconstruct Samye monastery, continue to protect the city for the benefit of all people.

Taking human form as the Nava Durga, they dance and are welcomed throughout the city with numerous offerings of food, alcohol, and animal sacrifice, in a series that begins with a buffalo sacrifice at the first of the Matrika shrines that ring and protect the city. (It is also from the riverbank at this eastern shrine that many people obtain the soil for their domestic pot of barley shoots.) Each of these eight shrines is visited in turn during the ten days of the festival, with visitors singing and chanting from local texts, playing the *dhime* drum that signals their initiation into adulthood, socializing with their neighbors, and worshipping the round aniconic goddess stones at the center of each shrine. It is through visits to and celebrations at these shrines that the body of the goddess is annually reconstructed.

The Nava Durga troupe dances amidst the presence of buffalo horns, another example of tantric binding during the goddess festival. Temples in Kathmandu sometimes display horns as reminders of the buffalo sacrificed there. This is especially true at temples to Nasadyo, the god of music, where the display of dozens of sets of horns memorializes the buffalo sacrifices that initiate young boys and girls into adulthood via their education in playing the *dhime* drum.

Anticipating the buffalo sacrifice on the final day of Dasain at the Nava Durga temple and commemorating Durga slaying the buffalo demon, drummers will affix buffalo horns to their drums, thus binding the fallen buffalo demon in place.

Binding also occurs on more mundane levels. Along with the *tika* mark received on the forehead as a visible marker that one has recently performed puja and the *bindi* that girls and women wear as a decorative mark, married women wear red *sindur* powder in the part of their hair.[11] Upon marriage, women also receive a thread worn around the neck, called either a *mangal sutra* ("auspicious thread") or *tali*.[12] This thread resembles many other threads that Hindus tie on their bodies in other ritual situations: worship at a goddess temple is often concluded by tying a red thread around one's wrist; during the summer festival of *raksha bandhan*, brothers present gifts to their sisters who respond by tying a protective *rakhi* thread around the wrists of their brothers; on that same day, Hindus in Nepal also celebrate *janai purnima* as priests provide blessings and tie a thread around the wrists of worshippers, while brahmins also, as they do at other times in South Asia, change the thread that they wear over their left shoulder.

With sindur in their hair and the sutra around their neck, married women are treated with all of the ambivalence of a goddess as we saw in *The Laws of Manu*. Symbolically bound to their husband, their *shakti* is brought under control and balanced by the *shri* that comes to define their married life. But this is hardly (and rarely has ever been) the only fate that women must endure.

In her powerful and controversial Elements trilogy, director Deepa Mehta uses film to show how women can take power for themselves despite historical and cultural structures that do not always work in their favor. The 1996 film *Fire* handles the sometimes stifling nature of the traditional Indian family, her 1998 *Earth* is set against the 1947 Partition of India and Pakistan, and her 2005 *Water* details the difficult lives of young widows. Similarly, Leena Manimekalai's 2019 film *Maadathy: an Unfairy Tale* takes up the issue of caste as the film's main character, the girl Yosana (bearing a green parrot on her shoulder in one scene in a subtle nod to the Tamil poetess Andal) passes down her story of caste and sexual violence for all to retell.

Like the women who tie threads during the Mother Ten *vrat* to Lakshmi, the same wedding tali that binds women in marriage can also more strongly connect women to the goddess. Girls, widows, or women enduring bad marriages have been known to rededicate themselves to the goddess by replacing their wedding tali with a new one from the goddess. These women, called *matamma, jogati*, or *devadasi* ("divine servants"), have had a range of experiences in their special status, from courtesan to temple dancer to female ascetic to secular artist.[13] For some women, however, the exchange of tali is just one way of acquiring shakti from the goddess, who "has given them the freedom to move across traditional social and spatial boundaries observed by many Hindu women in similar stages of life" (Flueckiger 2013: 213).

Embodiment

Seeking divine protective blessings through any of these strategies facilitates experiences of embodiment, the third major component of prosaic tantra. Embodiment represents the phenomenon of gods and goddesses physically manifesting in social space. These manifestations are always made in ways that are culturally recognizable: reading signs and omens in nature, witnessing the goddess in the sometimes violent movements of wooden chariots that bear her image, and even experiences of possession.

As part of the larger cultural connection with yoga and the South Asian health sciences of ayurveda, many tantric goddesses are associated with illnesses and the wellness of the body. Traditionally connected to smallpox, until its virtual eradication in the twentieth century, Shītalā and Yellamma are goddesses who now manifest as fever or measles or other similar ailments, their appearance seen as her blessing. Easily heated, their fever manifestations can be cooled through a ritual application of turmeric, often also applied to icons of the goddesses. These goddesses not only cool fever and smallpox but also relieve their worshippers from a variety of socially disempowering situations, such as poverty, famine, social discord, or childlessness.[14]

While goddesses are frequently housed in temples similar to those of any other deity, the fierce gods who are the subject of this chapter often find residence in a different type of sacred space. These shrines, often referred to as her Shakti Pīṭh (pronounced /peet/), house powerful rounded aniconic stones associated with the goddess Satī, the wife of Shiva. Sati makes her primary appearance in the story in which Shiva decapitates his father-in-law Daksha and replaces his head with that of a goat. Embarrassed at her husband's murder of her father, Satī, the "woman of truth," dies of shame. Distraught at his wife's death, Shiva wanders the earth carrying his wife's corpse and allowing the world to fall into disorder. Fearing a tragic end to the entire world due to Shiva's lack of attention, the gods send Vishnu to cut up her body with his discus and to encourage Shiva to get over his grief.

Variously connected to this narrative, shrines to goddesses are regularly venerated in sets. Sati's fifty-one body parts – corresponding to the fifty-one letters of the Sanskrit alphabet – land across India, each enshrined as a seat of her physical shakti. Among her most prominent shrines are those in Kalighat in Calcutta where her toes fell; at Tarapith where her third eye fell; and in Kamakhya in the state of Assam where her *yoni* vulva is venerated.[15]

Whether in single temples to the circle of sixty-four Yogini or sets of shrines where any number of fierce Shakti, Yakshi, or Dākini reside, these sets exemplify multiplicity and the fine lines between human, divine, and demonic. The eight Shakti Pith that surround the cities of the Kathmandu Valley, including Bhaktapur where the Nava Durga dance, are similarly open-air shrines rather than enclosed temples. Visited serially during the ten days of Dasain, they sit in a protective stance outside the city, where non-brahmin officials regularly direct animal sacrifices to the row of aniconic stones that house the power of the goddess.

Possession

When we speak of a goddess embodying a person, rather than an object or place, we cross over from embodiment to possession. A regular feature of the Hindu tradition from very early on, possession is often denoted in text and practice with a consistent vocabulary that tells us much about how it is understood. The term *pravesha* (entrance) communicates the penetration of a person by an external force, while *āroḍha* (to ride) and *līlā* (to play) both communicate the extraordinary physical and emotional intimacy of the possessing deity with the person possessed.[16]

Occasionally, it is a male deity such as Bhairav who possesses, as he is seen throughout the Himalayan region as a "god of justice" for those who have been wronged (Sax 2009: 32–37). More typically, however, it is forms of the goddess who animate the bodies of the possessed. While potentially dangerous, possession events are typically seen as a blessing of the deity's grace, a gift rather than an unwanted demonic invasion from the outside as we typically see it in the West (Erndl 1993: 106). Rather than requiring an exorcism to purge the possessing spirit, the possession event becomes an opportunity to venerate a living divine form.

But possession also exists on a spectrum. Possession appears in the prosaic tantra of rituals and festivals, where masked dancers are escorted by two human guardians who attach themselves to the dancer's outstretched arms. The frenzy of such a festival replete with singing, drumming, and worship can also spontaneously incite possession, or at least trance, as devotees exhibit signs at the close contact with these dancers or even just the sight of their masks. For some, possession represents a goal that they concentrate on and seek to manifest, as a local priestess might gain a reputation for speaking the words of the goddess, even within an urban middle-class Indian setting.[17]

One prominent example that sits in between embodiment and possession is Nepal's "living goddess" Kumari. Balancing *shri* and *shakti*, Kumari manifests female divinity by simultaneously embodying Durga, the local royal goddess Taleju, and the Buddhist Vajradevi in the form of a young girl.[18] Reinforcing the authority of the king and the military might of the Vedic warrior Indra, Kathmandu's Indra festival connects her power to that of the Hindu king. For centuries, Kumari has processed the perimeter of the city in a large chariot alongside those of her brothers Ganesh and Bhairav. In most other places, however, she makes her grand appearance during the goddess festival of Dasain, where she is the center of the many representations of Durga's multiple Shakti assistants who together represent the body of Durga.[19]

Kumari's royal power reflects certain restrictions, however, as on the final day of the Indra festival when Hindus enter her house to receive her blessing, non-Hindus are prevented from receiving this blessing. Such a restriction occurs at other times and places and for other reasons as well. It is only on the day of Vijaya Dashami that Hindus are allowed to enter Kathmandu's temple to the royal goddess Taleju. Entrance of non-Hindus is completely restricted in other places such as the Jagannath temple in Puri in India. These restrictions are due to a combination of factors: the power of the deity who resides within, a tradition of qualification and sectarian initiation, colonial structures that often restricted Indians from British spaces in India, and the problems resulting from an influx of tourists to active religious spaces. Along these same lines, Hindu temples also frequently restrict wearing shoes and leather objects such as belts and from taking photography inside sacred spaces.

In goddess temples among Caribbean Guyanese communities in Queens, New York, possession by the goddess – or "invocation," as they refer to it – represents a standard activity. Although only the main priestess truly invokes Mariyamman, many others participate and welcome the goddess. Resembling forms of Pentecostal Christianity in the American South, these weekly services in honor of the goddess, set against a backdrop of sharp Caribbean percussion and the presence of both universal and village deities, include wild dancing, eating fire, and repeatedly pouring water over those who welcome the presence of the goddess.[20]

Particularly powerful, however, are instances of spontaneous possession. Often occurring within the context of a puja, a woman who becomes possessed by the goddess exhibits a standard set of gestures that community members quickly recognize: her eyes glaze over, she shakes or whirls her head around, her bound hair comes loose, and she may stand up to dance frenetically. In some cases, fellow worshippers may get out of the way to give her space, while in others they may gather around her seeking their own intimacy with this human manifestation of the goddess.

Many women manifest possession amidst situations of loss and tragedy. Most common are circumstances of women's infertility, a biological and cultural condition that produces "phantoms, demons, and village goddesses [who] have a horrifying agency and ontological characteristics of their own" (Ram 2013: 86).[21] In other words, rather than viewing divine beings as entities that are fundamentally separate from the humans who speak about them, we should consider them as agents or co-agents who operate along with the women who host them. In one particularly poignant example, a village woman who continues to miscarry and is possessed by a witch visits a priest possessed by Bhairav. A sort of last-ditch effort as these situations regularly are, her husband watches on, increasingly frustrated, as they conclude their dialogue with the wife/witch plaintively asking the priest/ Bhairav, "What should I do?" (Gold 1988/2000: 181–185).

Conclusion

These two chapters have presented the goddess in her multiple forms along the *shri-shakti* spectrum. With some of her forms representing more of her feminine glory and others more of her tantric power, the goddess also overlaps with the full spectrum of female experience. These cultural forms are hardly universal, however, as they change with the times. Recalling the nationalist novel

Anandamath and its dual presentation of Lakshmi and Durga, we will conclude with one historical note on the transformation of the goddess in eighteenth-century Bengal, in whose capital of Kolkata the British established the base of their Indian empire.

Transcending the strictly *shakti* form that she had embodied, Kali began to be seen as fully becoming the mother: Mā Kālī or Kālī Mā. Venerating her with increasingly standard devotional forms such as those directed to goddesses who present as *shri*, the Bengali devotional poet Kamalakanta Bhattacharya fully engaged Kali's multiplicity and extraordinary fluidity. Identifying her ability to change form and gender, he identified the Bengali Kali with Krishna from his homeland in Braj/Vraja:

> She who terrifies demons
> With her disheveled hair and brandished sword
> Occasionally visits Vraja,
> Captivating the cowherd women's hearts
> With the sound of his flute.
> (McDermott 1995: 67)

But the significant historical transition in the Bengali Kali is in her identity as both destroyer and Mother, a shift that several hundred years later is now essentially complete. In one of his other poems, Kamalakanta marks this complex identity of The Dark Lady.

> Tell me, Śyāmā,
> How could it hurt you to look at me
> Just once?
> You're a mother;
> If you see so much pain,
> But aren't compassionate,
> What kind of justice is that?
> I have heard from the scriptures
> That you rescue the fallen.
> Well? *I* am such a person –
> Wicked and fallen!
> You are famed as a deliverer of the wretched.
> If it pleases you,
> Take Kamalākānta across.
> (McDermott 1995: 72)

The softening of Kali that we see in Kamalakanta's poetry reverberated throughout Bengal and India, forever changing the complex ways that we see Hindu goddesses. But this poet was hardly alone in these accommodations. Rather, he was only one agent of large-scale social and cultural change largely emanating from the state of Bengal whose *bhadralok* middle class was negotiating its own place in an increasingly globalized world.

The next two chapters will trace the many ways that Hinduism changed following its negotiations with both Islam, which had entered India in the first few centuries following the death of the prophet Muhammad in the seventh century, and with the beginning of the British Empire in the eighteenth century. Although this story of religious reform is often rooted in interactions with the British Empire and the Bengali *bhadralok*, the next chapter will begin on the other side of the subcontinent in the western state of Gujarat and with the charismatic figure of Swaminarayan.

Notes

1 In temples and in shops, offerings and money are given and received with the right hand, often with the left hand underneath the right.
2 In Sanskrit, these terms are, respectively: madya, māṃsa, matsya, mudrā, maithuna.
3 This text is also called the *Durgā Saptashati* ("The Durgā 700"), the text of Durga in seven hundred verses. See Coburn 1991 for a full translation of the *DM*.
4 Another fierce tantric goddess, Chinnamastā ("She who cuts off her own head"), self-decapitates making an offering of her own blood to her female devotees.
5 Among the Newars of Kathmandu, the festival is called Mohani, named after the ash produced in a clay cup on the final day.
6 Medieval statues of this event can be found at many museums, including a ninth-century one at the Metropolitan Museum of Art in New York City, entitled "Goddess Durga Slaying the Demon Mahisha" (www.metmuseum.org/art/collection/search/719420).
7 These final four days (7–10) are called Kālrātrī (the Black Night), Mahāshtamī (the Great Eighth), Mahānavamī (the Great Ninth), and Vijaya Dashamī (the Victorious Tenth).
8 Animal sacrifice is part of a larger tantric imagery surrounding death that also includes the repeated imagery of skulls in text, image, and practice: Aghori renouncers finding and preparing a skull, Kali wearing a garland of skulls, and Bhairav holding a skull(cap) meant to hold the blood or alcohol he receives as an offering.
9 Mills 2003: 279.
10 A more complete version of this story can be found in Levy and Rajopadhyaya (1990: 503–505).
11 A married woman's first application of sindur is at her *sīmāntonnayana*, one of her *saṁskāra* rites of passage.
12 The word *sūtra* is related to the English word suture that also refers to the threads used to tie together the pages of a traditional text, also called a *sūtra*.
13 See Soneji 2012 for more on women, dance, and gesture.
14 See Ferrari 2015 for more on medicine and healing in South Asia.
15 See the chapter on Tara at Tarapith from "The Lady Twilight" chapter in Dalrymple 2010. The Buddhist Tara regularly appears in twenty-one different forms (Keul 2013).
16 Erndl (2006) discusses the terms *āroḍha* and *līlā*.
17 A woman who "speaks prophecy" from the goddess while keeping *kolu* often does so from within the middle class of Tamil south India (Ilkama 2021: 166–169).
18 See Gairola and Ranganathan 2023a and 2023b for Himalayan examples of the worship of goddesses, especially in the form of a young girl.
19 During the festival to Pachali Bhairav in Kathmandu that occurs during Dasain, three local elders are possessed by Bhairav, Ganesh, and Taleju. Processing from the cremation grounds on the banks of the Bagmati River, a buffalo is sacrificed at their destination at the royal palace in full view of Kumari.
20 Padma 2013.

21 See Ram 2013 and Bloomer 2018 for more on women, goddesses, and possession in contemporary India, including examples from south Indian Christianity where women are possessed by and speak through Mary, the mother of Jesus.

References

Balkaran, Raj. 2019. Visions and Revisions of the Hindu Goddess: Sound, Structure, and Artful Ambivalence in the Devī Māhātmya . *Religions* 10 (5): 322.

Hüsken, Ute, Vasudha Narayanan, and Astrid Zotter (eds.). 2021. *Nine Nights of Power: Durga, Dolls, and Darbars*. Albany: State University of New York Press.

White, David Gordon. 2000. *Tantra in Practice*. Princeton, NJ: Princeton University Press.

Key terms

buffalo demon
embodiment and possession
Durga
Durga Puja/Dasain festival
Kali
shakti
Tantra: esoteric and prosaic; purity and pollution
Texts: Shrī Kālī Chālīsā, Devī Māhātmya, Abhinavagupta's poetry

Persons

Abhinavagupta
Kamalakanta Bhattacharya
Kumari
Leena Manimekalai
Deepa Mehta

Study questions

1 What are the relationships – sympathetic and antagonistic – between domestic (*shri*) and powerful (*shakti*) forms of the goddess?
2 How have some contemporary Indian films continued to experiment with the intrinsic relationships between Hindu goddesses and women?
3 What are some of the many ways that the texts and practices of the autumnal Durga festival display and venerate forms of Durga?

7 Swaminarayan and *seva*

Service, spirituality, and reform in the British Empire

For nearly two weeks in the middle of August 2014, the Swaminarayan temple in Robbinsville, New Jersey, hosted Pramukh Swami, the head guru of its global Hindu community. This journey constituted a regular part of his *vicharan* travels that brought him to teach throughout India as well as to the United Arab Emirates, Europe, and the United States as early as 2000. Pramukh Swami was no stranger to the New Jersey area, having already visited the Swaminarayan community in New Jersey at another temple a half-hour north in the town of Edison. But this trip to America would be particularly special.

Coming with Pramukh Swami were the icons that he had consecrated two years earlier in Ahmedabad, a city in India's western state of Gujarat, and the home of the Swaminarayan *sampradaya*. Displayed in the Vicharan photo section of the organization's extensive website, these rites were performed on July 22, 2012, during Pramukh Swami's months-long residency in Ahmedabad. While there, he would perform *murti pratishtha vidhi*, the rites for consecrating icons, for images that would travel to thirteen other new temples in India and the United States, including those destined for Washington, DC, and Jacksonville, Florida. His performance of the installation rites on August 10, 2014, simultaneously established the deity images in the temple and inaugurated the Robbinsville temple as one of the sampradaya's twelve major temples worldwide. These two events were brought together as the temple artisans carved a depiction of Pramukh Swami performing the consecration rites in India onto the exterior of the temple itself.

But Pramukh Swami's visit meant just as much to the members of the Swaminarayan temple and the large South Asian community in the area. At age ninety-four and having served as guru for some forty-five years, Pramukh Swami had been the face of the organization for several generations of devotees.

Knowing that this would be his final visit before passing on the leadership of the community to the next guru, the community relished every moment they had with him. Thousands of people met him at the temple for his one a.m. arrival with chants of "Pramukh Swami Maharaj ki jay!" – *Glory to the great king Pramukh Swami!* – and returned to take daily darshan of him both inside and outside the temple.[1] (Pramukh Swami died in 2016 at the age of ninety-six, passing on the leadership of the community to the guru who would come to be named Mahant Swami and who was also present at the 2014 Robbinsville vicharan.)

DOI: 10.4324/9781003475033-8

As with the previous pair of chapters on Hindu goddesses, and the pair of chapters previous to those on the two main avatars of Vishnu, the current and following chapter will form their own pair. With India's 1947 independence from the British Empire marking a loose boundary between these two chapters, the following chapter will examine the migration of Indian families and communities to virtually every country in the world and the rise of local and global *guru* teachers who accompanied them and have since attended to both Indian and non-Indian communities.

This first chapter will begin at a previous crossroads in the history of India, and hence in the history of the Hindu tradition. Taking as its historical starting point the British acquisition of land and power near the city of Kolkata (formerly Calcutta) in the state of Bengal in 1757, this chapter will consider the interactions between local Indian thinkers and officials of the global British Empire. Frequently referred to as part of a reform movement within Hinduism, the intercultural dialogues that were part of this process represent a significant moment in the meeting of East and West.

Key to these dialogues was Swaminarayan himself, the person who lends his name to the sampradaya introduced in the vignette above. Born in 1781 and living much of life in Gujarat hundreds of miles west of Kolkata, Swaminarayan will serve as the lens through which these two chapters will view larger segments of the Hindu tradition as a whole: namely, through practices of devotional *sevā* service to gurus within the context of transnational movements and global organizations. More than just being part of the global conversations around reform in British India, Swaminarayan established a school that has since spread across the globe and that represents one of the fastest growing religious denominations in the twenty-first century.

Fully in line with the other chapters of this book, the figure of Swaminarayan exemplifies the theme of multiplicity: he is present as a human being who lived in historical time and who, in the different phases of his life, is given completely different names; he appears as a fully divine being who resides in the heavenly abode of Akshardham; and he is eternally accompanied by a series of human beings who take the form of the gurus of the Swaminarayan tradition. This simultaneous set of human and divine forms makes more clear the outpouring of devotion and emotion at Pramukh Swami's final presence at the Robbinsville temple.

Hinduism and the British Empire

The sixteenth and seventeenth centuries are often referred to as the Age of Discovery, as Europeans ventured far beyond their borders. Their destinations were lands throughout Asia, Africa, and the Americas, but their goals were much more economic than they were "discovery" for its own sake. In addition to extracting human and material resources for their financial gain, European kings and merchants often fell into the business of governance of these foreign lands. India exemplifies this colonial trend like no other.

Beginning in the early 1600s, the Dutch, French, and Portuguese came to govern and trade in local regions in India, each trying to corner the spice market. In 1757, the British East India Company acquired – through military might, economic power, and political duplicity – a plot of land at Plassey. The nearby city of Calcutta would soon become the capital of British India, the "crown jewel" of the global British Empire. Eventually, they would wrest control of north India from the Mughals who ruled from Delhi and Agra and come to govern all of India.

In the eighteenth century, Calcutta served not only as the political capital of India but also as a major cultural hub. Similar to how some 2,500 years earlier the urban center of Varanasi provided a setting where the exchange of diverse ideas assisted in the formation of the major religions of Hinduism, Buddhism, and Jainism, the city of Calcutta brought together customs, languages, and ways of being from two different worlds. We refer to these interactions with the term "Orientalism," a concept that necessarily entails a stark difference in power, always to the advantage of the colonizer over the colonized.

In his 1979 book *Orientalism*, Edward Said emphasized how the role of power in such colonial contacts, wherever we might find them, results in the European construction of "the East". Said wrote:

> The Orient is not only adjacent to Europe; it is also the place of Europe's greatest and richest and oldest colonies, the source of its civilizations and languages, its cultural contestant, and one of its deepest and most recurring images of the Other. In addition, the Orient has helped to define Europe (or the West) as its contrasting image, idea, personality, experience.
>
> (Said 1979: 2).

Ruling from an office of the British East India Company in London, officers in the early British Empire were initially sympathetic to the religious and cultural traditions they encountered in India. The Orientalist William Jones saw Indian culture and Sanskrit language as the foundation of all of the world's cultures, even penning his own hymns to the Hindu gods. A judge by trade but a skilled linguist by hobby, Jones translated from the Sanskrit, as we saw in an earlier chapter, *The Laws of Manu*, a text that British judges would use, as Indians never had before, to adjudicate court cases.

The Company's Charter Act of 1813 even called for the financial support of Persian and Sanskrit languages in "the revival and improvement of literature and the encouragement of the learned natives of India, and for the introduction and promotion of a knowledge of the sciences among the inhabitants of the British territories in India." British support of Indian education was not completely benevolent, of course, but was intended to create an educated class in service of the British and their colonizing mission.

In later years, however, and under the partial influence of Christian missionaries whom the Company had previously banned from working in India, these previously positive British attitudes towards Indian languages and culture began to wane. In his 1835 "Minute on Indian Education," the British official Thomas Macaulay famously asserted that "a single shelf of a good European library was worth the whole native literature of India and Arabia." Advocating English as the sole medium of Indian education, Macaulay sought to create among educated Indians "a class who may be interpreters between us and the millions whom we govern – a class of persons Indian in blood and colour, but English in tastes, in opinions, in morals and in intellect."

Macaulay's policy was easier to idealize than to enforce, as local languages such as Bengali remained in effect throughout the region. His infusion of English-language education, however, quickly altered virtually every facet of social and cultural life in India. Moving beyond William Jones's academic and romantic respect for the ancient and transcendent culture of "the Orient," these new policies sought to train the Indian populace as low- to mid-level clerks, scholars, and government officials within the ever-expanding imperial infrastructure.

This Western-educated and English-speaking Bengali *bhadralok* middle class had indeed imbibed the tastes, morals, and intellect that Macauley had desired. Occasionally converting to Christianity, the *bhadralok* were forced more regularly to navigate Bengali and English languages and cultures in ways that would become common to people throughout the British Empire. Exposed to consistent British critiques that portrayed Hinduism as backward, polytheistic, and generally speaking negatively exotic (as opposed to the positive exoticism of the earlier generation of Orientalists like William Jones), Bengalis responded in a variety of ways.[2]

The stories of Radha and Krishna can serve as a lens through which we can see changing social and political attitudes. As we saw in a previous chapter, Chaitanya, the sixteenth-century Bengali devotee of Krishna, developed a new devotional orthodoxy that located the love of Radha and Krishna in the land of Vrindavan, which became a pilgrimage place for Hindus from across India. In Chaitanya's Bengali homeland, however, his orthodoxy reinforced gender, class, and caste hierarchies. His reduction of a story of a playful and sexually charged illicit love affair to a simple theological longing for the divine eventually became stretched thin. By the nineteenth century, this same story of Radha and Krishna began to reflect the plight of young couples in the culture of urban Calcutta: of wealth and poverty, hopes and fears, and romance and betrayal.[3]

From within this skilled and educated Bengali middle class emerged a number of authors, poets, and thinkers whose place of prominence would allow them to have a significant effect on changing Indian attitudes. Wrestling with British critiques of Indian society and religion, this group would generally come to be known as Indian reformers. Among later reformers is the author Bankim Chandra Chattopadhyay, who in 1882, as we saw in an earlier chapter, published the nationalist novel *Anandamath* (*The Abbey of Bliss*). Its focus on Bharat Mata (Mother India) was part of a larger focus on goddess worship in Bengal that, with its beginnings partially in a response to famines in the late 1700s, continues as a prominent feature of the Durga Puja today.[4]

At the beginning of this line of reformers stands the figure of Ram Mohan Roy, "the father of modern India." Born into a wealthy and upper-class brahman family in 1774, Ram Mohan studied Tibetan Buddhism, the mystical branch of Sufi Islam, Christian ethics, as well as the Hindu scriptures that were part of his family's culture. This broad study of religion, set against the background of the British Empire, encouraged him to question the foundations of all of them, even "calling in question the validity of the idolatrous system of the Hindūs" (Hay 1988: 20).

His rejection of the veneration of "idols" speaks to a larger questioning of Hindu culture, as he sought to apply the essence of these philosophical teachings to social and political causes. To this end, Ram Mohan founded the Brahmo Samaj organization in 1828, one of whose primary issues was the rights of women. Negotiating a complex set of issues that found the organization allied in some ways with officials in the British Empire, Ram Mohan worked to reform such thorny issues as setting a minimum age for the marriage of girls; *sati*, the sacrifice of widows upon the funeral pyres of their husbands among some ultraorthodox communities; and widow remarriage.

The issue of widow remarriage is one that would for decades continue to divide more conservative Hindu communities who relied upon the Sanskrit dharma texts from more progressive communities siding with the more democratic ideals advocated by the British. (For some perspective, Britain finalized its Slavery Abolition Act in 1833, which freed slaves throughout the entire empire.) A strong advocate of widow remarriage, the Calcutta-based reformer Ishvarchandra Vidyasagar published his treatise, *Hindu Widow Remarriage*, in 1855. Disputing the strictly conservative position of the dharma texts, he railed against those who would "prevent the promotion of widow remarriage out of slavery to local custom and at the expense of the injunctions of the authoritative treatises" (Hatcher 2012: 202).

The rejection of idolatry serves as a theme that runs through many of Ram Mohan's writings, leading him to translate into English and Bengali several of the Hindu Upanishads whose non-dual philosophy represents a core of his body of work. The name of the Brahmo Samaj and its focus on the Upanishads recall brahman, the universal impersonal principle by whom the entire world operates. The organization's emphasis on brahman precludes attention to individual Hindu deities and especially their icons, one of the group's main religious tenets, as it directs attention instead to a unity that underlies the entire universe.

The return to brahman and the Upanishads by the Brahmo Samaj was mirrored by another organization, the Arya Samaj, that offered another response to Christian monotheism. Originating across the country in the western coastal city of Bombay, the Arya Samaj founded by Dayanand Saraswati in the 1870s represents one of the earliest and most notable modern applications of the Vedas. In his essay "Of Mice and Idols," Dayanand writes of how he watched a mouse wander across the statue of Shiva during the festival of Shivratri. He concluded that it was impossible "to reconcile to the idea of an omnipotent, living god, with this idol which allows the mice to run over his body and thus suffers his image to be polluted without the slightest protest."[5]

Both a critique of Hindu temple ritual and a synthesis with Western monotheism, this story grounds the Arya Samaj conception of God as "formless, omniscient, just, merciful, unborn, endless, unchangeable, beginning-less, unequaled, the support of all, the master of all, omnipresent, immanent, unaging, immortal, fearless, eternal and holy, and the maker of all. He alone is worthy of being worshiped." The combination of these factors led Dayanand to advocate a return to the Vedas, texts that were coming into a new prominence with their recent translation by European scholars.[6]

Returning to older forms of Hinduism – the impersonality of brahman and the texts of the Vedas – often entailed connections with Hindu nationalism. As with Chattopadhyay who used images of the goddess for nationalistic purposes in *Anandamath*, Debendranath Tagore, a subsequent leader of the Brahmo Samaj, made similar connections: "Our Motherland is dear to us, but Religion is dearer, Brahma is dearest of all, dearer than son, dearer than riches, supreme over everything else" (Hay 1988: 44). Later writers more clearly combined themes of religion and nationalism, drawing close connections between the nation of India and the religion of Hinduism, often at the expense of Western Christianity and, despite its millennium-long presence in India, Islam whose traditions do not as easily map onto the landscape of India.[7] Vinayak Damodar Sarvarkar pushed this connection to its limits. In a text initially composed while a political prisoner, Sarvarkar published in 1923 the principles of Hindutva, the idea of a pure "Hindu-ness" devoid of any connections with or sympathy to Islam or the West. In service of this Hindu ideal, Savarkar asserted India's long history, the presumed homogeneity of its people(s) and culture(s), and the "perfect" and ancient language of Sanskrit.

The new formulations of Hinduism introduced by these many reformers produced a new strain of Hinduism, sometimes called neo-Hinduism. Less than "reforming" Hinduism, these authors responded to the dominant rhetoric of British imperialism in a number of consistent ways that are still felt today.

Socially, Hinduism became a significant means to build regional, national, and global communities. Beyond building on the geographically Indian roots of Hinduism found in *māhātmya* texts that glorify cities, regions, and natural features of the environment, political parties in contemporary India have frequently galvanized sections of the population by asserting some form of the nationalistic Hinduism asserted by these reformers. Through less overtly politically means, organizations such as the Arya Samaj have sent missionaries to Hindu populations in such places as South Africa and the Caribbean to regulate and define "proper" notions of what it means to be Hindu.

Philosophically, the return to the most ancient forms of Hinduism reflected (and frequently continues to reflect) trends in the field of Religious Studies where the most ancient textual form of a tradition is perceived to be its most authentic. By focusing on the Vedas and the non-dualistic portions of the Upanishads, neo-Hindu authors helped to construct new ways of speaking about Hinduism, both in India but especially globally: that Hinduism is a "way of life" and not a "religion," or that Hinduism is a monotheistic religion in which all of the gods and goddesses are facets of the singular brahman.

Theologically, the work of the reformers reinforced a renewed focus on Vishnu, a process often called Vaishnavization. As we have seen throughout this book, the Hindu pantheon is roughly divided into Shaiva, Vaishnava, and Shākta categories. Whereas Shaiva practices tend to emphasize renunciation and Shākta practices lean towards tantra, Vaishnava practices reflect the domestic maintenance of dharma. Often replacing animal sacrifices with vegetarianism, local texts and languages with Sanskrit, and the worship of local goddesses with forms of Vishnu, the process of Vaishavization recognizes the ways that communities focus on forms of Vishnu as strategies to increase their respectability and suitability among diverse middle-class communities.[8]

The main topic of this chapter, the Swaminarayan sampradaya, brings all of these themes together. Reinforcing the ancient guru–shishya (teacher–student) relationship, the Swaminarayan school has deep roots in the historical era of the British Empire and Hindu reform as described above. More than a philosophical school contending with Western ideas, the Swaminarayan school has established a global Hindu community based on Vaishnava stories, rituals, and values.

Swaminarayan

Living across the country in the western region of Gujarat at the same time that Ram Mohan Roy was working in Calcutta – thus between what have sometimes been called India's medieval and modern periods – the man who would come to be known as Swaminarayan began to incorporate similar themes into his own new form of Hinduism. According to his hagiographical story well known to his millions of followers worldwide, Swaminarayan was born in 1781 with the name Ghanshyam in north India. At the age of eleven, and now known as Nilkanth Varni, he began a life of itinerant renunciation, traveling throughout South Asia for seven years learning, studying, and teaching. Ending up in Gujarat, he was initiated into an ashram led by one Ramanand in 1799, given the new name of Sahajanand Swami, and named the ashram's new guru a short two years later.

Like the Bengali reformers, Sahajanand was involved in social, political, and religious reform until his death in 1830 at the age of forty-nine. His campaigns against female infanticide and *sati* widow burning won him support from British officials in the Western regions of India that were just then coming under imperial control. Whether or not the region was as lawless as his hagiography claims, he instituted many other religious reforms that resembled those changes being made by the Bengali reformers: against lewd and bawdy songs during festivals, animal sacrifice and meat eating, sexual license in general but especially within tantric practice, and imbibing alcohol and other intoxicants. A puritanical code maintained by both laypeople and the many sadhus he would initiate throughout his lifetime, this ethical system laid the groundwork for the global Swaminarayan community that continues to this day.

Sahajanand and subsequent swamis established their code of conduct and practice in a series of texts that comprises the Swaminarayan scriptural canon and that shows us much about the school's historical and cultural development.

The *Vachanamrut* is a collection of 273 discourses delivered by Swaminarayan between 1819 and 1829. Compiled by four of his disciples, these discourses are arranged chronologically and geographically, according to his travels through the various towns and villages throughout Gujarat where he delivered them. Delivered within the format of a question-and-answer session as with many classical Sanskrit texts, the *Vachanamrut*, the first major prose text in the Gujarati language, represents the core text of the Swaminarayan tradition by which its theology has been established.

The *Swamini Vato* is a collection of sayings and stories by Gunatitanand Swami, Sahajanand Swami's primary disciple who manifests as the eternal student Akshar. Serving as a practical commentary on the *Vachanamrut*, this Gujarati text serves as an accessible guide for translating Vedantic philosophy into the everyday life of the community.

The Satsangi Jivan is a large five-volume work whose devotional life story of Sahajanand resembles that of Vishnu and his avatars, especially Krishna, in the Bhagavata Purana. The *Satsangi Jivan* similarly begins at the beginning of the world and culminates in the narrative life of Sahajanand, from the well-known stories of his childhood, to his life as a renouncer in Ramanand's monastery in Gujarat, to the ethical life of laypeople, women, and the many renouncers who interact within his newly established school of Swaminarayan Hinduism. All members, whether they are householder or renouncer, practice vegetarianism, humility, and devotion within a Vaishnava idiom.

And the *Shikshapatri*, a 212-verse work written by Sahajanand, provides a set of moral precepts for the community. Composed in Sanskrit and duplicated in some of the later portions of the *Satsangi Jivan*, this concise text has recently come into focus in the contemporary community. Due to its composition and brevity, it can be relatively easily memorized, both in the original Sanskrit and in its Gujarati and English translations, even by young children in their introduction to the tradition's foundational texts.

Bringing together the traditional with the innovative, these texts represent a microcosm of the entire Swaminarayan tradition that, as Raymond Williams states, "provides a case study of the historical and social process of adapting religious tradition to create new identities in response to evolving social, economic, and political changes" (2019: xviii). An independent religious school rooted in the classical textual canon, Swaminarayan Hinduism also clearly reflects a Vaishnava devotional identity.

Virtually every Swaminarayan temple contains images of Krishna and/or Radha-Krishna. The earliest Swaminarayan temples, those built by Sahajanand himself, display images of Krishna in their main shrine; icons of Sahajanand himself only come later and occupy a secondary place. In contemporary temples, however, images of Swaminarayan come to occupy the main shrine, with (Radha and) Krishna ceding their place of prominence. This difference in temple iconography reflects a series of historical changes by which Sahajanand came to supersede Krishna as the school's primary human manifestation of divinity. In this process of replacement, stories, images, and festivals of Krishna have also been adopted and adapted to fit those of Sahajanand. For example, the story of Krishna stealing butter becomes interpreted as the child Ghanshyam playing with the moon.

This process of Vaishnavization draws heavily on the style of worship prominent in the Gujarati Pushti Marg school with which Sahajanand was quite familiar. Members of this school focus on acts of devotional *sevā* (service) to forms of Krishna, "to be understood as the spontaneous expression of the devotee's love for [Krishna] and the desire to put the happiness of God before one's own personal desires" (Shah 2014: 140). Pushti Marg devotees adorn, feed, and entertain icons of Krishna in lavish displays similar also to traditions of the south Indian Shri Vaishnava school. For large Swaminarayan temples, these displays include five daily pujas to the central icons with larger and more elaborate pujas on festival days. An internet image search of Swaminarayan service to Krishna on the day of Govardhan Puja, the fourth day of the Diwali festival when Krishna lifted up the mountain against Indra's storms, reveals some truly amazing displays of Annakuṭ, mountains of food and sweets, presented to the central icon of Swaminarayan.

Central to essentially all Vaishnava devotional schools is the tenth-century *Bhagavata Purana*. With its own archaic language connecting it to ancient Vedic schools and traditions, this text provides a template for contemporary schools to innovate around concepts and practices devoted especially to Krishna. Inspiring the text of the *Satsangi Jivan*, the *Bhagavata Purana* also prescribes the tradition of devotional *sevā* service to Krishna. Similar to the five *bhāva*s (attitudes towards God) that inform the devotional traditions in Radha and Krishna's Govinddevji Mandir in Jaipur, nine actions comprise the body of Krishna's devotional service:

1. *shrāvaṇa* – listening to stories;
2. *kīrtana* – singing;
3. *smaraṇa* – remembering;
4. *pād-sevāna* – massaging feet;
5. *archana* – performing puja;
6. *vandana* – bowing respectfully;
7. *dāsya* – acting as a servant;
8. *sākhya* – behaving as a friend;
9. *ātma-nivedana* – unconditionally offering everything, including one's self.

As with the many ways that the Swaminarayan tradition has adapted traditional Vaishnava actions towards different ends, so also has it redirected this *sevā* towards the person of Swaminarayan. In no place has this process of adaptation been more clear than in the Swaminarayan BAPS school. Rooted in the soil of Gujarat in western India, the BAPS school (Bochasanwasi Akshar

Purushottam Swaminarayan Sanstha) split off from mainstream Swaminarayan Hinduism in 1907 and has grown exponentially ever since. The homepage of its website describes the global organization as follows: "The BAPS Swaminarayan Sanstha is a spiritual, volunteer-driven organization dedicated to improving society through individual growth by fostering the Hindu ideals of faith, unity, and selfless service."

Although the final letter of this acronym aligns it with the larger school of Swaminarayan Hinduism, its first three letters distinguish it both from the mainstream school and from other subsequent schools. Locating its geographical center in the town of Bochasan, rather than in either of the two towns of Vadtal and Ahmedabad that marked the twin headquarters of the mainstream school, BAPS established itself as an independent school.

The middle two letters further distinguish the BAPS school and its particular lineage of gurus. Eternally co-present as devotee and deity, respectively, Akshar and Purushottam embody the two persons represented by virtually identical icons in the central shrine of every Swaminarayan temple worldwide: Gunatitanand Swami, the spiritual successor of Sahajanand and the first guru in the BAPS lineage, and Swaminarayan himself. BAPS theologians assert the eternal co-presence of Akshar and Purushottam with the dual term *akshara-brahmana* that appears in the classical texts that Vaishnava theologians have long commented on: the Upanishads, *Bhagavad Gita*, and the Brahma Sutras. Traditionally translated as "the eternal brahman," akshara-brahmana is read in the BAPS community as the joint appearance of these two central figures. Transcending the material world, Akshar regularly incarnates in the lineage of human gurus beginning with Gunatitanand; Purushottam appeared just once in the form of Sahajanand.

Placing itself within a qualified non-dual lineage where human beings remain separate from Vaishnava forms of the divine, BAPS posits Akshardham as the heavenly abode that is the destination of all human beings enmeshed in the material world. Akshar and Purushottam work together to "release seekers of spiritual liberation from their ignorance and elevate them to an enlightened state, finally granting them an eternal place in Akṣaradhāma, his transcendental abode" (Paramtattvadas 2017: 71).

Akshardham takes its most majestic forms in the three massive earthly Akshardham temples, each of which serves, according to the website of the New Delhi Akshardham, as "an abode of God, a Hindu house of worship, and a spiritual and cultural campus dedicated to devotion, learning and harmony." Built in 2005, the temple in New Delhi was preceded by the first Akshardham near the homeland of Swaminarayan in Gandhinagar, Gujarat (1992), and followed by another in Robbinsville, New Jersey, USA (2023).

In addition to the features found in large Swaminarayan temples worldwide, the Akshardham in Delhi contains a number of features intended to draw large audiences even from outside of the BAPS community. The half-hour nightly water show is set outdoors at a step-well directly in front of the temple. Complete with lasers, music, video projections, and live actors, the water show tells a version of the story of the battle between the gods and demons from the Kena

Upanishad. In this rendering, the Vedic gods again emerge defeated, though here it is Swaminarayan in the form of an abstract lotus flower and the statue of the child Nilkanth Varni who preside over the show.

The temple complex also contains three large exhibition halls, each displaying elements of Swaminarayan Hinduism. The first, the "Hall of Values," portrays through a number of media many of the community's ethical standards: non-violence, vegetarianism, and family harmony, illustrated through depictions of the youthful forms of Swaminarayan. The second hall reinforces sacrifice and service through a film version of young Nilkanth's travels across South Asia. And the third, the Cultural Boat Ride, portrays a history of India via its many contributions to the world: yoga, chess, eye surgery, and medieval university life.

Combining elements of a temple, an amusement park, and a historical museum, the Delhi Akshardham repeatedly communicates the connections of this relatively new form of Swaminarayan Hinduism with ancient India. The Cultural Boat Ride displays a Vedic market, the Hall of Values allows visitors to experience "timeless messages of Hindu culture," and the water show explicitly refers to the texts of the Upanishads.

Also regularly appearing in Swaminarayan productions are the related themes of nationalism and patriotism. Their short film "Our India, My India" (*hamārā Bhārat, merā Bhārat*), a production about the fairly mundane topics of driving safety, littering, and energy use, is suffused with these themes. Performed in Ahmedabad and pinned to the homepage of the BAPS website, this half-hour program begins by following a group of soldiers in formation as they head into battle and plant the Indian flag in front of an image of Bhārat Mātā (Mother India). As characters in the film's three episodes invoke such key terms as *swacchatā* (cleanliness), *vikās* (development), *surakshā* (protection), and *desh* (the nation), the narrator tells its audience how by performing regular careful actions towards family and the environment, we all become soldiers for India (*ham bhi Bhārat ki sainak haiṁ*) and follow Pramukh Swami's statement: "We should follow the rules of whichever nation in which we live" (*jis desh meṁ rahte haiṁ, us desh ke niyamoṁ kā avashya pālan kareṁ*).

Unlike many other temples in the West that operate relatively independently, BAPS, the largest of all Swaminarayan schools, operates some 1,100 temples and 3,850 centers, with five international centers in Ahmedabad, Gujarat, India; Robbinsville, New Jersey, USA; Nairobi, Kenya; Sydney, NSW, Australia; and Neasden, London, England. In addition to its three Akshardham temples, BAPS recognizes three other types of temple (*mandir*), listed here in increasing size.

Reflecting the centrality of the ultimate goal of Akshardham, many BAPS families maintain a home temple (*ghar mandir*), as they provide daily worship to the images of Akshar-Purushottam installed there (Kim 2014).

The *hari mandir* temples serve a relatively small community where worship is carried out only twice daily, as opposed to five times in larger temples. The first BAPS *hari mandir* in America was built in the Flushing neighborhood of Queens, New York. Built in 1974 and with its newest images consecrated in

2004, it preceded the construction of the large and unrelated Ganesh temple just down the street. Although much of the community has since shifted to the diverse Jackson Heights neighborhood in the heart of Queens and elsewhere, the Flushing *hari mandir* has served as the anchor for much of the BAPS community residing in Queens.

The largest style of temple is the *shikharbaddha mandir*, which contains many elaborate artistic and architectural features – especially multiple prominent *shikhar* steeples – whose construction could only be financially supported by much larger congregations. The large *shikharbaddha* temple in Robbinsville, New Jersey, inaugurated in 2014, provided the base for its large Hindu community as well as for the massive Akshardham temple consecrated a few years later (Figure 7.1).[9]

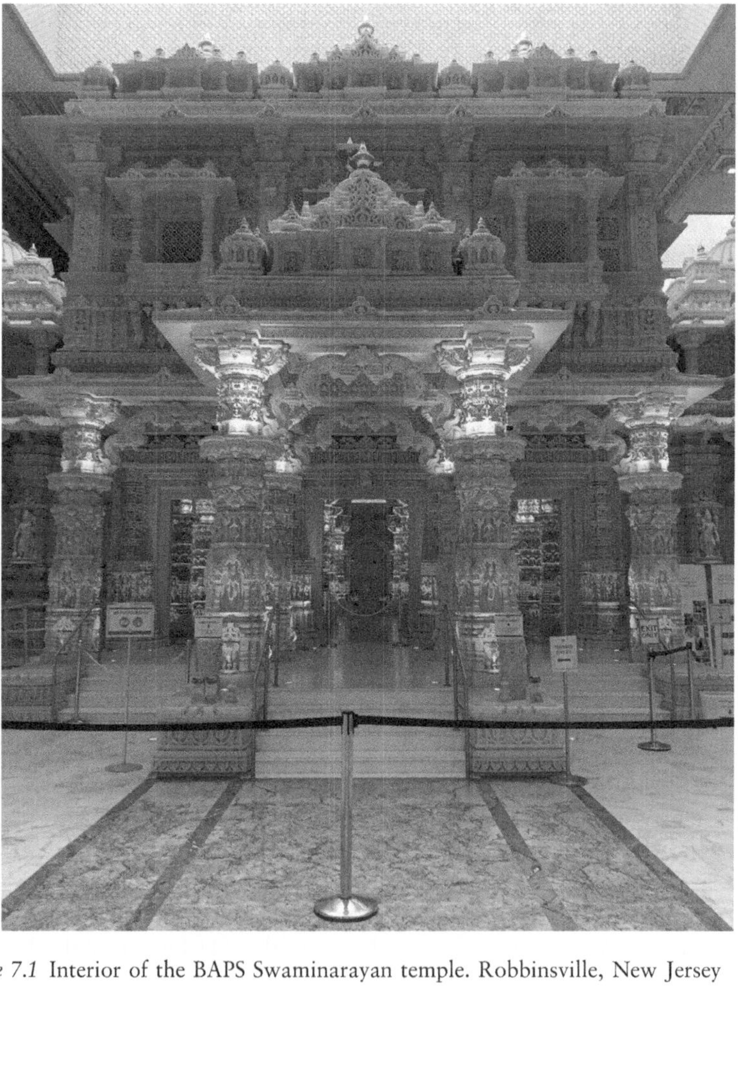

Figure 7.1 Interior of the BAPS Swaminarayan temple. Robbinsville, New Jersey

The layout of these temples resembles that of many other global Hindu temples. Rather than focusing on just one deity as temples in South Asia often do, Hindu temples outside of India frequently display the icons of a number of gods and goddesses, as they accommodate devotees and their deities from all over South Asia. For example, the prayer hall at the Hindu Temple of Minnesota houses each of its many deities in their own shrine that represents the architecture of that place, even including a separate shrine for the small Jain community that practices there. The temple closest to me as I write this book is in the small town of Kaukauna, Wisconsin; like many Hindu temples in America, it does not identify itself with any single deity – it is called the "Hindu Temple of Northeast Wisconsin" – while it displays on its main altar small shrines to seven different deities or groups of deities.

Somewhat different from these global Hindu temples, however, BAPS temples focus solely on the twin icons of Akshar and Purushottam. The *shikharbaddha* temple in Robbinsville is fairly representative of Swaminarayan temples around the world, though it is larger and much more elaborate. Immediately outside the temple stands a forty-nine-foot-tall bronze image of Nilkanth Varni, Swaminarayan in his form as the teenage itinerant renouncer. Standing on one foot with his hands raised above his head, this image depicts the difficult *tapas* that he performed during his seven years traveling India.

In an adjacent room just inside the temple complex, worshippers regularly perform *abhishek* – anointing with water – to a metal image of the renouncer Ghanshyam, the youngest form of Swaminarayan. The inner walls of this room contain a colorful frieze of the young Ghanshyam sitting in a tree with his friends as he points to the west, a sort of premonition of his travels west to Gujarat and even farther west to his eventual New Jersey home.[10]

Entering the main temple, one walks past icons of the Ram family on the left (Ram, Sita, Lakshman, and Hanuman) and the Shiva family on the right (Shiva, Parvati, Ganesh, and Skanda). These two families represent complementary Vaishnava and Shaiva concepts, grounding the temple in a recognizable Hindu culture that brings together aspects of both householdership and renunciation. These deities represent preliminary stages, however, to the central forms of Swaminarayan displayed at the very center of the entire temple complex.

Three small connected shrines sit at the front of the temple, where five times daily the congregation gathers to participate in the pujas that priests perform to the icons contained therein. Numbering anywhere from fifty to one hundred – more during the three mid-day pujas, fewer during the earliest and latest – devotees sing and chant along with piped-in recorded music. Some devotees process closely past the icons in acts of quiet meditative darshan, while others will fully circumambulate the three shrines during and after the puja. And still a few others perform individual acts of *danda pranam*, fully prostrating themselves on the ground towards the icons like a stick (*daṇḍa*). The right-most of these three shrines contains a single image of Ghanshyam. The left contains icons of Radha and Krishna alongside another childhood form of Swaminarayan, Harikrishna Maharaj, whose face and body are made of metal rather than of stone.

The central shrine contains the two figures of Gunatitanand Swami and his teacher, Swaminarayan. These icons represent and reinforce the eternal unity of devotee and deity (Akshar-Purushottam), their duality repeated throughout the temple: twin *dwarapals* (door protectors) flank entryways; the deities Ram with Sita, Krishna with Radha, and Shiva with Parvati sit in their own shrines; and images of numerous pairs of deities and their ideal devotees are carved onto the walls of the temple (Nar-Narayan, Balaji-Padmavati, Lakshmi-Narayan, and Vithoba-Rukmini). A number of framed murals displaying events from the life of Swaminarayan also hang around the interior of the temple and reinforce his central position.

The final set of icons displayed in the temple are those of the gurus who comprise the BAPS lineage. One of the primary ways that BAPS established its own identity was with its construction of a line of gurus distinct from that of mainstream Swaminarayan Hinduism. Reinforcing the basic concept of multiplicity, these gurus are present throughout the temple, with their most central position in a separate shrine on the wall adjacent to the temple's three central shrines. Here, the four gurus following Gunatitanand appear as life-sized icons with the current guru appearing in a framed photograph. The gurus appear together also in icons, posters, and postcards, as well as in the several books they have authored, all available for purchase in the bookstore and gift shop within the larger temple complex. Finally, they are also embodied in the numerous swamis who, wearing simple orange robes, reside in the temple complex. Administering the day-to-day operations of the temple, they are responsible for performing daily puja to the temple's icons, preaching sermons throughout the year, and receiving the respect of the congregation – often with a salutation of "Jay Swaminarayan" and by touching their feet – as they move throughout the temple.

Temples throughout the Hindu world are not only places of worship. Depending on the size of the temple, they might also hold language classes that cater to the regional communities that worship there (typically including Sanskrit, the language of many core Hindu texts), courses on particular texts such as the *Bhagavad Gita*, and yoga and meditation classes. The Swaminarayan temple in Robbinsville is no different. Complete with a large kitchen, bookstore, and snack stall, it also includes a wing of classrooms that support instruction in various facets of South Asian culture. Building on the domestic *ghar mandir*, many children attend Saturday (or Sunday) *sabha*, a sort of Hindu Sunday school or Catholic CCD.[11] Separated by age and gender, Swaminarayan children of all ages do art projects, watch videos, and hear stories about the gurus, both in English and Gujarati. This educational program might inspire some members to embark upon the BAPS Satsang examination program that assists "in enriching and enlightening thousands of devotees, young and old, with the knowledge of Vedic, cultural and Satsang values." A temple's *sabha* day typically ends with a large *satsang* gathering of the community with presentations, lectures, sermons, and readings by one or more of the resident swamis.

Seva

One of the primary ways that BAPS members give back to their community and work to attain their ultimate place in Akshardham is through spiritual service. Shifting their attention from the nine actions of divine devotional service to practical acts of volunteerism that benefit the community, members from across the country commit thousands of hours to the Robbinsville temple. As part of my research for this book, I visited the Swaminarayan temple in Robbinsville and talked with dozens of BAPS members about their seva. Inspired by the generosity related in the many *prasang* stories of BAPS gurus, they told me their own stories of giving back to the community. Among the many people who shared their stories with me, the following especially illustrate this sense of seva.

Two women who immigrated to the United States in 1998 have long served in the temple kitchen offering food, as they told me, to the divine in everybody.

Recalling the 1991 Cultural Festival of India held in Edison, New Jersey, before the temple there was built, one woman told me how her work in the kitchen removes the sense of her own ego; in tears, she related stories of the guru and especially of her presence at Pramukh Swami's 2014 visit to Robbinsville.

One man got his crane operator's license in order to work on the construction of the new Akshardham.

A group of women traveled from California assuming they would spend their time cleaning or working in the kitchen; instead, they were taught how to drill and grind stones for the temple. One of these women said that she felt peace in her heart and the guru working through her during her one opportunity to perform seva here.

A group of young ladies in high school and college told me of all the skills they acquired in the Saturday *sabha*: public speaking, organizing events, computer coding, cooking, and even changing a car tire. A fun opportunity that they wouldn't trade for anything, they acquired core values and morals that became for them a personal choice more than a religious command.

And finally, the husband of the family that hosted me in their home told me how he helped to clean dust from several of the pillars in the interior of the temple during its construction; taking ownership over that small part of the temple, he exclaimed as he showed that pillar to me, "This is my home!"

Among these and many other conversations – with electricians, architects, dentists, restauranteurs, students, and housewives – several common themes emerged. Although not articulated by any one person, these stories highlighted the intimate connections between the three main themes of Hinduism: action, knowledge, and devotion. Their individual and collective acts of service reflect the acts of devotion to Swaminarayan, supplementing the theological knowledge taught by the gurus.

A second theme is the construction of a South Asian community abroad. Whether first- or second-generation, and whether having immigrated from India, England, or Nairobi, BAPS members are aware of their cultural and religious difference within American society. As with many non-Christian religious institutions throughout America, the temple provides members the opportunity to practice the culture and reflect the values of their community within a setting that is comfortable and makes sense to all. By learning traditional South Asian artistic forms such as singing, playing the tabla drum, and speaking Gujarati language with family, friends, and relative strangers, members have created a new place of belonging with roots in India.

Finally, these acts of service are rooted in the action and inspiration of the lineage of gurus. Everybody I spoke with referred to the gurus in one way or another, with nearly all referring specifically to Pramukh Swami whose 2014 visit and 2016 death were still very much on everyone's mind almost a decade later. Frequently coming up in conversation were the many letters that members had written to him seeking advice on personal and potentially life-changing events, such as whether or not to start their education, take a new job, or start a family. Although a renouncer without personal concern for the trappings of the householder life, Pramukh Swami became an intimate friend and confidant whose personal advice in all of these matters members explicitly sought.

Beginning in 2021, BAPS began its extensive Centennial Celebrations of the one-hundredth anniversary of the birth of Pramukh Swami, called PSM100 for short and, in Gujarati, "Pramukh Swami Maharaj Shatabdi Mahotsav." Amidst cultural programs worldwide, its online store also clearly showed the impact of Pramukh Swami and the desire for BAPS members to remember him. A new line of T-shirts commemorated his birthday with such messages of his as "Live with Love, Faith, Humility"; "Giving, Compassion, Unity, Faith"; and "Eat, Play, Pray, Stay Together." This final message was a part of Pramukh Swami's domestic Ghar Sabha Initiative whose intention was to extend the organization's general message of Samp (togetherness) to families and homes throughout the global community. Many of the descriptions in the online store connect each item to the life of Pramukh Swami, ending with the phrase, "May we be inspired by his humble, peaceful, friendly and spiritual life," and including his oft-quoted statement, "In the joy of others lies our own."

Conclusion

This chapter focused on Swaminarayan Hinduism and its guru with roots in both traditional Hindu devotional schools and traditions of reform emerging from imperial contact within the British Empire. The next chapter will move on to the role of individual gurus whose Indian roots are more modern. Although not directly connected to India's 1947 independence from the British, the global reach that these gurus attained could only have occurred with the presence of technological modernity, especially in forms of convenient and rapid forms of communication and transportation. More than catering to the spiritual needs of people of South Asian descent – whether they live in India or abroad – many of these gurus, many of whom are women, continue to attract audiences that cross global boundaries of nationality, ethnicity, homeland, and religious identity.

Notes

1 Videos of the events in Robbinsville can be found on social media sites with the title Guruhari Darshan, 5–6 August 2014, Robbinsville, NJ, USA. Images of Pramukh Swami's consecration of the Robbinsville images in India can be found on the organization's website here: www.baps.org/Vicharan/2012/27-July-2012-3927.aspx.

2 Muslim communities in India also responded to local culture in a variety of ways: Sufi mystics expressed sympathy with Hindu devotional attitudes towards the divine while conservative Salafi movements insisted upon a return to the earliest Islamic texts.

3 Banerjee 2010.

4 Hatcher (2012) questions the use of the term "reform," arguing that it both unduly critiques the Indian past while impossibly predicting its future. I retain this word throughout this chapter while accounting for Hatcher's apt criticisms.

5 The Bharat Sevashram Sangha represents a similar organization. Devoted to tribal welfare, spiritual harmony, healthcare services, education programs, and relief work, the organization was founded by the guru Swami Pranavananda (1896–1941) in Bengal in 1917. Many decades after his death, Swami Pranavananda continues to be venerated in Hindu temples throughout the global Hindu world, including by Caribbean Hindu communities at the Hindu Milan Mandir in Minnesota.

6 Max Muller's editing of the Sacred Books of the East series, begun in 1879, was preceded by his translation and publication of the Rig Veda in 1874, work sponsored in part by the British East India Company.

7 Not only have nationalist writers excluded Islam as an Indian religion, but they have also absorbed others – Jainism, Buddhism, and Sikhism – within the nebulous category of "Hinduism."

8 Liechty (2003) details a secular variation of this process among Kathmandu's modernizing population at the beginning of the twenty-first century.

9 See the essays in Williams and Trivedi 2016 for more on Swaminarayan temple architecture.

10 The temple was consecrated in 2014; the *abhishek* image of Ghanshyam in 2017; and the Nilkanth Varni image in 2021.

11 Not affiliated with BAPS, this same focus on education within Swaminarayan Hinduism is extended to a full boarding school in the Shree Swaminarayan Gurukul International School, an educational system with more than a dozen centers in India and eight in the United States.

References

Banerjee, Sumanta. 2010. *Logic in a Popular Form*. London: Seagull Books.

Paramtattvadas, Swami. 2017. *An Introduction to Swaminarayan Hindu Theology*. Cambridge: Cambridge University Press.

Williams, Raymond Brady and Yogi Trivedi (eds.). 2016. *Swaminarayan Hinduism: Tradition Adaptation and Identity*. New Delhi: Oxford University Press.

Key terms

Akshar-Purushottam
BAPS
seva

Persons

Swaminarayan: Ghanshyam, Harikrishna Maharaj, Sahajanand
Gunatitanand Swami
Thomas Macaulay
Ram Mohan Roy
Dayanand Saraswati
Vinayak Damodar Sarvarkar
Debendranath Tagore

Study questions

1 How do practices of seva reinforce fundamental points of Hindu doctrine and practice?
2 In what ways does Swaminarayan Hinduism represent a prominent example of Global Hinduism?
3 How does Swaminarayan Hinduism represent a much different type of "reform" than the contemporary Bengali thinkers of the early to mid-nineteenth century?

8 Amma and the *guru*

The dynamics of Global Hinduism

In her 2004 novel, *These Foolish Things*, English author Deborah Moggach writes of a group of older white English residents who travel to India to live out their final years together in a retirement hotel.[1] Many of the new residents remember their lives as part of the British Empire, with India as its crown jewel; some were even born in India and lived their childhoods there. Their own children who have accommodated their parents' travel to India and come to visit them have no such memories, however; for them, India represents something very different: a bundle of contradictions with its contrasting poverty and wealth, tradition and modernity, and familiarity and exoticism.

India's inherent spirituality is a nuanced theme that runs throughout the book, as many of the British guests encounter India's cultures and religions for the first time. One character, Theresa, navigates her distant relationship with her mother Evelyn, one of the hotel's residents. To balance out this tension as she enters middle age, she regularly visits India in order to find meaning in her life. Although stating that she has found "the real India" down a dank back alley in the bustling south Indian city of Bangalore, she has really embarked upon a spiritual quest to the ashram of Amma, "the Hugging Mother." Between unsuccessful visits to other gurus, one of whom was away on a visit, ironically, to Europe when Theresa arrived in India, her visit to Amma helps her finally confront and resolve (at least some of) her lifelong tensions with her biological mother[2] (Moggach 2004: 206, 215, 238).

This chapter will focus on the global Hindu guru in all of their multiplicity. The Sanskrit term *guru* originally referred to the "heavy" as opposed to the *laghu* "light" syllable of a Vedic verse. As it has been used in more common language since, it refers to a teacher, a spiritual master who has acquired the heavy knowledge and expertise that makes them qualified to take on students, to lead a community, and to establish schools of thought and practice.

Just like many themes covered in previous chapters of this book, the concept of the global guru also exists on a spectrum. The style of each guru depends upon a variety of contributing factors: the historical presence of the British Empire; immigration laws in countries outside of India; each guru's place of origin, destination, and headquarters; the extent to which the guru's community is primarily of South Asian descent; and, on the other hand, the efforts that the guru has made to accommodate their message to a Western audience.

DOI: 10.4324/9781003475033-9

As with previous pairs of chapters in this book, this chapter forms a pair with the previous one. The preceding chapter focused on Swaminarayan, a *guru* teacher who lived at a key time in the British imperial history of India and marked a transition from late medieval to early modern India. Like those who led the reform movements that emerged out of Calcutta and the Bengali Renaissance, Swaminarayan adapted classical Indian traditions amidst newly dominant Western patterns of thought and governance. Whereas Swaminarayan Hinduism continues to use *bhakti* devotion as its primary form of practice, Amma and other contemporary global gurus, similarly living and working in a dynamic period of great social and cultural change, operate from within a much less explicitly Hindu framework that opens the door for a more global audience.

We might locate the BAPS community of Swaminarayan Hinduism at one end of this spectrum. Operating across a number of Hindu categories, the person of Swaminarayan is regarded as a *swami*, a guru, and a reformer, as well as a manifestation of the divine. In his position as the head of a religious lineage – first of Ramanand's monastery and then of his own new lineage – he cultivated feelings of devotion and inspired acts of *seva* service in his followers. Ministering to an almost completely South Asian, and a majority Gujarati audience, the subsequent gurus of the Swaminarayan tradition have visited and been venerated by BAPS communities from across the globe from Nairobi to New Jersey.

The Hugging Mother is located at the other end of this spectrum. Most commonly known simply as Amma, "The Mother" has cultivated a global audience based on the hug. Using this simple gesture that she began practicing as a young girl in her village, Amma has connected with millions of people throughout the world who seek greater meaning in their lives, often through spiritual techniques outside of those they grew up with.

This chapter will begin by presenting several generations of related gurus from late medieval India before moving outwards to explore those gurus who, arriving in America in three waves beginning in the 1890s, brought new versions of these earlier messages to a ready and willing global audience.

The South Asian guru

Like Swaminarayan, many contemporary gurus living and working in India draw on forms of Vaishnava devotion. The most global of these gurus, however, draw on less explicitly Hindu language and ritual. Distancing oneself from overt forms of Hinduism in this way has a significant precedent in Indian religion. In the several centuries preceding Swaminarayan (sixteenth–eighteenth centuries), many notable *sant* poets ("those who ARE") sought more united religious communities by disavowing any sole identity with any single religion. We will attend first to this earlier wave of gurus before turning to the global gurus of the past century.

These earlier gurus and *sant* poets might be distinguished from one another by the fundamentally different ways they saw and described the divine. Some operated in a *nirguna* environment as they saw the divine "without qualities," while others (the *saguna* poets) spoke of God *with* particular (Hindu) names and forms. Among the *sant* poets of the *saguna* variety, we earlier met Tulsidas, the author of the Hindi Ramayana, and Mirabai, who devoted her life to Krishna.

Regardless of how they depicted the divine in their work, all of these poets participated in a broad and socially inclusive movement. Somewhat like the ancient renouncers who, from the Upanishads up until the present day, have questioned the reality of their world, the medieval *sant* poets challenged established social, political, religious, and gendered ways of being. Building bridges across sectarian boundaries with poetry and music – especially devotional *bhajan* and *kirtan* songs – these early bhakti *sant*s engaged with Bengali Baul, Punjabi Sikh, and Muslim Sufi communities.

For the *nirguna sant* poets, the divine is transcendent, unable to be contained within the beliefs, texts, icons, and social taboos of any particular cultural form. From a low-caste group of weavers, the sixteenth-century poet Kabir questioned the great lengths to which religious people (Hindus and Muslims) went as they asserted a religious identity that differentiated themselves from others. He wrote:

> Why bump that shaven head on the earth,
> why dunk those bones in the water?
> Why wash your hands and mouth, why chant
> with a heart full of fraud?
> Why bow and bow in the mosque, and trudge
> to Mecca to see God?
> Search in the heart, in the heart alone:
> there live Ram and Karim!

Describing his poetry with such words as *blunt* and *simple*, scholar Linda Hess quotes this passage as an example of the "rough rhetoric" that Kabir, a "shouting illiterate" often used (1987: 143). A social reformer at least as much as a poet, Kabir calls out religious fraud on all sides in order to see that the Hindu gods and the Muslim Allah are all one. Often claimed by both contemporary Hindus and Muslims, Kabir very clearly situated himself outside of either tradition.

The poet Ravidas, a Dalit outcaste from a low leather-working caste, similarly criticized those who clung too tightly to cultural traditions. Addressing universal issues of social equality through a distinctly South Asian vocabulary, Ravidas attended especially to the social construct of caste. In one story, a group of upper-caste brahmins are revolted at the thought of having just eaten a meal with him. Showing them that he indeed belongs, Ravidas peels back his skin and shows them the golden brahmin thread that lay across his left shoulder, an inner and permanent part of his person rather than their temporary thread that must be regularly replaced.

Considering the body to be "a scaffold made of grass" and the world "a house of tricks," Ravidas refers to the four classes of the Hindu *varna* system, establishing their equality with several categories of Dalits:

> Priests or merchants, laborers or warriors,
> Half-breeds, outcastes, and those who tend cremation fires –
> Their hearts are all the same.
>
> (Hawley and Juergensmeyer 2006: 212–3)

This passage, along with much of the earliest work of both Kabir and Ravidas, is contained in the Adi Granth or Guru Granth Sahib, the central sacred text of the Sikh tradition. Founded by Guru Nanak a generation after Kabir, Sikhism is based on the simple and similar premise that there ultimately is no Hindu and no Muslim, an insight revealed to Nanak at his moment of transformation.[3]

The Radhasoami community represents one current guru-led movement that explicitly draws on the work of these *sant* poets, especially that of Guru Nanak. Its founder is Shiv Dayal Singh, whose later adopted name Soamiji Maharaj incorporates the titles of both religious leadership (Swami: teacher) and royalty (Maharaj: great king). Founded in Agra (the city of the Taj Mahal) in the 1860s and with Punjabi roots connecting it to Guru Nanak and Sikhism, the Radhasoami community has been so regularly rent by schism that each of its multiple sects currently operating in north India sees itself as the authentic lineage.[4]

In the Radhasoami tradition, people are referred to as *pind*, the same word for the temporary ritual balls of rice flour placed in the river during funeral rituals. Residing in a cycle of transmigration, these human *pind* must seek shelter in the guru. Desiring to ultimately reside in the heavenly abode of Radhasoami, initiated members practice *surat-shabda-yoga*, a meditation on sound. This yoga draws on tantric concepts and practices that allow practitioners to engage with the subtle unstruck sound (*shabda*) that permeates the universe. In a three-part process that includes the remembrance and repetition of the name Radhaswami, the contemplation of the divine form, and meditative listening to the ultimate divine sound, practitioners ascend on their path toward salvation.

Despite certain differences in theology, ritual, means of initiation, and lineage, the core of the greater Radhasoami community focuses on the guru who embodies the ultimate sonic principle of the universe. One category of Radhasoami song is the Shabad, a poem that resembles devotional songs from other *sant* poets. (The Hindi and Punjabi term Shabad is equivalent to the Sanskrit *shabda*, meaning "authoritative sound.") The earliest of these Shabad were written by the founder Soamiji Maharaj, whose many poems – like the guru himself – instantiate the Sound of the universe.[5] One such Shabad, "Dhannya Dhannya Dhan Dhannya Pyaare" (O dear one, exalted, truly exalted, is Shabad!), urges people to heed the call of this sound:

dhun ghaṭ meiṅ har dam ho rahi | kyoṅ sune na bānī shabad kī ||
The divine Melody perpetually resounds within – why don't you listen to the call of Shabad?

In another ("Satguru Khojo Ri Pyaari"), the poem repeats the virtue and centrality of the guru in its refrain:

satguru khojo ri pyāri | jagat meiṅ durlabh ratan yahi ||
Search for a true Guru, my dear friend – he is the rarest jewel in the world.

Later in that same song, the poet sings:

Shabad bheda aur Shabad kamāī | jin jin kīnhī sār lāī |||
Whoever is initiated into the secret of Shabad and meditates on Shabad will attain the Essence.

Embodying both the being Radhaswami and the Shabad sound, the guru is the center of a number of ritual transactions, versions of which are common throughout Hinduism. Devotees take the guru's visual *darshan* in life and view his relics and *samadhi* grave in death; they touch his feet and perform acts of *seva* service to ensure his every comfort; and they receive *prasad* blessings as they consume the leftover food from his plate and water from rinsing his mouth and from washing his feet. Performing all of these actions brings devotees into intimate physical contact with the guru as they replicate the hierarchy that exists between teacher and student while reinforcing traditional notions of purity and pollution.

The *nirguna* stance of Kabir, Ravidas, and Nanak mixed with the devotional notes of Radhasoami highlight the vast spectrum of modes of worship and practice present in guru traditions throughout the Hindu world. Appealing to a cosmopolitan audience comprised of both Western and Indian devotees, many contemporary gurus reduce if not eliminate those Hindu elements seen most frequently in traditional Indian religious communities: the language of caste, the names and images of particular gods and goddesses, the practice of puja and other rituals, and the social, cultural, and educational needs of South Asian communities often provided in Hindu temples in the West.

Overlapping with the rise of yoga in the twentieth century, Indian gurus have adjusted their missions to be less overtly Hindu, incorporating meditation, chanting, ethical values, and *seva* service within a loose structure of non-dual Advaita Vedanta. Despite the relative absence of these overt markers of the Hindu religion in their physical and virtual spaces, gurus still foster an attitude of bhakti in their devotees. Often by directing devotion towards themselves, gurus place themselves on a spectrum between human and divine and cultivate a sense of mysticism often desired by their followers.

Orientalism and the global guru

As we saw in Chapter 2, a student, following a minimum four-year period of studying the Vedas with their teacher, may become a householder, renouncer, or the guru of their own school. Few if any contemporary gurus follow that traditional Vedic path, instead adopting the mantle of guru through a variety of other means. Typically dependent upon an association with a previous guru, modern gurus are powerful figures who may be initiated, designated, descended by birth, or even be seen as the reincarnation of a former guru (Copeman and Ikegame 2014: 6).[6]

Living as a renouncer, the guru is detached from standard middle-class behavior and the material things of this world, maintaining purity of mind, body, and spirit without self-interest. Devotees from both South Asia and the West who attach themselves to a guru may then participate in a society whose spiritual master replicates some of the classical behaviors associated with an ancient Asian tradition. Although some of their behavior might frustrate some followers – for example, dietary restrictions such as not eating meat, garlic, and onions – their ascetic agenda sets them apart and plays into the audience's expectations of an Indian guru who experiences a universal divine reality that they reflect to their audience.

The Western appeal for Indian gurus is partly rooted in the concept of Orientalism. A concept we met in the previous chapter as scholars and officers within the Calcutta-based British Empire saw India as their "contrasting image," we might generally define the term simply as the construction of "the East" by and for a Western audience. The global British Empire reaffirmed previous Western scholarly and artistic ideas about "the East" and made India – rather than China from a previous era – its crown jewel. Separating East from West, imperial scholars and officers designated Britain as the seat of technology, democracy, and political power, while India was the seat of spirituality.

James Hilton's 1933 novel *Lost Horizon* presents a fictional account of Orientalism, here in a Tibetan Buddhist context. In a dangerous and tenuous world situated between two world wars, its four Western characters are kidnapped and taken to a Buddhist monastery in Tibet – a mysterious place that does not appear on any map – where they exhibit four typical Western responses: capitalism, conversion, fear, and acceptance. What J. J. Clarke writes in his book *Oriental Enlightenment* applies to *Lost Horizon* specifically, where "The East [...] represents a tendency in the West to escape from its current ills and to seek solace, however unrealistic and evanescent, in imaginary worlds elsewhere..." (2006: 19).

As gurus traveled to the West, they adapted their message even more for a Western audience that sought an escape from a cultural system that no longer worked for them. Not steeped in a Hindu culture, they sought refuge in a non-dual message that offered several advantages over a traditional bhakti devotional approach. The absence of overtly Hindu ritual and deities highlights more abstractly spiritual messages, such as the ultimate identity between the individual practitioner and the entire universe. Many Westerners who casually follow an Indian guru might desire to maintain their own tradition, often Judaism or Christianity, or might also – and equally casually – follow local or global Buddhist teachers. This non-dual approach allows them to downplay distinctions between religions and to consider all religions to be simply different paths up the same mountain.

Catering to, accommodating, and, as some skeptics would say, exploiting the Orientalist desires of Western audiences, gurus continue to portray India as a font of unique ancient, spiritual, and sometimes occult wisdom unavailable in the West. The absence of reality in these portrayals of the mystical East has not deterred Western seekers but has rather stoked their imagination by presenting the exotic as an attractive alternative to their ordered lives.[7] In his book *American Veda*, Philip Goldberg writes of the rising influence of Indian religious practices in America and, especially during and after the 1960s, the fluid ways that Americans began to alter their religious identities in relationship to these practices: "It added up to a watershed moment in the meeting of East and West. For the first time in history, the possibility of having a fruitful spiritual life outside conventional religion had become a distinct possibility for everyone. It was, arguably, the birth of 'spiritual but not religious'" (Goldberg 2010: 169).

These new religious identities did not necessarily entail a conversion to Hinduism. Those Americans and Europeans who previously identified as Christian or Jewish crossed lines of religion, spirituality, and self-help by combining a variety of techniques they learned from their gurus or (Western or Indian) teachers initiated by those gurus: attending lectures, reading new popular magazines, and practicing breath control and yoga at weekend retreats, at visits to meditation centers, and in the comfort of their own home.[8] Although the 1960s represented a key moment in the history of East–West crossover, the influence of India on the West began much earlier.

Gurus in America

In the 1830s, the American Transcendentalists – including Ralph Waldo Emerson, Henry David Thoreau, and, several decades later, Walt Whitman – began discussing and writing about the self, nature, and the world in ways that were uniquely American. Affiliated with the Unitarian Church, though only modestly "religious," these new patterns of thought drew explicitly on Hindu ideas, especially from the translations of the Upanishads and *Bhagavad Gita* that were becoming available in English for the first time. On the cusp of a counter-cultural wave that anticipated a similar and more familiar wave in the 1960s, Margaret Fuller wrote of her own generation in the 1840s: "Disgusted with the vulgarity of a commercial aristocracy, they become radicals; disgusted with the materialistic working of rational religion, they become mystics."[9]

Building on the slow spread of Indian ideas that began with the Transcendentalists, three waves of Indian gurus arrived on American soil beginning in the late nineteenth century. Roughly speaking, these waves came in the 1890s, the 1960s, and after the 1970s, with each wave expressing unique facets of the American culture that received and accepted it. In no way could this chapter provide a comprehensive description of all the gurus who arrived in each of these three eras, but it will describe a number from each wave: the means by which they ascended to their position, their unique place within the Indian and Western cultures of that era, and their relationships with Hindus and non-Hindus in South Asia and abroad.

> All of the contemporary gurus, as well as the surviving communities from many past gurus, continue to maintain thorough websites that provide the primary means by which they communicate their stories and missions to the world. Readers of this book should supplement this reading by seeking out those websites as well as relevant audio and video clips widely available on the Internet and social media.

The first wave: Swami Vivekananda

On September 11, 1893, Swami Vivekananda addressed the World's Parliament of Religions at the World's Fair in Chicago. Housed in the "White City" built especially for the global event, the World's Columbian Exposition, as it was called, celebrated the 400th anniversary of the American myth of Columbus "discovering" America. The Exposition as a whole contributed to this mythology as it placed its unique combination of American patriotism and Christian theology within a setting of neo-classical Greco-Roman architecture.

Although the fair trumpeted a set of universalist ideals, it only did so against a depiction of American exceptionalism. Adjacent to the fair's primary place of the White City that heralded American progress and technology, the secondary place of the Midway contained displays of peoples from all over the world – Africa, the Middle East, Asia, and from across Europe. While housing local peoples from those cultures and thus producing some sense of authenticity, these villages and their inhabitants highlighted their exoticism and otherness, sometimes described as barbaric, savage, and primitive, exemplifying a process of cultural evolution that placed America at the apex of global urban development as a New Rome, a New Greece, or the New Jerusalem (Seager 1995: xxxii).

Furthering the fair's universal ideals, the World's Parliament of Religions gathered together diverse religious leaders from around the world with its stated goal, "to unite all religion against all irreligion" (Seager 1995: xxvii). Again, and like the fair as a whole, however, the Parliament placed the world's religions in relationship to the religion most familiar to its participants. American Protestant Christianity operated as the default tradition to which all others were compared, and, for some, where all other religions were to find their ultimate resting place. Nearly completely excluding Native Americans, Muslims, and American Blacks, the Parliament presented the religions of the world as stepping stones to the ultimate truth.

Swami Vivekananda, whose new Raja Yoga we saw in a previous chapter, was the Parliament's main representative of Hinduism. In his address, Vivekananda presented the Parliament with an intriguing obstacle, delivering a message that reflected the Parliament's goal of universality, though setting it not within American Protestantism but squarely within the Hindu tradition. Eschewing the ecstatic goddess-based mysticism of his teacher Ramakrishna, he began his talk by addressing his "Sisters and Brothers of America," registering his opposition to "sectarianism, bigotry, and its horrible descendant, fanaticism." Arguing that the Hinduism of his native India represented instead "tolerance and universal acceptance," he asserted, speaking for all of Hinduism, "We believe not only in universal toleration, but we accept all religions as true."[10]

In a subsequent lecture on the relationships between multiple religions, Vivekananda similarly inquired into "the common centre to which all these widely diverging radii converge [...] the common basis upon which all these seemingly hopeless contradictions rest." In supporting this argument, Vivekananda twice paraphrases quotations from Hindu scripture, both times resembling quotations of Krishna from the *Bhagavad Gita*. First, from the perspective of Arjuna being confronted by the majesty of the divine, Vivekananda states: "As the different streams having their sources in different places all mingle their water in the sea, so, O Lord, the different paths which men take – through different tendencies, various though they appear, crooked or straight – all lead to Thee!" Shortly thereafter, and referring directly to the Parliament itself as "a declaration to the world," Vivekananda quoted Krishna from the *Gita*: "Whosoever comes to Me, through whatsoever form, I reach him; all men are struggling through paths which in the end lead to Me."

Vivekananda established the Vedanta Society in New York in 1894, followed by another major center in San Francisco in 1900. Here, in the American west, the Vedanta Society constructed what might be deemed the first American Hindu temple a few years later and a quaint peaceful monastery (Shanti Ashram) a few years after that. Still operational, the Vedanta Society continues to minister to a contemporary community at these and many other locations, espousing its ecumenical message: "Vedanta holds that all religions lead to the same goal. Further, Vedanta reveres all great teachers and prophets, such as Jesus Christ, Buddha, and Sri Krishna, and respects their teachings as the same eternal truth adapted to the needs of different times and peoples."

The second wave: Prabhupad

Whereas the first wave of Indian gurus to America was almost solely defined by Vivekananda, each of the two subsequent waves includes numerous gurus who, though operating independently, provided similar messages to an interested public.[11] Discovering an America that seemed always religious but never in quite the same way, Indian gurus filled various niches as they differently catered to the spiritual needs of Westerners. Beginning to arrive in 1965 once the American government relaxed its restrictive immigration laws, the second wave of Indian gurus catered to Americans who, though raised in mainstream Jewish and Christian traditions, engaged in the counter-cultural movements of the time. Building on Vivekananda's message of religious tolerance, these gurus successfully drew on parallel and sometimes overlapping cultural undercurrents in both India and the West.

One of the most famous East–West encounters from this era was that between the Beatles and Maharishi Mahesh Yogi. Traveling to India in 1968, the Beatles and their entourage spent several months in Rishikesh, a pilgrimage town on the Ganges River in north India where they learned the techniques of Maharishi's Transcendental Meditation. A formative experience especially for George Harrison, the Beatles' time in India resulted in much of their monumental self-titled double-album often called "The White Album."

The Maharishi's work influenced changing attitudes towards Eastern religions for generations of average Americans. Intersecting with the hippie counter-culture of the 1960s, Maharishi rejected the drug-induced liberation advocated by Timothy Leary and his crew, many of whom also spent time in India: Allen Ginsberg, one of the most prominent Beat poets; Aldous Huxley, famous for writing *Brave New World* and, more relevantly for their experiments with LSD, *The Doors of Perception*; and Richard Alpert, who as the guru Ram Dass would write *Be Here Now* (published in 1971), one of the most important books for the growing American meditation movement. Teaching meditation as a simple technique that can help everybody, Maharishi's influence continues to this day, through the universities he set up: the Maharishi Institute of Management in India's capital of New Delhi and Maharishi International University in Fairfield, Iowa, that offers such degrees as Regenerative Organic Agriculture; Consciousness and Human Potential; and Art, Consciousness, and Creative Practice.[12]

One global Hindu organization that sits somewhat outside the meditative *nirguna* mold is the International Society for Krishna Consciousness (ISKCON). An organization with roots in the devotional Gaudiya Vaishnava tradition of Bengal, ISKCON focuses intently on the person of Krishna and his female consort, Radha. Embodying the abstract universal impersonal principle prominent in Advaita Vedanta, Krishna takes the form of a person reflected in each individual: "As drops of ocean water have the ocean's qualities in minute degree, our forms and personalities are infinitesimal samples of the infinite Supreme Person" ("God is a Person"). And just like the Govindadeva temple in the city of Jaipur that we visited in Chapter 4, ISKCON temples throughout the world lavishly depict and venerate Krishna in his three main forms: as child, lover of Radha, and universal deity (Figure 8.1).

As Chaitanya and his Gosvami disciples traveled to Braj in the sixteenth century to re-establish the ponds, hills, and forests where Radha and Krishna played, Swami Prabhupad traveled to America in 1966 to establish Krishna devotion in a new place. Prabhupad established a meeting space on the lower east side of Manhattan in New York City, now known as the Bhakti Center, where devotees continue to attend workshops on spirituality, practice yoga, and sing together.[13] While in the presence of the center's central icons of Radha and Krishna (as well as of Prabhupad himself) and accompanied by drums and other musical instruments, its audience of largely non-Indian Americans sings

Figure 8.1 Offering milk, fruit, and flowers to Radha and Krishna on the occasion of Krishna's birthday at the ISKCON Sri Sri Radha Govinda Mandir. Brooklyn, New York

weekly kirtan songs, repeatedly chanting the Mahamantra with varying intensity: "Hare Krishna, Hare Krishna, Krishna Krishna, Hare Hare. Hare Rama, Hare Rama, Rama Rama, Hare Hare."[14]

Larger ISKCON temples host celebrations of major Hindu festivals just as we would see them in India. The Sri Sri Radha Govinda Mandir in Brooklyn, New York, for example, hosts celebrations of Krishna and Radha in the late summer – Krishna's birthday (Krishna Janmashtami) and Radhashtami – that are presided over by the Brooklyn Borough President. Complete with acts of visual *darshan* of the temple's large central image of Radha-Krishna, *katha* storytelling, participatory *abhishek* anointing with water of smaller festival icons, and dancing and *kirtan* singing of the Mahamantra until past midnight, the temple attracts hundreds of devoted guests from all walks of life.

An even larger festival, the Chariot Procession (Rath Yātrā) replicates the famous procession of Krishna in his form of Jagannath, the Lord of the World, in the coastal town of Puri in the eastern part of north India. The three chariots of Krishna, his brother Balbhadra, and sister Subhadra process the streets of cities worldwide, including, for example, on the beach during the Easter holiday in Durban, South Africa.[15]

More than just a Hindu school whose temples host devotional rituals dedicated to Krishna, ISKCON runs a number of other related projects. It is possibly most well known for its Bhaktivedanta Book Trust, which has published many translations of Vaishnava literature. Among its most famous publications are Prabhupad's *Bhagavad-Gītā As It Is*, a translation and commentary on this most central of Krishna devotional texts, and his Śrīmad-Bhāgavatam, a translation and commentary on the tenth-century Bhagavata Purana.

The ISKCON-run New Vrindaban in Moundsville, West Virginia, is an "intentional spiritual community in the foothills of Appalachia" whose goal is "to give Westerners an alternative to the materialistic way of life and to teach a lifestyle based on the principle of 'simple living and high thinking.'" Founded by Prabhupad in 1968, its architectural focus is its Krishna temple and Prabhupad's Palace of Gold. Its simultaneous focus on nature, however, more clearly replicates the natural surroundings of Krishna's forests in Vrindaban and the Braj region in north India. Here, community members grow their own food and flowers in several gardens, go on hikes through the approximately 2,500-acre space, and care for a herd of healthy and ailing cows as an act of *go-seva* (cow service or cow protection).

Finally, and associated with some of the approximately one thousand ISKCON temples present throughout the world is Govinda's restaurant whose strictly vegetarian dishes are all "ethically-sourced and karma-free." Adhering to ISKCON's dietary guidelines – no meat, alcohol, or onions, garlic, and mushrooms – its meals are "first offered to Lord Krishna" and then returned to the diner as a *prasad* blessing. Like a Lutheran potluck or a Sikh langar, these restaurants foster community through food that reflects the values of those who cook, eat, and share it.[16]

The third wave: Satya Sai Baba

The third wave of gurus includes, like the second, an amorphous collection of gurus who developed a large global audience. Beginning in the 1970s, these gurus continued to fill the spiritual niche – some might say, the spiritual vacuum – that Western science, technology, and rationalism had created. Thus, despite the end of the hippie and civil rights movements in the 1970s, Americans – and increasingly people of Indian and non-Indian descent living across the globe – sought to practice the yoga and meditation advocated by this third wave of gurus. In many cases, they did this by combining various paths: whereas Indian gurus taught techniques of yoga and meditation associated with the Path of Knowledge, the gurus themselves became to greater or less degrees central figures as in the Path of Devotion.

One of the most famous gurus of this era is Sathya Sai Baba (1926–2011).[17] Easily recognizable by his sizable afro hairstyle, Baba, as his devotees often refer to him, had only once left India. His headquarters are in his native village of Puttaparthi, near the modern city of Bangalore in south India. The organization that now continues his work – the Sri Sathya Sai International Organization – has established centers in 110 countries worldwide.

His unique name refers to his self-identification as a reincarnation of Shirdi Sai Baba (1838–1918), a guru who died in western India a decade or so before the latter Sai Baba's birth.[18] His simple message of *shraddhā sabūrī* ("Faith and Patience") resembles the previous messages of Kabir, Ravidas, Guru Nanak, and Radhasoami. This cross-cultural yet still very Indian statement reflects their common message of religious tolerance; after the deaths of many such figures, both Hindus and Muslims identified with and claimed them as their own. In his *Shirdi Diary*, the devotee Abdul Baba writes of Shirdi Sai Baba:

> God is our Beloved and takes the name of Sai Baba.
> In the two worlds the name of Sai Baba resounds.
> Sai Baba embodies the Vedas, as also Allah.

Many contemporary Indians both at home and abroad continue to venerate Shirdi Sai Baba as he provides "an alternative, more inclusive vision of Indian identity than that found in Hindu nationalist rhetoric."[19]

> There are some fifteen Shirdi Sai Baba temples in the United States, including one in Flushing, Queens, New York City, near the large Ganesh temple we encountered in Chapter 4 and the BAPS Swaminarayan temple in Chapter 7.

Shirdi Sai Baba's earlier message of multifaith tolerance came to inform Sathya Sai Baba's subsequent work in the late twentieth century. With a small following outside of India, his main audience has been primarily members of India's English-educated middle class who seek a sense of spirituality and social cachet within their modern lives. Helping people to "realize the Divine Principle innate in every human being," Sai Baba advocates meditation on and practice of "the five universal human values of Truth, Right Conduct, Peace, Love, and Nonviolence." Like many gurus, he also advocates *seva* service through supporting education, health care, and humanitarian relief.

This *seva* is rooted both in universal ideas of the innate divinity of all people as well as in devotional practices. Citing Hindu texts such as the *Bhagavad Gita* throughout his voluminous discourses, he repeats several basic themes throughout, connecting ethics with spirituality:

> Where Truth and Righteousness go together like the positive and negative, there will be Peace; where there is Peace there will be love. There will be no

> scope at all for violence when a human being is surcharged with the current of Love ...
>
> God is not separate from you. You are not separate from God. You and God are only one.
>
> (Be United In Divine Love | Sri Sathya Sai Speaks)

In active groups, these talks are followed by the singing of *bhajan* devotional songs, many of which are written by and dedicated to Sathya Sai Baba himself. Among the hundreds of such songs, many reiterate the community's multifaith tolerance while reinforcing the guru as an embodiment of divinity. One such Hindi-language *bhajan* runs as follows (I have added religious identifications in square brackets into the translation):

> Allah tum ho Eshwar tum ho
> Tum hi ho Ram Rahim
> Yesu tum ho Nanak tum ho
> Zohrashtra bhi ho Mahavir tum ho
> Gautama Buddha Karim
> Mere Ram Mere Ram Ram Rahim.
> You are Allah [Muslim] and you are the Lord [Hindu],
> You are Ram [Hindu] and Rahim [Muslim],
> You are Jesus [Christian] and you are Guru Nanak [Sikh],
> You are Zoroaster [Parsi] and you are Mahavira [Jain],
> Gautam Buddha [Buddhist] and Karim [Muslim].
> My Ram, my Ram, Ram, Rahim.[20]

One devotee among Sai Baba's community in Trinidad, a place he himself never actually visited, attributed his own conversion to just such a *bhajan*, saying, "And the singing of these bhajans rang through me like a current. I could not believe myself what was going on with myself [...] I knew whomsoever there, is directed by – must have been – an avatar of the Lord – must!" (Klass 1996: 145).

Just as the grave of his namesake Shirdi Sai Baba continues to serve as a pilgrimage place visited by people who seek to be healed, to be relieved of their suffering, and to conceive children, so also has the person of Sathya Sai Baba served as a center for healing and miracles, even after his death.[21] Building upon the teachings and songs that identify him as divine, Sathya Sai Baba regularly displayed his charisma through miracles. Devotees have regularly been amazed and told stories of his ability to heal the sick and read the minds of those who come to him for advice.

It is his penchant for materializing objects out of thin air, however, that has long defined his career as a guru. Jewelry, icons, sweets, and copies of the *Bhagavad Gita* are among the objects that Sathya Sai Baba is attested to have physically manifested as part of his *lila* play. Drawing on the ritual that Shirdi Sai Baba regularly performed in a previous generation in which he distributed ash from his ritual fire, and connecting him to Shiva who presides over the cremation ground, Satya Sai Baba distributes ash to his devotees that he seems to produce out of thin air. In 1975, the Canadian writer Paul William Roberts visited the Puttaparthi ashram as a proposed skeptic and left a lifelong devotee. He wrote the following about the experience of one particular devotee, typical of many, with Sathya Sai Baba "suddenly revolving his right hand in a curious polishing motion and producing, seemingly from nowhere, a small quantity of whitish powder which he placed in her outstretched palms."[22]

Whatever we think of these miracles, we must account for them as part of Sai Baba's larger project. More than miracles for their own sake, they are tools that generate what one scholar refers to as "intellectual surrender," the capacity for rational actors to acknowledge that their personal experience – their "thirst for the extraordinary" – eclipses their dependence upon dispassionate science.[23] The guru-focused pushback against the reliance upon modern science and technology has long been a draw for both Indian and Western audiences who have sought to incorporate some sense of spirituality into their rational lives.

The third wave: Mātā Amṛtānandamayī Mā

For many devotees, it is the spirituality associated with Indian women and goddesses that is a particular draw. Like women in religious and cultural traditions throughout the world, Hindu women may occupy any place between householder and renouncer, as we have seen throughout this book: the ascetic Brahma Kumari movement (Chapter 2); devotional poets such as Andal and Mirabai (Chapters 3 and 4); the variety of devotional *vrat* vows that women perform for themselves and their families (Chapter 5); the divinized form of the child goddess, Kumari (Chapter 6); and the many female devotees who perform *seva* service within the Swaminarayan (Chapter 7) and ISKCON communities (Chapter 8).

Male gurus throughout the three waves outlined in this chapter were frequently accompanied by powerful and charismatic women. Vivekananda's teacher Ramakrishna was attended by his wife Sarada Devi whom he considered a manifestation of the divine Mother. Aurobindo bequeathed to his collaborator Mother Mirra Alfassa, a woman of non-Indian heritage, the leadership of his ashram over which she presided until her death in 1973. And in the 1980s, Ma Anand Sheela played an outsized role at the Oregon-based ashram of Bhagwan Shree Rajneesh, before he returned to India and became Osho.

Many female gurus began to operate on their own within this third wave. One of the most popular female gurus was Ānandamayī Mā ("The Mother of Bliss") or just Ma. Like the relationship between Ramakrishna and Sarada Devi, Ma was married but her marriage with her husband was never consummated. Instead, as a manifestation of divinity she was the object of his devotion. Many other women visited and lived at her ashram near the banks of the Ganges River at the pilgrimage town of Dehradun until her death in 1982, venerating her as a woman, saint, guru, and avatar (Hallstrom 1999).

Many other female gurus in this period gained followings in India, some of whom then also moved to America.[24] But none of them gained the popularity of

Śrī Mātā Amritānandamayī Mā ("The Mother of Immortal Bliss") or simply Amma.[25] The object of Theresa's search in the fictional *These Foolish Things*, Amma is one of the most popular and beloved gurus in the contemporary world. Born in the small fishing village of Amritapuri in south India in 1953, Amma resembles Sathya Sai Baba and many other such gurus. As a young girl, she displayed signs of her future status as a guru through feelings of sympathy and mystical abilities: meditating for hours on end, composing and singing devotional songs, healing sick cows, and helping others.

Initially identifying herself with Krishna, her visions of the Goddess led her to fully identify as a form of the divine Mother, the Goddess whose graceful and powerful forms populate the Hindu pantheon. Never initiated by a guru, she gradually amassed a following at the Amritapuri Ashram built on the location of her family's home, before setting up major MA Centers in nine major cities throughout America and numerous others throughout India and the rest of the world. The MA Center closest to me as I write this is their 140-acre site in Chicago's western suburb of Elburn, where with the assistance of a regional swami their year-round activities include "spiritual programs, scriptural classes, guided meditation sessions, youth programs, selfless service projects, and our restoring harmony in nature initiatives."

Smaller *satsang* communities meet in private homes and community centers throughout the world. The *satsang* in Portland, Oregon, meets to chant the 108 names of Amma and the 1,000 names of the Goddess. Contributing to the nearly universal theme of *seva* service, they participate in the Mother's Kitchen program cooking and distributing thousands of meals annually, partnering with non-profits throughout the Portland area. All of these activities provide to devotees and to the larger communities where they live "emotional solace, spiritual guidance, and concrete solutions to their problems," as her website describes. It is from this global base that her charisma generates the miracles that her devotees regularly report.

But it is the *darshan* that Amma gives that distinguishes her from all other gurus. With a literal translation of the sacred sight, vision, or glance of the deity, Amma's *darshan* consists of a full physical embrace. At the conclusion of her lectures and before devotees wander through the gift shop and head home, and even with large gatherings of thousands of people, Amma gives physical *darshan* to all who attend, sometimes until the early hours the following morning – hence, "the Hugging Mother." Such an embrace could only occur in a global context, in which the strict Hindu norms that govern physical contact and that would typically prevent such intimacy would be relaxed.[26] Borrowing from but transcending the physical contact practiced within the nine modes of devotional *seva* towards deities and gurus, Amma's embrace establishes a physical intimacy that approaches equality and thus defies cultural restrictions on physical contact around gender, morality, and caste purity (Raj 2004).

Embodied in her hug, and spread across a large and interconnected virtual network, Amma's many projects display her message of a universal love that transcends any particular religion. She supports yoga and meditation through her holistic Integrated Amrita Meditation (IAM) Technique, with in-person silent meditation retreats at Amritapuri Ashram and virtual Amrita Yoga trainings and sessions. The humanitarian projects Embracing the World and Amrita Serve reiterate her motto of "Love, Nature, Service, Practice" from the homepage of her website, such that, "When people pour out their hearts to Amma, she offers them emotional solace, spiritual guidance, and concrete solutions to their problems." These projects engage the concept of *seva* through fundraising and direct service on such issues as education, healthcare, the environment, and the uplift of people in rural India. Finally, and like many other female gurus, she has empowered women to actively participate in traditional religious roles. By working to train women for the Hindu priesthood, a status nearly universally occupied by men, she has troubled traditional hierarchies among gurus, priests, devotees, and students.[27]

Conclusion

The office of Hindu guru has represented a significant component of Hinduism since its earliest days. A semi-divine poet, seer, and teacher, the guru is a multitasker who brings together in one person many of the facets that define the religion of Hinduism. Kabir and the *sant* poets advocated unity with God over sectarian division as they questioned the efficacy of particular religious practices, especially those rites that sowed division and created hierarchy within the tradition.

Contact with the West via the British Empire beginning in the 1700s and with the movement of Hindu populations out of India beginning in the 1800s – and especially to America after 1965 – did not fundamentally alter the centrality of the guru. Maintaining practices of puja, darshan, yoga, and meditation, three waves of global gurus extended their mission to Western populations whom the gurus saw, and who often saw themselves, as steeped in science and rationality but lacking in spirituality. And it was Indian spirituality, filtered through the Orientalist acceptance of Hinduism and Buddhism, that was frequently seen as providing the most available and efficient techniques for this infusion of spirituality.

The trails blazed over the past century by such gurus as Vivekananda, Prabhupad, Sathya Sai Baba, and Amma Ma ensure a bright future not just for forthcoming gurus from India but for further interreligious dialogue across the East–West divide.

Notes

1 The novel was republished in 2012 and its title changed to *The Best Exotic Marigold Hotel* to coincide with the release of a major Hollywood film that bore this new title. The movie's sequel, released in 2015, bears little relationship to the original novel.

2 The novel (and film) *Eat Pray Love* opens with a similar conceit as the female head of the American monastery that Liz visits is away, her absence leading Liz to visit her monastic headquarters in India and to travel further.

3 McLeod (2018) translates a number of stories from the Sikh tradition, each of which shows Nanak's critiques of those who adhere to the strict ritual details of Hinduism and Islam.

4 Babb 1986 (Chapters 1–3). Two of the main organizations that maintain a virtual presence on the Internet are the Radha Soami Satsang Beas (RSSB) in the Punjab town of Beas and the Radhasoami Satsang, Soami Bagh, Agra.
5 The recitations, transcriptions, and translations of many Shabad can easily be found on the Internet. The poems I quote here can be searched by their first line.
6 Within the Tibetan Buddhist world, such spiritual inheritance often takes place via the *tulku*, the reincarnation of a monk or nun who assumes leadership of an individual lineage. One of many such *tulku* is the Dalai Lama (the Tibetan word *lama* is a translation of the Sanskrit *guru*), the fourteenth in a human lineage that extends back to the early fifteenth century. Another facet of the Dalai Lama's spiritual lineage is the tradition that sees him as a manifestation of Avalokitesvara, the divine bodhisattva of compassion.
7 Beginning in 1875, the Theosophical Society extended the popularity of occult matters into the Western approach to Asian religions.
8 In his study of American Buddhism, Thomas Tweed coined the term "nightstand Buddhists" to refer to sympathetic Americans who are drawn to Buddhism through reading accessible English-language books by the Dalai Lama, the Vietnamese monk Thich Nhat Hahn, and other popular Buddhist authors. Such Buddhists might also casually practice Zen, attend local lectures, visit Buddhist websites, and decorate their homes with Buddhist artifacts. Their relatively superficial participation in Buddhism – they have no intention of devoting themselves to the tradition by taking monastic vows – may or may not lead them to actually refer to themselves as "Buddhist" (Tweed 2002: 17–33).
9 Goldberg 2010: 32.
10 A special issue of the *International Journal of Hindu Studies*, "Swami Vivekananda as a Cosmopolitan Thinker", contains seven articles that detail new approaches to the diverse thought of Vivekananda (issue 27 (1), 2023).
11 Arriving in California in the 1930s, Yogananda and his Self-Realization Fellowship (SRF) carried many of the same messages as Vivekananda and served as something of a bridge between the first and second waves of Hindu gurus.
12 In 2002, the portion of Fairfield, Iowa, affiliated with the university became its own city, Vedic City, that issued its own currency, the Raam Mudra.
13 The current head priest of the Bhakti Center is Vasudeva Das, a young white man from the Netherlands.
14 The informal name of ISKCON as "the Hare Krishna movement" is based on their repetition of this mantra.
15 Kumar 2008.
16 The Temple Canteen at the Ganesh temple in Flushing, Queens, was rated #96 in the 2023 *New York Times* list of the 100 best restaurants in New York City.
17 Babb 1986 (Chapters 7–8).
18 Sathya Sai Baba also spoke of a third and future incarnation, Prem Sai Baba.
19 McLain 2016. The remembrance of Shirdi Sai Baba is part of a larger process of memorialization of saints (see Accardi 2018, an introduction to issue 22.3 of the *International Journal of Hindu Studies* on this topic). The Sufi Muslim guru Meher Baba (1894–1969) was also influenced by the work of Shirdi Sai Baba.
20 For many of these songs, arranged alphabetically on the organization's website, visitors can access the audio and/or video. The text for this song is slightly adapted from the original, its audio available here: Allah Tum Ho Eshwar Tum Ho.
21 The *Shri Sai Satcharitra*, one of the few texts describing the life of Shirdi Sai Baba, opens with a tale of the miracle by which the *sant* prevented cholera from entering the village of Shirdi by sprinkling flour that he himself ground in the town's mosque around its perimeter.
22 During the festival of Mahashivaratri (detailed in Chapter 2), Sathya Sai Baba, as a manifestation of Shiva, produces a glowing green crystal linga from his own mouth.

Residing at the Puttaparthi ashram for months, Paul William Roberts wrote about his witnessing of this event: "I would not have believed any of this last year either. Baba is essentially a personal experience, not something that can be written or even talked about." Sathya Sai Baba (from Vogue Magazine – Canada Edition, December 1975) | Sri Sathya Sai International Organization.

23 Babb 1986: 182.

24 See Pechilis (2004) for a collection of essays on Amma and many other female gurus in America.

25 In literature through approximately the 2010s, the shortened form of her name was officially "Ammachi," a south Indian title that is still used in some places throughout her organization.

26 See "My Eight Seconds With the 'Hugging Saint'" for a journalist's account of her embrace with Amma. The global pandemic at the beginning of the 2020s required that Amma pull back from her focus on hugging, both in her worldwide travels and at Amritapuri Ashram. As a result, she continues to diversify the means by which she spiritually engages with devotees. www.pbs.org/newshour/nation/embracing-amma-my-eight-seconds-with-the-hugging-saint#:~:text=Eight%20seconds.-,Eight%20seconds.,why%20everyone%20looked%20so%20happy.

27 Raj 2004: 215. See Dempsey 2006 for another example of women being trained as priests, at the Sri Vidya temple in Rush, New York.

References

Goldberg, Philip. 2010. *American Veda: From Emerson and the Beatles to Yoga and Meditation: How Indian Spirituality Changed the West*. New York: Harmony Books.

McLain, Karline. 2016. *The Afterlife of Sai Baba: Competing Visions of a Global Saint*. Seattle and London: University of Washington Press.

Raj, Selva. 2004. Ammachi, the Mother of Compassion. In Karen Pechilis (ed.), *The Graceful Guru: Hindu Female Gurus in India and the United States*. New York: Oxford University Press, 203–218.

Key terms

American Transcendentalists
International Society for Krishna Consciousness (ISKCON)
Lost Horizon
Orientalism
Radhasoami
World's Parliament of Religions

Persons

Kabir, Ravidas, and Nanak
Ānandamayī Mā ("The Mother of Bliss", Ma)
Śrī Mātā Amritānandamayī Mā ("The Mother of Immortal Bliss", Amma)
Maharishi Mahesh Yogi
Prabhupad
Sathya Sai Baba
Shirdi Sai Baba
Swami Vivekananda

Study questions

1. How did the early *nirguna sant* poets (Kabir, Ravidas, and Nanak) pave the way for the three subsequent waves of gurus to the West?
2. How are the three waves of gurus to America and the West similar to and different from each other?
3. How might female Indian gurus appeal to Americans in ways that male gurus don't? And vice versa? Why might some gurus become more successful in the West than others?

9 Conclusion

Kamadhenu: the Hindu cow, politics, and the environment

In the early 1900s, Mahatma Gandhi launched his *satyagraha* ("truth force") movement that sought Indian independence from the British Empire. Among the political and economic strategies that comprised this movement, Gandhi advocated for rural uplift and economic sustainability through small-scale agriculture and the local production of *khadi* cloth woven on the family *charkha* wheel. Reflecting the non-violence (*ahimsa*) that permeated his entire strategy, and drawing upon existing rhetoric of reform from the previous century, Gandhi insisted upon the protection of the cow as one of the movement's central ethical tenets. Referring to the cow as "a poem of pity" and "the mother to millions," Gandhi went so far as to state in his 1921 essay, "The Cow in Hinduism": "The central fact of Hinduism is cow protection.... Cow protection is the gift of Hinduism to the world. And Hinduism will live so long as there are Hindus to protect the cow" (King 2012: 182).

If there is one thing that people in the West know about Hinduism, it is that "the cow is sacred." But what does this really mean, and how is it applied in an everyday sense among Hindu communities? This conclusion will bring together and extend elements from the previous chapters in this book to address this question of the cow. Rather than treating her as simply a passive symbol, however, it will consider the cow as a living animal who embodies Hindu multiplicity through the many ways she has traditionally been thought about. As one author writes of its centrality in Hindu thought, the cow's associations with time, space, and the creation of the world means that "the cow not only reflects Hindu reality but also embodies and defines it" (Korom 2000: 193). The cow's reflection of Hindu reality has made it a key symbol of Hindu identity.

In India today, Hindus will honor the cow by touching it, as one would respectfully touch any other sacred object such as the icon of a deity. But the cow was a powerful image as early as Vedic times. In various creation hymns of the Rig Veda, Indra releases the cows from the grip of the serpent Vṛtra and from the Vala cave guarded by the Panis. In these Vedic stories, the audience of the hymn seeks these same cattle as evidence of their wealth, as the cows are equated to the rays of the morning sun the original waters of the universe, and the flames of the sacrificial fire.

DOI: 10.4324/9781003475033-10

Elements of natural, feminine, and maternal life-giving fertility, cows are also associated with the goddess of wealth, Lakshmi. Celebrated during her autumnal Diwali festival, cows continue to symbolize wealth as people light lamps in order to invite Lakshmi, the incarnation of *shri* glory, to support and protect their homes and businesses. Cows also appear alongside the crow and dog during Diwali, together venerated as animal vehicles who convey the spirits of the recently deceased to the world of the ancestors.

Numerous other cows appear throughout images and narratives of classical Hinduism. Emerging from the Churning of the Cosmic Ocean alongside the vessel of immortality, the mother cow Kamadhenu embodies all of the life-giving qualities typically attributed to cows. In some devotional images, she contains within herself all of the gods and goddesses, just as Krishna does in the *Bhagavad Gita*. Her medical and purificatory qualities are often embodied in the five products of the cow (*pancha-gavya*): milk, butter, curd, urine, and dung. Krishna is regularly depicted with cows, especially under his names Gopala (the cow protector) and Govinda (pleasing to cows), his rural personae in which he is associated with Radha and the other female gopis. And in the land of Braj, Krishna redirects the festival of Indra to Mount Govardhan and the brahmins and cows who live nearby.

The powerful symbolism of the cow has resulted in a contemporary sense of cow protection, with the prohibition of cow slaughter even written into the Indian Constitution (Article 48). More than an ancient symbol, the cow continues to communicate power in modern democratic and capitalist India. The Hindu American Foundation, an educational and advocacy organization, has extended this respect for the cow to the global Hindu community, asserting: "The cow thus represents Hindu values of selfless service, strength, dignity, and ahimsa (non-harming). Though not all Hindus are vegetarian, for this reason many traditionally abstain from eating beef."[1]

Anthropologist Claude Levi-Strauss wrote that animals are "good to think with," especially as they highlight structural oppositions within and across cultures. Within global Hindu communities, the cow operates as just such a sign, used by groups who support conservative nationalism and/or progressive environmentalism.

This conclusion will handle two facets of the protection of the cow, a Hindu symbol that draws on Gandhi's perspective in the opening vignette. The first part will discuss how cow protection, like yoga and the image of Mother India, has long been a deeply political issue; fitting within the context of Hindu nationalism and sectarian violence, cow protection has challenged India's cultural, religious, and linguistic diversity. The second part will consider the ways that individuals, communities, and organizations use traditional images of and care for the cow in service of animal rights and environmental sustainability.

Both of these perspectives apply images, stories, and practices that we have seen throughout this book towards practical ends. Although some readers might be tempted to oppose these two applications of politics and sustainability – as violent/peaceful, regressive/progressive, improper/proper, novel/traditional, bad/good, etc. – I urge you to refrain from making such judgments and instead analyze how communities continue to apply images of the cow to changing conditions in contemporary South Asian life.

Hindu nationalism

Hindu nationalism challenges India's history as a deeply multi-religious country whose many Hindu, Muslim, Sikh, and *sant* poets have worked hard to negotiate its various traditions using particularly Indian styles of interfaith dialogue. I am reminded of the man whom William Dalrymple interviews in his documentary *Sufi Soul*, who says that the thirteenth-century Islamic Sufi shrines of the saint Nizammudin Auliya and the musician and poet Amir Khusrau in Delhi are beacons of light for people of all faiths. He says: "What's nice about this place is no one is Hindu, Muslim, Sikh or Christian. All faiths pray together. I've found a lamp of love here for all religions" (Broughton 2008).

Although India's majority religion of Hinduism is followed by approximately 80 percent of its billion-plus citizens, the nation's inherent diversity led writers and editors of India's Constitution to describe the country as explicitly "secular." This legal emphasis on secularism is an ideal, however, that is not lauded by all of India's citizens. Despite Vivekananda's speech at the World's Parliament of Religions, in which he registered his opposition to "sectarianism, bigotry, and its horrible descendant, fanaticism," Hinduism has been used by some to oppose the "universal toleration" he advocated.

> The original Constitution defines India as a "sovereign democratic republic" (in 1947), though its forty-second amendment (in 1976) expanded that description to "sovereign socialist secular democratic republic." These words are in all capital letters in the text. Article 25.2b, under its "Right to Freedom of Religion" section, includes the only significant description of Hinduism, where it legally equates it with other religions of South Asian origin: "the reference to Hindus shall be construed as including a reference to persons professing the Sikh, Jaina or Buddhist religion, and the reference to Hindu religious institutions shall be construed accordingly."

Similar to the Christian religious right in America, Jewish Zionism in Israel, Buddhist violence in Myanmar, and Islamic fundamentalism radiating outwards from countries on the Arabian Peninsula, Hinduism, as the dominant religion in India, can also generate conservative and even violent attitudes and actions. We have seen some of the seeds of Hindu nationalism already throughout this book in the form of texts, narratives, and practices that undergird political power, especially in times of great social change and especially within the context of the British Empire in the nineteenth century.

In Chapter 2, we saw how Vivekananda and Aurobindo constructed forms of yoga to build national pride. In Chapter 5, nationalist writer Bankim Chandra Chattopadhyay used the Hindu image of Bharat Mata (Mother India) to rally Indians against the British. And in Chapter 7, Swaminarayan and other reformist writers and activists deployed distinctively Hindu language to formulate what they considered more modern Hindu positions on women, science, and the physical representations of the gods.

Chapter 3 is most relevant to the political issue of cow protection, however. In that chapter, we saw many of the texts and practices devoted to the god-king-avatar Ram. While for most Hindus, texts of the Ramayana, performances of the Ram Lila festival, and viewings of the TV Ramayana (the original in the 1980s and rebooted twice since) are religious experiences that present living manifestations of Ram and Sita. For some, however, these media have fueled nationalist feelings and anti-Muslim sentiments that have erupted into communal violence.

More importantly, however, it is necessary to consider these nationalist manifestations of Ram as part of Indian history. Like the Ganesh festival more than a century later in western India, and like the TV Ramayana in the late 1980s, the Ram Lila is hardly an ancient timeless festival but was rather born out of a certain set of political circumstances. The late 1700s saw the decline of the Islamic Mughal empire as well as the rise of the British Empire. Royal sponsors of the Ram Lila saw these changing social, political, and religious times as an opportunity to patronize this more explicitly Hindu festival, whose performances highlight Ramraj – "the kingdom of Ram" – and the overthrow of the demonic kingdom of the ten-headed Ravana.[2] For many, the latest wave of Hindu nationalism is meant to culminate in the building of a Ram temple on the site of the Babri Masjid in Ayodhya, which will begin a new era of Ramraj.

The cow has re-emerged in this newest wave of Indian nationalism. Writing on the "myth of the holy cow," author Dwijendra Narayan Jha questions the timeless symbol of the Hindu cow. Referring to the sacred cow as "elusive" throughout the millennia, Jha shows how the strict non-violence of Buddhism and Jainism combined with earlier Vedic texts, as they did in a variety of ways, to gradually sacralize the cow. Emerging over time, the sacredness of the cow has become a divisive facet of Indian sectarianism and nationalism and a "tool of mass political mobilization" (2002: 18).

The roots of organizational cow protection are in 1870s Bombay, when Dayanand Saraswati founded not only the Arya Samaj but also the Gorakshini Sabha (Cow Protection Society). During the late 1800s, numerous riots over the cow occurred at festivals, often at celebrations of the festivals of Eid, when Muslims sacrifice and consume animals as part of the feast. These conflicts over cow protection reflected other social, political, and economic conflicts between Hindus and Muslims in British India, but most of all represented a threat to the majority Hindu population (Walsh 2011: 161).

Cow protection has taken the more recent and extreme form of cow vigilante violence. Especially in the mid- to late 2010s, numerous informal organizations were established, with many groups operating with minimal structure. Most examples followed the same trend. A Muslim or Dalit was accused (though rarely with sufficient evidence) of having killed, stolen, or smuggled a number of cows; in other cases, they were only found in possession of meat that their accusers said was beef. The accused were then beaten and in some cases killed. Such violence used the cow and cow protection as an extremist weapon deployed against non-Hindus, with tactics that were relatively rare but whose images of extraordinary violence spread quickly through news agencies and social media.

Considering the flexibility of culture in general and the notion of multiplicity within Hinduism in particular, we will look in the following section at how many (and many more) Hindus draw on similar images and ideas of the cow as the foundation for a modern notion of ecological sustainability.

Hindu environmentalism

In the early eighteenth century, Abhay Singh, the Maharaja of Jodhpur, entered the village of Khejarli in the western deserts of the state of Rajasthan. In search of lumber for a new palace, he dispatched his soldiers to cut down all the khejari trees in the area. To prevent this act of deforestation, the local woman Amrita Devi confronted the soldiers and hugged the trees in order to prevent their felling. Joined by other villagers from the surrounding area who similarly offered their own heads in place of the trees, Amrita Devi was one of 363 villagers beheaded that day. Inspired by the tenets of the fifteenth-century Bishnoi movement and inspiring the contemporary Chipko "tree-hugging" movement, the Khejarli massacre continues to be remembered as a key moment in the modern Indian environmental movement.[3]

In his pioneering 1967 study of religion and environmentalism, Lynn White argues that Christian thought in medieval Europe fostered the cultural perception, one that has become the dominant mode of thought in the modern world, that human beings operate independently of nature. This perceived separation between humans and nature has resulted in humanity's very real scientific and technological power to exploit nature. No longer acknowledging the local spirits that were traditionally seen to inhabit and protect local elements of nature – rivers, trees, stones, and mountains – humans have developed a sense of anthropocentrism whereby they see themselves as the center or apex of biological life on Earth and as even having fully transcended nature. One might recognize an example of this in the biblical creation story at Genesis 1.28, where God tells Adam, the first man, to (depending on the translation) "rule over / subdue / have dominion over" the newly created world. Responding indirectly to this biblical injunction, White proposes a solution that concludes his essay: "Since the roots of our trouble are so largely religious, the remedy must also be essentially religious, whether we call it that or not" (White 1967: 1207).

The second part of this conclusion will consider White's solution within the framework of Hindu concepts and practices of environmental sustainability. When we discuss sustainability, we are referring to a concept that arose in the

1960s, amidst many other cultural revolutions. Spurred on especially by Rachel Carson's *Silent Spring*, the environmental movement began to account for the chemical pollutants, widely used by many multinational corporations, detrimental to the clean air, plants, and water necessary for a healthy life on planet Earth.

Since that time, religious organizations around the globe have become more proactive in becoming part of the solution. In different ways, various religious communities retrieve, reevaluate, and reconstruct their own stories, systems of ethics and doctrine, and practices in order to align themselves with modern notions of sustainability.[4] David Haberman outlines four core interrelated concepts that ground Hindu environmental perspectives: all elements of the world are part of an interconnected reality; deities fully manifest themselves in elements of nature; as parts of that divinity, nature deserves loving and devotional service (*seva*); and that devotion creates a deep loving connection with the object of service (Haberman 2017).[5] This focus on devotional service allows us to avoid making broad generalizations about the relationships between Hinduism and sustainability. Rather than simply asserting that "Hinduism is an inherently environmentally friendly religion," our attention to acts of devotional service highlights a distinction from ascetic traditions focused on Shiva in which renouncers transcend this temporary world of suffering and move on to the next. Such distinctions can be found within all religious traditions that have acquired, over a long period of time, various complementary ways of being in the world.

Numerous Hindu organizations engage in various facets of this work, on local and global levels, and with varying emphasis on devotional service. I will highlight several of them here.

Bhumi Global refers to itself as "The Hindu Movement for Mother Earth," and has as its mission, "to engage, educate, and empower people and communities to address the triple crisis of climate change, biodiversity loss, and pollution. Our work is based on Hindu principles of environmental care."

Other organizations represent interests more local to India. Named after the wish-granting tree of Hindu myth, Kalpavriksh organizes around issues of land conservation throughout India, reporting on such issues as local agriculture, eco-tourism, community forests, protected lands and wildlife, oil drilling, and elephant, tiger, and lion deaths.

Based in Laporiya, a village in the western state of Rajasthan, the Gram Vikas Navyuwak Mandal, Laporiya (GVNML) (the Youth Organization for Village Development) maintains an up-to-date website detailing the many ways that they are "transforming the relationship and values upheld by the community towards their natural resources," especially as they relate to establishing safe and equitable drinking water throughout the villages of the region.

From the west Indian city of Pune, eCoexist combines social uplift programs – for women farmers, prisoners, rag pickers, and people with disabilities – with nature programs that connect local citizens, especially children, to experiences with wilderness, nature, gardening, and animals. They also produce and sell eco-friendly vegetable (rather than chemical) colors for playing Holi and to paint their reusable statues made of natural and reusable clay, papier mâché, or cow dung for the Ganesh festival.

Finally, Navdanya is one of the most famous sustainability organizations in the world. Led by their equally famous founder, Vandana Shiva, Navdanya (a Sanskrit word that means both "Nine Seeds" and "New Gift") describes itself as "an Earth Centric, Women centric and Farmer led movement for the protection of Biological and cultural Diversity." One of its main tasks is conserving seeds, which contributes to an intersectional set of tasks that includes "conserving biodiversity, conserving knowledge of the seed and its utilization, conserving culture, conserving sustainability." Navdanya's Seed University, based near the north Indian city of Dehradun near several major Hindu pilgrimage towns on the Ganges River, runs courses for locals and devoted tourists such as Eco-feminism, Sacred Ecology, and Gandhi, Globalisation and Earth Democracy.

All of these organizations consider elements of nature as inherently valuable. Where they draw on more explicitly Hindu principles, these elements of nature also become inherently sacred, in ways that are virtually impossible within Western traditions.

ISKCON, the global Hindu organization devoted to Krishna that we met in the previous chapter is rooted in traditional notions of the Hindu cow, and thus is often connected to both nationalism (typically in India) and environmentalism (typically abroad). ISKCON's founder, Prabhupad, upheld the cow as sacred in much the same way that Gandhi did. Similar to Gandhi's statement, "The central fact of Hinduism is cow protection," Prabhupad stated in his commentary on Krishna's life story in the *Bhagavata Purana*, "Cow protection means feeding the brahminical culture, which leads towards God consciousness, and thus perfection of human civilization is achieved" (King 2012: 184).

ISKCON applies cow protection in a variety of ways through the organizations it operates and supports. Its many Govinda's restaurants prepare a strictly vegetarian and "ethically-sourced and karma-free" menu; its Krishna-inspired intentional spiritual community of New Vrindaban in West Virginia practices *go-seva* (cow protection); Food for Life promotes "the art and science of food yoga" in its vegan hunger relief programs and the International Society for Cow Protection (ISCOWP) in Gainesville, Florida, and Care For Cows Society in Krishna's Indian homeland of Vrindaban protect cows as one would protect one's mother. Although not without difficulties in executing some of its programs, especially in the West with its different relationships towards animals and animal products, these many global programs reflect the basic Hindu virtue of cow protection, whose focus "is the lens through which ISKCON is able to critique the cruelties of commercial farming and animal exploitation" (King 2012: 197).

The general divinity of the cow, sometimes embodied in the mother cow Kamadhenu, is reflected in the many other aspects of nature that take on particularly divine forms in the Hindu world. Among stones and mountains that reflect masculine forms of divinity – the Himalayan mountain range is the father of Shiva's wife Parvati – trees embody different Hindu divinities. The *pipal* tree is venerated as a manifestation or residence of Vishnu, though also of the dangerous ghosts of the recently deceased and of the inauspicious planet Saturn (Shani) whom worshippers avoid at night. The *neem* tree manifests as the Goddess who provides helpful medicinal products, and – to return to one of the central metaphors of Hinduism where this book began – the massive *banyan* tree, often considered the indestructible or immortal (*akshaya*) form of Shiva, is the residence of the multiple gods and goddesses who reside in the shrines built for them under the tree's massive canopy (Haberman 2013) (Figure 9.1).

Finally, and as we have seen throughout this book, rivers are particularly significant and often divine. As the term "Hinduism" translates as "the religion of India," its geographical connection to rivers – via *sindhu*, the general Sanskrit term for river – also renders the term Hinduism metaphorically as "the religion of rivers." Echoing the significance of the Seven Rivers in

Figure 9.1 Protected by a separate shrine to Hanuman, an image of Ram, Sita, Lakshman, and Hanuman sits at the base of a tree. Varanasi, India

the Rig Veda, the Yamuna and Ganges Rivers are sisters and goddesses who feed and nurture the hundreds of millions of people who live within reach of them in north India.[6]

In his study of the pollution of the Yamuna River in north India, David Haberman contrasts standard Western anthropocentric approaches to the environment with those from the Hindu devotional tradition. He writes, "The aspects of Hinduism most invested in the worship of natural forms as divine beings seem to provide the greatest resource for environmental care" (2006: 179). Chemical pollution and human waste, the by-products of modernity everywhere, are threatening the existence of rivers in India. The identity of rivers as goddesses means that not only are viable sources of drinking water under threat, but so also are the goddesses who embody them. Accounting for this intimate connection between free-flowing rivers and beneficial goddesses, Haberman offers three possibilities for the future of the Yamuna River (and by extension other Indian rivers, such as the Ganges): the death of the river as a goddess, her transformation to another divine identity with a different function, or the restoration of both the river and the goddess. The particular identity of rivers also as mothers presents a unique opportunity for additional motivation to maintain their purity, as devotees consider them to be clean, pure, nurturing, forgiving, loving, sometimes dangerous, and always worthy of our protection (Figure 9.2).

Conclusion

I once taught in a Religious Studies department with a colleague who, in their World Religions course in which they taught surveys of all major religions, refused to teach Hinduism. It was too complicated and didn't make sense, they said. Their students, of course, received an incomplete education from a faculty member who couldn't conceive of the world outside of the box into which they were born and raised.

I introduced the concept of multiplicity early in this book and returned to it often as a way to conceive of the complexity of Indian thought. The banyan tree that provides a metaphor and serves as a natural object that encompasses multiple gods and goddesses; the multiple avatars of Vishnu who maintain dharma in all the world's cyclical eras; the simultaneity of Hindu practice by those who, especially associated with Shiva, practice austere renunciation and intense devotion apart from society; goddesses who marry and remain single, create and destroy, and whose femininity is displayed in domestic grace and independent power; and the cow who inspires some to defend an ideal Hindu nation and others who seek to sustain a healthy planet.

These sets of multiples and repetitions reinforce a way of thinking that is different from dominant modes of thought in the West. Specifically, its myth of monotheism has long been an obstacle to understanding, or even approaching Hinduism, hence my colleague's difficulty. With its many texts, creation stories, and deities, Hinduism reflects the many communities that live underneath its banyan tree. I hope that this book has provided a sufficient introduction that

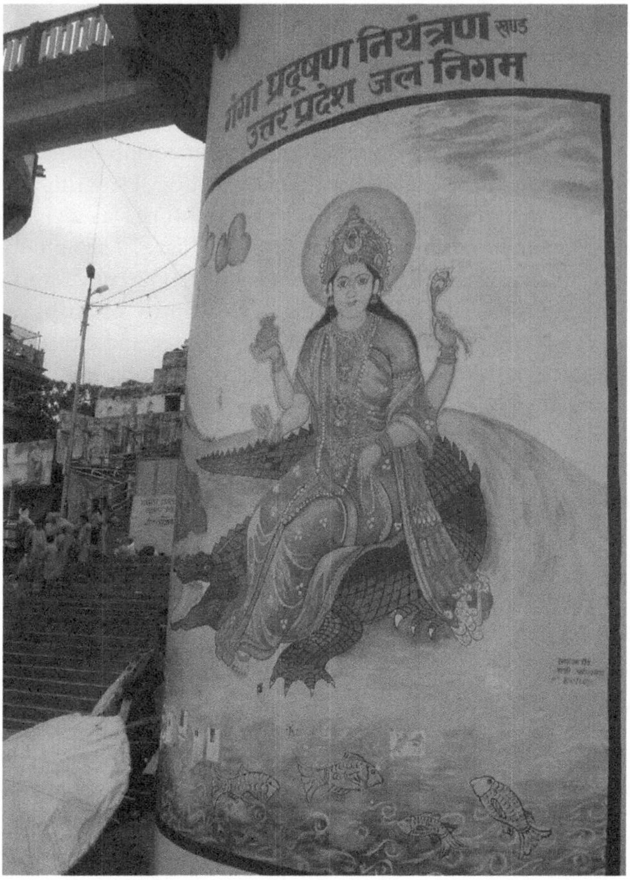

Figure 9.2 Painting of the river goddess Ganges on a bridge pillar support for the Ganga Pollution Board and Uttar Pradesh Water Project, with sadhus nearby. Varanasi, India

communicates the wide diversity of voices within the global Hindu tradition and encourages readers to seek out additional texts and translations, social media platforms and posts from across the virtual world, and local and living Hindu temples and communities whose notorious hospitality – "Guest is God!" – enlivens cities, towns, and neighborhoods everywhere.

Notes

1 Media Toolkit – Hindu American Foundation.
2 Hess 2006 and Lutgendorf 1992.
3 See Darlington 2012 for an account of the centrality of trees in the Thai Buddhist environmental movement. See Jain 2011 for studies of the Bhil, Bishnoi, and Swadhyay environmental movements.

4 This concept of retrieval, re-evaluation, and reconstruction comes from Tucker and Grim 2018, the introductory essay from the *Routledge Handbook of Religion and Ecology*. This essay, along with much additional information on religion and sustainability – primary sources and statements, engaged projects, and other links and media – are available on the website, Forum on Religion and Ecology, hosted by Yale University's School of the Environment (https://fore.yale.edu).

5 Respectively, these four Sanskrit terms are *sarvatma-bhava, svarupa, seva*, and *sambandha*.

6 In the Hindi language, this expansive and densely populated region is called the *doāb*, the region of the two rivers.

References

Haberman, David L. 2017. Hinduism: Devotional Love of the World. Yale Forum on Religion and Ecology. https://fore.yale.edu/World-Religions/Hinduism/Overview-Essay.

Jha, D. N. 2002. *The Myth of the Holy Cow*. London: Verso.

King, Anna S. 2012. Krishna's Cows: ISKCON's Animal Theology and Practice. *Journal of Animal Ethics* 2 (2): 179–204.

Key terms

cow protection
Hindu nationalism
Hindu environmentalism
Indian constitution

Persons

Mahatma Gandhi

Study questions

1 How is Hindu nationalism related to Hindu concepts and deities seen throughout this book?
2 How is Hindu environmentalism related to Hindu concepts and deities seen throughout this book?
3 In what ways does the cow intersect with both Hindu nationalism and environmentalism?

Bibliography

Accardi, Dean. 2018. Introduction to Special Issue: Making a Hindu Saint. *International Journal of Hindu Studies* 22: 379–384.

Allocco, Amy. 2014. Snake Goddess Traditions in Tamilnadu. In P. Pratap Kumar (ed.), *Contemporary Hinduism*. London: Routledge, 191–203.

Ashraf, Ajaz. 2015. Modi's yoga celebration is a mix of cultural nationalism, commercialisation and subtle coercion. Scroll.in. https://scroll.in/article/732049/modis-yoga-celebration-is-a-mix-of-cultural-nationalism-commercialisation-and-subtle-coercion.

Babb, Lawrence A. 1986. *Redemptive Encounters: Three Modern Styles in the Hindu Tradition*. Berkeley: University of California Press.

Baier, Karl. 2019. Swami Vivekananda: Reform Hinduism, Nationalism and Scientistic Yoga. *Interdisciplinary Journal for Religion and Transformation in Contemporary Society* 5: 230–257.

Balkaran, Raj. 2019. Visions and Revisions of the Hindu Goddess: Sound, Structure, and Artful Ambivalence in the Devī Māhātmya . *Religions* 10 (5): 322.

Baltutis, Michael. 2023. *The Festival of Indra: Innovation, Archaism, and Revival in a South Asian Performance*. Albany, NY: SUNY Press.

Baltutis, Michael. 2014. The Indrajatra Festival of Kathmandu, Nepal. In P. Pratap Kumar (ed.), *Contemporary Hinduism*. London: Routledge, 83–96.

Baltutis, Michael. 2009. Renovating Bhairav: Fierce Gods, Divine Agency, and Local Power in Kathmandu. *International Journal of Hindu Studies* 13 (1): 25–49.

Banerjee, Sumanta. 2010. *Logic in a Popular Form*. London: Seagull Books.

Beal, Timothy K. 2014. *Religion and Its Monsters*. Hoboken, NJ: Routledge.

Bellamy, Carla. 2011. *The Powerful Ephemeral: Everyday Healing in an Ambiguously Islamic Place*. Berkeley: University of California Press.

Biernacki, Loriliai. 2013. Miming Manu: Women, Authority and Mimicry in a Tantric Context. *South Asia: Journal of South Asian Studies* 36 (4): 644–660.

Birkenholtz, Jessica Vantine. 2018. *Reciting the Goddess: Narratives of Place and the Making of Hinduism in Nepal*. New York: Oxford University Press.

Bloomer, Kristin C. 2018. *Possessed by the Virgin: Hinduism, Roman Catholicism. and Marian Possession in South India*. New York: Oxford University Press.

Bose, Mandakranta. 2010. *Women in the Hindu Tradition: Rules, Roles, and Exceptions*. Routledge.

Brereton, Joel and Stephanie Jamison. 2020. *The Rigveda: A Guide*. New York: Oxford University Press.

Broughton, Simon (dir.). 2008. *Sufi Soul: The Mystic Music of Islam*. Riverboat Records/ World Music Network.

Brown, Karen McCarthy. 2001. *Mama Lola: A Vodou Priestess in Brooklyn*. Berkeley: University of California Press.

Bryant, Edwin F. 2003. *Krishna: The Beautiful Legend of God: Śrīmad Bhāgavata Purāṇa Book X: With Chapters 1, 6, and 29–31 from Book XI*. London: Penguin.

Caṭṭopādhyāya, Baṅkimacandra. 2005. *Ānandamaṭh, Or the Sacred Brotherhood*. Translated by Julius Lipner. New York: Oxford University Press.

Chapple, Christopher Key and Mary Evelyn Tucker (eds.). 2000. *Hinduism and Ecology: The Intersection of Earth, Sky, and Water*. Cambridge, MA: Harvard University Press.

Clarke J. J. 2006. *Oriental Enlightenment: The Encounter between Asian and Western Thought*. London: Routledge.

Coburn, Thomas B. 1991. *Encountering the Goddess: A Translation of the Devī-Māhātmya and a Study of Its Interpretation*. Albany: State University of New York Press.

Coleman, Tracy. 2010. Viraha-Bhakti and Strīdharma: Re-Reading the Story of Kṛṣṇa and the Gopīs in the Harivaṃśa and the Bhāgavata Purāṇa. *Journal of the American Oriental Society* 130 (3): 385–412.

Comeau, Leah Elizabeth. 2020a. *Material Devotion in a South Indian Poetic World*. London: Bloomsbury.

Comeau, Leah. 2020b. Garlands for Gods in Southeast India. The Jugaad Project, June 7, www.thejugaadproject.pub/home/garlands-for-gods-in-southeast-india.

Copeman, Jacob and Aya Ikegame (eds.). 2014. *The Guru in South Asia: New Interdisciplinary Perspectives*. London: Routledge.

Craddock, Elaine. *Siva's Demon Devotee: Karaikkal Ammaiyar*. Albany: State University of New York Press, 2010.

Crane, George. 2000. *Bones of the Master: A Buddhist Monk's Search for the Lost Heart of China*. New York: Bantam Books.

Dalrymple, William. 2010. *Nine Lives: In Search of the Sacred in Modern India*. New York: Alfred A. Knopf.

Darlington, Susan M. 2012. *The Ordination of a Tree: The Thai Buddhist Environmental Movement*. Albany: State University of New York Press.

Davis, Richard H. 2015. *The Bhagavad Gita: A Biography*. Princeton, NJ: Princeton University Press.

DeNapoli, Antoinette E. 2013. Vernacular Hinduism in Rajasthan. In P. Pratap Kumar (ed.), *Contemporary Hinduism*. London: Routledge, 97–113.

Dempsey, Corinne G. 2006. *The Goddess Lives in Upstate New York: Breaking Convention and Making Home at a North American Hindu Temple*. Oxford: Oxford University Press.

Doniger, Wendy. 1981. *The Rig Veda: An Anthology*. London: Penguin.

Doniger, Wendy. 1975. *Hindu Myths: A Sourcebook*. Harmondsworth: Penguin.

Dutt, Yashica. 2019. *Coming Out as Dalit: A Memoir*. New Delhi: Aleph.

Eck, Diana L. 2013. *India: A Sacred Geography*. New York: Three Rivers.

Eck, Diana L. 1998. *Darśan: Seeing the Divine Image in India*. New York: Columbia University Press.

Erndl, Kathleen M. 2006. Possession by Durga: The Mother Who Possesses. In John Stratton Hawley and Vasudha Narayanan (eds.), *The Life of Hinduism*. Berkeley: University of California Press, 158–170.

Erndl, Kathleen M. 1993. *Victory to the Mother: The Hindu Goddess of Northwest India in Myth Ritual and Symbol*. New York: Oxford University Press.

Erndl, Kathleen M. 1989. Rapist or Bodyguard, Demon or Devotee? Images of Bhairo in the Mythology and Cult of Vaiṣṇṇo Devī. In Alf Hiltebeitel (ed.), *Criminal Gods and Demon Devotees*. Albany: State University of New York Press, 239–250.

Falk, Nancy Auer. 2006. *Living Hinduisms: An Explorer's Guide*. Belmont, CA: Thomson Wadsworth.

Ferrari, Fabrizio M. 2015. *Religion, Devotion and Medicine in North India: The Healing Power of Śītalā*. London: Bloomsbury.

Fisher, Elaine M. 2017. *Hindu Pluralism: Religion and the Public Sphere in Early Modern South India*. Oakland: University of California Press.

Flood, Gavin. 1996. *An Introduction to Hinduism*. Cambridge: Cambridge University Press.

Flueckiger, Joyce Burkhalter. 2020. *Material Acts in Everyday Hindu Worlds*. Albany: State University of New York Press.

Flueckiger, Joyce Burkhalter. 2015. *Everyday Hinduism*. Chichester: Wiley-Blackwell.

Flueckiger, Joyce Burkhalter. 2013. *When the World Becomes Female: Guises of a South Indian Goddess*. Bloomington: Indiana University Press.

Frazier, Jessica. 2010. Arts and Aesthetics in Hindu Studies. *The Journal of Hindu Studies* 3 (1): 1–11.

Fuller, C.J. 2004 [1992]. *The Camphor Flame: Popular Hinduism and Society in India*. Princeton, NJ: Princeton University Press.

Gairola, Vineet, and Shubha Ranganathan. 2023a. The Divine as a Child and the Mother Goddess: On the History and Practice of Kunwarikā Devī Worship in the Garhwal Himalaya. *HIMALAYA* 42 (1): 98–117.

Gairola, Vineet, and Shubha Ranganathan. 2023b. Worship in Transition: An Encounter with the Rājrājeshwarī Devī of the Garhwal Himalaya. *HIMALAYA* 42 (1): 118–140.

Geertz, Clifford. 1993 [1973]. Religion as a Cultural System. In *The Interpretation of Cultures: Selected Essays*. New York: Basic Books, 87–125.

Gold, Ann Grodzins. 2000 [1988]. *Fruitful Journeys: The Ways of Rajasthani Pilgrims*. Prospect Heights, NY: Waveland Press.

Goldberg, Philip. 2010. *American Veda: From Emerson and the Beatles to Yoga and Meditation: How Indian Spirituality Changed the West*. New York: Harmony Books.

Goldman, Robert P. 2016. *The Rāmāyaṇa of Vālmīki: An Epic of Ancient India. Vol. 1: Bālakāṇḍa*. Princeton, NJ: Princeton University Press.

Goldman, Robert P. and Sally J. Sutherland Goldman. 2021. *The Rāmāyaṇa of Vālmīki: The Complete English Translation*. Princeton, NJ: Princeton University Press.

Gonda, Jan. 1974. *The Dual Deities in the Religion of the Veda*. Amsterdam: North-Holland Publishing Company.

Gross, Rita M. 2000. Is the Goddess a Feminist? In Alf Hiltebeitel and Kathleen M.Erndl (eds.), *Is the Goddess a Feminist? The Politics of South Asian Goddesses*. New York: New York University Press, 104–122.

Gupta, Sanjukta. 1972. *Lakṣmī Tantra: A Pāñcarātra Text*. Leiden: E.J. Brill.

Haberman, David L. 2017. Hinduism: Devotional Love of the World. Yale Forum on Religion and Ecology. https://fore.yale.edu/World-Religions/Hinduism/Overview-Essay.

Haberman, David L. 2013. *People Trees: Worship of Trees in Northern India*. Oxford: Oxford University Press.

Haberman, David L. 2006. *River of Love in an Age of Pollution: The Yamuna River of Northern India*. Berkeley: University of California Press.

Haberman, David L. 1994. *Journey through the Twelve Forests: An Encounter with Krishna*. New York: Oxford University Press.

Hallstrom, Lisa Lassell. 1999. *Mother of Bliss: Ānandamayī Mā (1896–1982)*. New York: Oxford University Press.

Hart, George L. and Hank Heifetz. 1989. *The Forest Book of the Rāmāyaṇa of Kampaṉ*. Berkeley: University of California Press.

Hatcher, Brian A. 2012. *Hindu Widow Marriage*. New York: Columbia University Press.

Hawley, John Stratton and Mark Juergensmeyer. 2006. A Dalit Poet-Saint: Ravidas. In John Stratton Hawley and Vasudha Narayanan (eds.), *The Life of Hinduism*. Berkeley: University of California Press, 199–217.

Hawley, John Stratton and Vasudha Narayanan (eds.). 2006. *The Life of Hinduism*. Berkeley: University of California Press.

Hay, Stephen (ed.). 1988. *Sources of Indian Tradition. Volume Two: Modern India and Pakistan*, 2nd ed. New York: Columbia University Press.

Heesterman, Jan. 1985. *The Inner Conflict of Tradition*. Chicago, IL: University of Chicago Press.

Hess, Linda. 2006. An Open-Air Ramayana: Ramlila, the Audience Experience. In John Stratton Hawley and Vasudha Narayanan (eds.), *The Life of Hinduism*. Berkeley: University of California Press, 115–139.

Hess, Linda. 1987. In Karine Schomer and W. H. McLeod, *The Sants: Studies in a Devotional Tradition of India*. Berkeley, CA: Berkeley Religious Studies Series, 143–166.

Hiltebeitel, Alf and Kathleen M. Erndl (eds.). 2000. *Is the Goddess a Feminist? The Politics of South Asian Goddesses*. New York: New York University Press.

Hiltebeitel, Alf (ed.). 1989. *Criminal Gods and Demon Devotees*. Albany: State University of New York Press.

Hilton, James. 1933. *Lost Horizon*. Harper Perennial.

Hüsken, Ute, Vasudha Narayanan, and Astrid Zotter (eds.). 2021. *Nine Nights of Power: Durga, Dolls, and Darbars*. Albany: State University of New York Press.

Huyler, Stephen. 2002. *Meeting God: Elements of Hindu Devotion*. New Haven, CT: Yale University Press.

Ilkama, Ina Marie Lunde. 2021. Female Agency during Tamil Navarātri. In Ute Hüsken, Vasudha Narayanan, and Astrid Zotter (eds.), *Nine Nights of Power: Durga, Dolls, and Darbars*. Albany: State University of New York Press, 165–190.

Jacobsen, Knut A. 2008. *South Asian Religions on Display: Religious Processions in South Asia and in the Diaspora*. London: Routledge.

Jain, Andrea R. 2015. *Selling Yoga: From Counterculture to Pop Culture*. New York: Oxford University Press.

Jain, Pankaj. 2011. *Dharma and Ecology of Hindu Communities: Sustenance and Sustainability*. Surrey: Ashgate.

Jamison, Stephanie W. 1996. *Sacrificed Wife/Sacrificer's Wife: Women, Ritual, and Hospitality in Ancient India*. New York: Oxford University Press.

Jamison, Stephanie and Joel Brereton. 2014. *The Rigveda: The Earliest Religious Poetry of India*. New York: Oxford University Press.

Jenkins, Willis, Mary Evelyn Tucker, and John Grim. 2018. *Routledge Handbook of Religion and Ecology*. Abingdon: Routledge.

Jha, D. N. 2002. *The Myth of the Holy Cow*. London: Verso.

Keul, István (ed.). 2013. *'Yoginī' in South Asia: Interdisciplinary Approaches*. London and New York: Routledge.

Kim, Hanna H. 2014. Devotional Expressions in the Swaminarayan Community. In P. Pratap Kumar (ed.), *Contemporary Hinduism*. London: Routledge, 126–137.

King, Anna S. 2012. Krishna's Cows: ISKCON's Animal Theology and Practice. *Journal of Animal Ethics* 2 (2): 179–204.

Kinsley, David R. 2004. Kālī. In Rachel Fell McDermott and Jeffrey J. Kripal (eds.), *Encountering Kali: In the Margins, at the Center, in the West*. Delhi: Motilal Banarsidass, 23–38.

Klass, Morton. 1996. *Singing with Sai Baba: The Politics of Revitalization in Trinidad*. Prospect Heights, NY: Waveland Press.

Knipe, David. 2015. *Vedic Voices: Intimate Narratives of a Living Andhra Tradition*. New York: Oxford University Press.

Knott, Kim. 2016 [2000]. *Hinduism: A Very Short Introduction*. Oxford: Oxford University Press.

Korom, Frank J. 2000. Holy Cow! The Apotheosis of Zebu, or Why the Cow Is Sacred in Hinduism. *Asian Folklore Studies* 59 (2): 181–203.

Kumar, P. Pratap (ed.). 2014. *Contemporary Hinduism*. London: Routledge.

Kumar, P. Pratap. 2010. Introducing Hinduism: The Master Narrative – A Critical Review of Textbooks on Hinduism. *Religious Studies Review* 36 (2): 115–124.

Kumar, P. Pratap. 2008. Rathayatra of the Hare Krishnas in Durban: Inventing Strategies to Transmit Religious Ideas in Modern Society. In Knut A. Jacobsen (ed.), *South Asian Religions on Display: Religious Processions in South Asia and in the Diaspora*. London: Routledge, 205–216.

Leslie, I. Julia. 1989. *The Perfect Wife: The Orthodox Hindu Woman According to the Strīdharmapaddhati of Tryambakayajvan*. Delhi: Oxford University Press.

Levy, Robert Isaac and Kedar Rāj Rājopādhyāya. 1990. *Mesocosm: Hinduism and the Organization of the Traditional Newar City in Nepal*. Berkeley: University of California Press.

Lewis, Todd, Subarna Man Tuladhar and Labh Ratna Tuladhar. 2000. *Popular Buddhist Texts from Nepal: Narratives and Rituals of Newar Buddhism*. Albany: State University of New York Press.

Liechty, Mark. 2003. *Suitably Modern: Making Middle-Class Culture in a New Consumer Society*. Princeton, NJ: Princeton University Press.

Lipner, Julius J. 1996. Ancient Banyan: An Inquiry into the Meaning of "Hinduness". *Religious Studies* 32 (1): 109–126.

Lutgendorf, Philip. 2007. *Hanuman's Tale: The Messages of a Divine Monkey*. Oxford: Oxford University Press.

Lutgendorf, Philip. 2006. A Ramayana on Air: "All in the (Raghu) Family," A Video Epic in Cultural Context. In John Stratton Hawley and Vasudha Narayanan (eds.), *The Life of Hinduism*. Berkeley: University of California Press, 140–157.

Lutgendorf, Philip. 1994. My Hanuman Is Bigger than Yours. *History of Religions* 33 (3): 211–245.

Lutgendorf, Philip. 1992. Ram's Story in Shiva's City: Public Arenas and Private Patronage. In Sandria B. Freitag (ed.), *Culture and Power in Banaras: Community Performance and Environment 1800–1980*. Berkeley: University of California Press, 34–61.

Marriott, McKim. 2006. Holi: The Feast of Love. In John Stratton Hawley and Vasudha Narayanan (eds.), *The Life of Hinduism*. Berkeley: University of California Press, 99–112.

McDermott, Rachel Fell and Jeffrey J. Kripal (eds.). 2004. *Encountering Kali: In the Margins, at the Center, in the West*. Delhi: Motilal Banarsidass.

McDermott, Rachel Fell. 1995. Bengali Songs to Kālī. In Donald S. Lopez (ed.), *Religions of India in Practice*. Princeton, NJ: Princeton University Press, 55–76.

McKendry-Smith, Emily. 2022. Public Household, Private Congregation: The Brahma Kumaris as a "Public Private" Space for Nepali Women. *Nova Religio: The Journal of Alternative and Emergent Religions* 25 (3): 32–56.

McLain, Karline. 2016. *The Afterlife of Sai Baba: Competing Visions of a Global Saint*. Seattle and London: University of Washington Press.

McLain, Karline. 2009. *India's Immortal Comic Books: Gods, Kings, and Other Heroes*. Bloomington: Indiana University Press.

McLeod, Hew. 2018. The Life of Guru Nanak. In Donald S. Lopez (ed.), *Religions of Asia in Practice: An Anthology*. Princeton, NJ: Princeton University Press, 109–121.

Michaels, Axel. 2004. *Hinduism: Past and Present*. New Delhi: Orient Longman.

Miller, Barbara Stoler. 2004. *The Bhagavad-Gita: Krishna's Counsel in Time of War*. New York: Bantam Books.

Mills, Martin A. 2003. *Identity, Ritual, and State in Tibetan Buddhism: The Foundations of Authority in Gelukpa Monasticism*. London and New York: RoutledgeCurzon.

Mines, Diane P. 2005. *Fierce Gods: Inequality, Ritual, and the Politics of Dignity in a South Indian Village*. Bloomington: Indiana University Press.

Mocko, Anne T. 2016. *Demoting Vishnu: Ritual, Politics, and the Unraveling of Nepal's Hindu Monarchy*. New York: Oxford University Press.

Moggach, Deborah. 2004. *These Foolish Things [or] the Best Exotic Marigold Hotel*. London: Chatto & Windus.

Mohammad, Afsar. 2014. The Sri Venkateswara Temple in Tirupati. In P. Pratap Kumar (ed.), *Contemporary Hinduism*. London: Routledge, 232–244.

Müller F. Max. 1976 [1878]. *Lectures on the Origin and Growth of Religion As Illustrated by the Religions of India: Delivered in the Chapter-House Westminster Abbey in April May and June 1878*. New York: AMS Press.

Muller-Ortega, Paul. 2000. On the Seal of Śambhu: A Poem by Abhinavagupta. In David Gordon White (ed.), *Tantra in Practice*. Princeton, NJ: Princeton University Press, 573–586.

Nagarajan, Vijaya. 2018. *Feeding a Thousand Souls: Women, Ritual, and Ecology in India: An Exploration of the Kolam*. New York: Oxford University Press.

Narayanan, Vasudha. 2007. Performing Arts, Re-forming Rituals: Women and Social Change in South India. In Tracy Pintchman (ed.), *Women's Lives, Women's Rituals in the Hindu Tradition*. Oxford: Oxford University Press, 177–198.

Olivelle, Patrick. 2008. *Upaniṣads*. Oxford: Oxford University Press.

Olivelle, Patrick. 2005. *Manu's Code of Law: A Critical Edition and Translation of the Manava-Dharmasastra*. Oxford: Oxford University Press.

Olson, Carl. 2007. *The Many Colors of Hinduism*. New Brunswick, NJ: Rutgers University Press.

Packert, Cynthia. 2010. *The Art of Loving Krishna: Ornamentation and Devotion*. Bloomington: Indiana University Press.

Padma, Sree. 2013. *Vicissitudes of the Goddess: Reconstructions of the Gramadevata in India's Religious Traditions*. New York: Oxford University Press.

Paramtattvadas, Swami. 2017. *An Introduction to Swaminarayan Hindu Theology*. Cambridge: Cambridge University Press.

Pariyar, Mitra. 2018. Caste Discrimination Overseas: Nepali Dalits in England. In David N. Gellner and Sondra L. Hausner (eds.), *Global Nepalis: Religion, Culture, and Community in a New and Old Diaspora*. London: Oxford University Press, 404–434.

Pati, George. 2014. Nambūtiris and Ayyappan Devotees in Kerala. In P. Pratap Kumar (ed.), *Contemporary Hinduism*. London: Routledge, 204–216.

Patton, Laurie L. 2005. *Bringing the Gods to Mind: Mantra and Ritual in Early Indian Sacrifice*. Berkeley: University of California Press.

Pechilis, Karen. 2012. *Interpreting Devotion: The Poetry and Legacy of a Female Bhakti Saint of India*. Abingdon: Routledge.

Pechilis, Karen (ed.). 2004. *The Graceful Guru: Hindu Female Gurus in India and the United States*. New York: Oxford University Press.

Prothero, Stephen R. 2003. *American Jesus: How the Son of God Became a National Icon*. New York: Farrar Straus and Giroux.

Raj, Selva. 2004. Ammachi, the Mother of Compassion. In Karen Pechilis (ed.), *The Graceful Guru: Hindu Female Gurus in India and the United States*. New York: Oxford University Press, 203–218.

Raj, Selva and William Harman (eds.). 2006. *Dealing with Deities: The Ritual Vow in South Asia*. Albany: State University of New York Press.

Ram, Kalpana. 2013. *Fertile Disorder: Spirit Possession and Its Provocation of the Modern*. Honolulu: University of Hawai'i Press.

Ramanujan, A. K. 2004. Three Hundred Rāmāyaṇas: Five Examples and Three Thoughts on Translation. In *The Collected Essays of A. K. Ramanujan*. Oxford: Oxford University Press, 131–160.

Ramanujan, A. K. 1981. *Hymns for the Drowning: Poems for Viṣṇu*. Princeton, NJ: Princeton University Press.

Ramanujan, A. K. 1973. *Speaking of Śiva*. Harmondsworth: Penguin.

Richman, Paula. 2008. *Ramayana Stories in Modern South India: An Anthology*. Bloomington: Indiana University Press.

Said, Edward W. 1979. *Orientalism*. New York: Vintage Books.

Samuel, Geoffrey. 2008. *The Origins of Yoga and Tantra: Indic Religions to the Thirteenth Century*. Cambridge: Cambridge University Press.

Sanderson, Alexis. 2015. Tolerance, Exclusivity, Inclusivity, and Persecution in Indian Religion During the Early Mediaeval Period. In *Honoris Causa: Essays in Honour of Aveek Sarkar, edited with a foreword by John Makinson*. London: Allen Lane, 155–224.

Sanford, A. Whitney. 2007. Pinned on Karma Rock: Whitewater Kayaking as Religious Experience. *Journal of the American Academy of Religion* 75 (4): 875–895.

Sax, William S. 2009. *God of Justice: Ritual Healing and Social Justice in the Central Himalayas*. New York: Oxford University Press.

Schomer, Karine and W. H. McLeod. 1987. *The Sants: Studies in a Devotional Tradition of India*. Berkeley, CA: Berkeley Religious Studies Series.

Seager, Richard Hughes. 1995. *The World's Parliament of Religions: The East West Encounter, Chicago, 1893*. Bloomington: Indiana University Press.

Shah, Shandip. 2014. Kṛṣṇa Devotion in Western India. In P. Pratap Kumar (ed.), *Contemporary Hinduism*. London: Routledge, 138–147.

Shaikh, Juned. 2021. *Outcaste Bombay: City Making and the Politics of the Poor*. Seattle: University of Washington Press.

Shrestha, Bal Gopal. 2006. The Svanti Festival: Victory over Death and the Renewal of the Ritual Cycle in Nepal. *Contributions to Nepalese Studies* 33 (2): 203–221.

Siegel, Lee. 2009. *Gītagovinda: Love Songs of Rādhā and Kṛṣṇa*. New York: New York University Press/JJC Foundation.

Simmons, Caleb, Moumita Sen, and Hillary Rodrigues. 2018. *Nine Nights of the Goddess: The Navaratri Festival in South Asia*. Albany: State University of New York Press.

Smith, Brian K. 1989. *Reflections on Resemblance, Ritual, and Religion*. Oxford: Oxford University Press.

Soneji, Davesh. 2012. *Unfinished Gestures: Devadāsīs, Memory, and Modernity in South India*. Chicago: University of Chicago Press.

Srinivasan, Doris. 1997. *Many Heads, Arms, and Eyes: Origin Meaning and Form of Multiplicity in Indian Art*. Leiden: Brill.

The World's Great Religions. 1957. New York: Time-Life Books.

Tucker, Mary Evelyn and John Grim. 2018. The Movement of Religion and Ecology: Emerging Field and Dynamic Force. In Willis Jenkins, Mary Evelyn Tucker, and John Grim (eds.), *Routledge Handbook of Religion and Ecology*. Abingdon: Routledge, 1–11.

Twain, Mark. 1989. *Following the Equator: A Journey Around the World*. New York: Dover Publications.

Tweed, Thomas. 2002. Who Is a Buddhist? Night-Stand Buddhists and Other Creatures. In Charles S. Prebish and Martin Baumann (eds.), *Westward Dharma: Buddhism Beyond Asia*. Berkeley: University of California Press, 17–33.

Viswanath, Rupa. 2014. *The Pariah Problem: Caste Religion and the Social in Modern India*. New York: Columbia University Press.

Venkatesan, Archana. 2010. *The Secret Garland: Āṇṭal's Tiruppāvai and Nācciyār Tirumoli*. New York: Oxford University Press.

Verma, Rahul. 2019. The TV show that transformed Hinduism. *BBC Culture*. www.bbc.com/culture/article/20191022-the-tv-show-that-transformed-hinduism.

Walsh, Judith E. 2011. *A Brief History of India*. 2nd ed. New York: Facts On File.

White, David Gordon. 2012. *Yoga in Practice*. Princeton, NJ: Princeton University Press.

White, David Gordon (ed.). 2000. *Tantra in Practice*. Princeton, NJ: Princeton University Press.

White, Lynn. 1967. The Historical Roots of Our Ecological Crisis. *Science* 155: 1203–1207.

Wilkerson, Isabel. 2020. *Caste: The Origins of Our Discontents*. London: Penguin Books.

Williams, Raymond Brady. 2019. *An Introduction to Swaminarayan Hinduism*. New York: Cambridge University Press.

Williams, Raymond Brady and Yogi Trivedi (eds.). 2016. *Swaminarayan Hinduism: Tradition Adaptation and Identity*. New Delhi: Oxford University Press.

Index

Note: *Italic* page number refer to *figures*.